Music, Dance and Translation

Also Available from Bloomsbury

Music, Text and Translation, edited by Helen Julia Minors
Theatre Translation, Massimiliano Morini
Sociologies of Poetry Translation, Jacob Blakesley
Celebrity Translation in British Theatre, Robert Stock
Translating For Singing, Ronnie Apter and Mark Herman
Music as Multimodal Discourse: Semiotics, Power and Protest, edited by Lyndon C. S. Way and Simon McKerrell

Music, Dance and Translation

Edited by Helen Julia Minors

BLOOMSBURY ACADEMIC
LONDON • NEW YORK • OXFORD • NEW DELHI • SYDNEY

BLOOMSBURY ACADEMIC
Bloomsbury Publishing Plc, 50 Bedford Square, London, WC1B 3DP, UK
Bloomsbury Publishing Inc, 1385 Broadway, New York, NY 10018, USA
Bloomsbury Publishing Ireland, 29 Earlsfort Terrace, Dublin 2, D02 AY28, Ireland

BLOOMSBURY, BLOOMSBURY ACADEMIC and the Diana logo are trademarks of
Bloomsbury Publishing Plc

First published in Great Britain 2023
Paperback edition published 2025

Copyright © Helen Julia Minors and Contributors, 2023, 2025

Helen Julia Minors and Contributors have asserted their right under the Copyright,
Designs and Patents Act, 1988, to be identified as Authors of this work.

For legal purposes the Acknowledgements on p. xiv constitute an extension of
this copyright page.

Cover design: Elena Durey
Cover image © Georgii Boronin/istock

All rights reserved. No part of this publication may be: i) reproduced or transmitted
in any form, electronic or mechanical, including photocopying, recording or by
means of any information storage or retrieval system without prior permission in
writing from the publishers; or ii) used or reproduced in any way for the training,
development or operation of artificial intelligence (AI) technologies, including
generative AI technologies. The rights holders expressly reserve this publication
from the text and data mining exception as per Article 4(3) of the
Digital Single Market Directive (EU) 2019/790.

Bloomsbury Publishing Plc does not have any control over, or responsibility for,
any third-party websites referred to or in this book. All internet addresses given
in this book were correct at the time of going to press. The author and publisher regret any
inconvenience caused if addresses have changed or sites have ceased to exist,
but can accept no responsibility for any such changes.

A catalogue record for this book is available from the British Library.

A catalogue record for this book is available from the Library of Congress.

ISBN: HB: 978-1-3501-7573-0
       PB: 978-1-3503-7160-6
       ePDF: 978-1-3501-7574-7
       eBook: 978-1-3501-7575-4

Typeset by RefineCatch Limited, Bungay, Suffolk

For product safety related questions productsafety@bloomsbury.com.

To find out more about our authors and books visit www.bloomsbury.com
and sign up for our newsletters.

Contents

List of Figures	vii
List of Examples and Tables	viii
Notes on Contributors	ix
Acknowledgements	xiv
Note on the Text	xvi

Part One Translation and Dance

1. Translation in Music and Dance Discourse
   Helen Julia Minors — 3

2. The Role of Translation in the Practice of Dance Reconstruction
   Helen Julia Minors, in conversation with Millicent Hodson and Kenneth Archer — 17

Part Two Gestures between Music and Dance

3. Points of Contact: Bases for Translations between Music and Dance
   Lawrence M. Zbikowski — 29

4. Interactions and Correspondences between Music/Sound and Dance/Movement as Permanent Negotiations of Translation Processes
   Stephanie Schroedter — 49

5. Collaborative Ballet Dialogues in Translation and Creating *La Parade* (1917) in Paris
   Helen Julia Minors — 63

Part Three Translation through Music-Dance Performance

6. Maurice Béjart's Variations on Wild's *Salome* and Kinetic Translation of Words and Music in *La Mort Subite* (1991) and *Boléro* (1960)
   Juliette Loesch — 81

7   The Music has Movement in It
    Lesley Main   99

8   Cranko's Reinvention of Pushkin's Text in his Ballet *Onegin* (1965)
    Anna Ponomareva   117

Part Four   Institutional Representation: Notation, Archives and the Museum

9   Two National Estonian Ballet Translations of Theodor Amadeus Hofmann's *Coppélia* to Leo Délibes' Music by Mauro Bigonzetti (2002) and Ronald Hynd (2010)
    Heili Einasto   133

10 Fruitful Intersemiotic Transfers between Music and Choreography in the National Ballet of Canada's *Romeo and Juliet*
    Denise Merkle   147

11 Dancing Symbols and Movement Notation as a Form of Translation
    Mary Wardle   163

Bibliography   179
Index   197

Figures

4.1 *Eadweard's Ear.* Instruments of the music ensemble: conductor's desk, working place of the bassoon soloist, the electric guitar player and the drummer — 58
7.1 *Passacaglia 14* MOMENTA Dance Company 2007 — 104
7.2 *Fugue 7* MOMENTA Dance Company 2007 — 105
7.3 Doris Humphrey as 'The Matriarch' — 109
7.4 Groups 1, 2, 3 in Section B, Middlesex University dancers, May 2015 — 111
9.1 *Coppélia.* Choreography by Ronal Hynd following the original ballet of 1870. Estonian National Ballet production of 2010 — 138
9.2 *Coppélia.* Choreography by Mauro Bigonzetti. Estonian National Ballet production of 2002 — 141

Examples and Tables

3.1 Antonio Vivaldi, *Gloria* (RV 589), 'Laudamus te', bars 17–27, soprano 1 and 2. Text translation: 'We praise thee, we bless thee' — 30
3.2 Georg Friedrich Handel, *L'Allegro, il Penseroso ed il Moderato* (HWV 55): No. 6, 'Haste thee nymph', bars 25–35 — 38
3.3 Wolfgang Amadeus Mozart, Piano Concerto No. 11 in F major (K. 413, first movement, bars 172–179 — 44
3.4 Wolfgang Amadeus Mozart, Piano Concerto No. 11 in F major (K. 413, first movement, bars 24–33 — 44
10.1 Full score of group dance. Mazurka from 'Coppélia' — 153
10.2 The notation includes details such as hand holds, many of which are not seen in a photo or video — 154

Table

7.1 Structure of Section A — 110

Contributors

Heili Einasto is Lecturer in Dance Theory at Tallinn University in Estonia, where she works in the Baltic Film, Media and Arts School. She has been an active dance critic in Estonia since 1991, and has taught dance and ballet history at Tartu University, Viljandi Cultural College and Tallinn University since 1997. She has an MA in gender and culture from the Central European University (CEU), Budapest, and a PhD in Cultural Studies from Tallinn University.

Juliette Loesch holds a PhD in English and Comparative Literature from the University of Lausanne (CH). Her PhD project, supervised by Prof. Martine Hennard Dutheil de la Rochère, analyses the transcreative dynamics of Oscar Wilde's Salome from the page to the stage, with an emphasis on Maurice Béjart's ballet adaptations. She has published several articles on related topics, including "Staging the 'Dance of the Seven Veils'. Three Variations on Oscar Wilde's Salomé by Maurice Béjart" (in Translate, Illustrate, Rewrite, Stage, 2023), and she co-edited conference proceedings on Traces et résonances. Ré-écrire, consigner, adapter la danse (2020) with Céline Gauthier and Lucas Serol.

Lesley Main is Head of the Department of Performing Arts at City, University of London. Formerly, she was Head of the Department of Performing Arts at Middlesex University, London. She danced in the United States with Ernestine Stodelle from 1985, is founder/director of the Doris Humphrey Foundation UK, and stages Humphrey's repertory for, amongst others, Arke Compagnia D'Arte (Italy) and MOMENTA Dance Company (Chicago), including *Water Study* (1928), *The Call/Breath of Fire* (1928/29), *Two Ecstatic Themes* (1931), *The Shakers* (1931), *New Dance* (1935), *With My Red Fires* (1936) and *Passacaglia* (1938). Main's publications include chapters and articles for a range of dance journals and conference presentations in the UK and internationally, and two books: *Transmissions in Dance: Contemporary Staging Practices* (2017) and *Directing the Dance Legacy of Doris Humphrey: The Creative Impulse of Reconstruction* (2012).

Denise Merkle is Department Head and Professor of Translation and Translation Studies (TS) at the Université de Moncton, Canada. She is a former president of the Canadian Association for Translation Studies (CATS), and is currently a member of the TS journal, *Traduction, terminologie, rédaction* (*TTR*) editorial board, as well as its book review editor. In addition, she is a member of other TS and French studies editorial boards and scientific committees, the FWO (Fonds Wetenschappelijk Onderzoek Vlaanderen) Review College (Belgium) and research group CLESTHIA – laboratoire de recherche : la neutralité du traducteur (Université Sorbonne 3, Paris, France), headed by Isabelle Collombat and Fayza El Qasem. Her research interests encompass censorship, official plurilingualism and minorities and their interactions with translation, along with the translating subject. She has co-edited refereed volumes of selected papers, including: 'Minority Languages, National Languages, and Official Language Policies' (2018) and 'Plurilinguisme et pluriculturalisme: Des modèles officiels dans le monde' (2016), both with Gillian Lane-Mercier and Jane Koustas; *Territoires de l'interculturalité* (2013) with Mourad Ali Khodja, Jean Morency and Jean-François Thibault; and *The Power of the Pen: Translation and Censorship in Nineteenth-Century Europe* (2010) with Carol O'Sullivan, Michaela Wolf and Luc van Doorslaer. Furthermore, she has (co-)edited thematic issues of *TTR*, *Meta*, *TranscUlturAl* and *Alternative francophone*. Among her publications are, 'Four French-Canadian Official Translators and Historians (1837–1927)', in M. Lin Moniz, I. Gil and A. Lopes (eds), *Era uma vez a tradução . . . / Once upon a time there was translation . . .* (2020), contributions to B. Banoun, I. Poulin and Y. Chevrel (eds), *Histoire des traductions en langue française, XXe siècle* (2019) and 'L'état des lieux de la formation en traduction professionnelle au Nouveau-Brunswick. La littératie au service de la formation en traduction' in *Forum* (2018).

Helen Julia Minors is Professor and the Head of the School of Arts at York St John University, UK. She was previously Associate Professor of Music and School Head of the Performing Arts Department at Kingston University, London. She is also Visiting Professor in Artistic Research at Luleå University of Technology, Sweden. Helen was the founder and first co-chair of EDI Music Studies Network UK. She is co-investigator of the Arts and Humanities Research Council funded Women's Musical Leadership Online Network. She has published the following volumes: *Music, Text and Translation*, as editor (2013); *Building Intercultural and Interdisciplinary Bridges*, co-edited with Pamela Burnard, Valerie Ross, Kimberly Powell, Tatjana Dragovic and Elizabeth Mackinlay (2016); *Paul Dukas: Legacies of a French Musician*, co-edited with Laura Watson (2019); *Artistic Research in Performance Through Collaboration*, co-written and co-edited with Martin Blain (2020); *Routledge Companion to Women's Musical Leadership*, co-written and co-edited with Laura Hamer (forthcoming 2023); and *Choreomusicology: Dialogues in Music and Dance*, co-edited with Samuel Dorf and Simon Morrison (forthcoming 2024). Recent articles have appeared in *London Review of Education* (2017, 2019) and *Tibon* (2021), and recent book chapters in *Historical Interplay in French Music and Culture* (2018), *Translation and Multimodality* (2019), *Opera in Translation* (2020), *Intersemiotic Perspectives on Emotions* (2022) and *The Routledge Companion to Applied Musicology* (2023).

Anna Ponomareva is Lecturer in Russian, Translation Studies and Comparative Literature at the School of Slavonic and East European Studies (SSEES)/School of European Languages, Culture and Society (SELCS), University College London (UCL), University of London, UK. She also teaches Russian at Imperial College London (ICL) in its Centre for Languages, Culture and Communication. She contributes to teaching undergraduate and postgraduate students as well as to supervising their dissertations and PhD theses. Anna's first degree is in Analytic Philosophy, Moscow State University, in which the study of language, personal identity and other minds are emphasized. Her MPhil was conducted at the University of Manchester, where Anna wrote her thesis on the influence of Indian culture on the development of Russian Symbolism, in particular on Andrei Belyi (1880–1934). Her PhD was written at UCL in the area of Translation Studies. The focus of Anna's PhD is on translation methods. In her thesis, she used data collected from the five recent translations into English of Alexander Pushkin's novel in verse *Eugene Onegin* (1830s). Anna's areas of research are translation theory, translation and music, Russian language, Russian symbolism, comparative literature and history of ideas. She is the author of several publications in Russian and English, including: 'Edvard Grieg and Andrey Belyi's Northern Symphony', (*Studia Musicologica Norvegica*) (2007) and 'Two Scheherazades, a Suite and a Ballet, as Cultural Translations of the Nights', *Médiévales* (2012). Anna has currently submitted her most recent article, 'Moulding the Music to the Text: Donizetti's Opera Lucia di Lammermoor (1835)', for peer review *Translating the World Transmedially* at the University of Tartu, Estonia.

Stephanie Schroedter worked at the Department of Musicology at the University of Salzburg, Austria, with an emphasis on music theatre and dance research, while completing her PhD on changes in the art of dancing from 'Affect' to 'Action'-based performances in the late seventeenth and early eighteenth centuries (awarded the Tanzwissenschaftspreis Nordrhein-Westfalen, 2001). Afterwards, she became Research Fellow at the Department for Music Theatre

Research, University of Bayreuth, Germany. Fellowships from the DAAD ('Maison des sciences de l'homme' programme) and the Deutsches Historisches Institut Paris (DHI) enabled her to pursue research in Paris for the development of a project on *Music in Motion: Dance Cultures of the 19th Century* (subsidized by the Deutsche Forschungsgemeinschaft, DFG). Additionally she worked on a project on artistic translation processes exemplified by co-productions of Pina Bausch's 'Tanztheater Wuppertal' under the direction of Professor Dr Gabriele Klein (Performance Studies at the Hamburg University). For her second monograph ('habilitation') entitled, *Paris qui danse. Bewegungs- und Klangräume einer Großstadt der Moderne* (*Movement and Sound Spaces in a Modern City*), she received a 'venia legendi' for musicology and dance studies from the Freie Universität Berlin (2015). Stephanie taught as visiting and substitution professor for musicology, dance studies, theatre and media studies and organized several international conferences focused on intertwinings of music, dance, theatre/performance and media art. In addition to her work as book editor and her contributions to collective volumes, journals and lexika, she gave talks in Europe as well as in the US and Canada. Her latest research project 'Bodies and Sounds in Motion' (again supported by the DFG) aims at theory-based methodical approaches to the analysis of intertwinings of music/sound and dance/movement in performances of the twentieth and twenty-first centuries. In 2021, she became Professor for Theories of Music and Movement at the University for Music and Performing Arts Vienna (MDW), Austria.

Mary Wardle is Associate Professor at the Sapienza University of Rome, where she teaches English Language and Translation Studies. Her academic interests include the phenomenon of retranslation, the study of paratextual elements, adaptation studies and translation as an embodied practice. Present projects include work on the reception of translations in the literary press and which/how nationlects are chosen for the 'English translation' of a foreign-language source text. Recent publications include papers on Umberto Eco, translation and the visual arts, Italian retranslations of *The Great Gatsby*, how readers choose among different (re)translations, intersemiotic translation from book to film to manga, the role of archives in translation studies, how translations are reviewed by literary critics and Englishes in translation. Forthcoming publications include book chapters on intercultural elements and translingual identity in the works of Jhumpa Lahiri; the paratextual elements framing Lahiri's production; and the English translations of the works of Primo Levi in a volume on the intersection between translation studies and memory studies.

Lawrence M. Zbikowski is Professor of Music at the University of Chicago. His research focuses on the application of recent work in cognitive science to a range of problems confronted by music scholars, including the nature of musical grammar, the relationship between music and movement, text-music relations and the structure of theories of music. He is the author of *Conceptualizing Music* (2002) and *Foundations of Musical Grammar* (2017). He has recently contributed chapters to *Performing Metaphoric Creativity across Modes and Contexts* (2020), *Music and Consciousness 2* (2019), *Music-Dance* (2017), *The Routledge Companion to Music Cognition* (2019), *Music in Time* (2020) and *The Oxford Handbook of Topic Theory* (2014). His articles and reviews have appeared in *Music Theory Online*, *Musicæ Scientiæ*, *Music Theory Spectrum*, *Music Analysis*, *Ethnomusicology*, the *Dutch Journal of Music Theory* and the *Journal of Musicological Research*. During 2020–1, he was Fellow at the Franke Institute for the Humanities at the University of Chicago at work on a new book, *The Nature of Musical Thought*.

Acknowledgements

This book began as a continuing process of questioning, following the first volume I edited, *Music, Text and Translation* (2013). My work has always covered both music and dance, and concerned collaboration, so it seemed natural and exciting to plan a further volume which focused on dance in this field of artistic translation. Since the first book, I worked alongside Professor Lucile Desblache (Roehampton University, UK) on the funded network of the Arts and Humanities Research Council, Translating Music (see www.translatingmusic.com) during 2013–14, and as part of it had the opportunity to talk to many colleagues internationally about this growing field of artistic translation. This developed into many questions and single-authored articles and chapters. But I was keen to foster a dialogue through an edited collection. I am especially grateful to the moral support of Stephanie Schroedter and Eddie Dobson, who have been constant voices of encouragement over the years, and likewise to my mentors and friends Professor Stephanie Jordan, Caroline Potter and Professor Richard Langham Smith.

This field of translation is interdisciplinary and intersectional, and as such I am grateful to the late Daniel Albright and Gunther Kress for the many conversations, offers of advice and support and guidance as my research career has developed. My other research articles and chapters in this field have all been supported by conference organizers and publication editors, there are many to name, and those supporting the development of this multimodal translation field include: Monica Boria, Angeles Carreres, Maria Noriega-Sanchez, Marcus Tomlin, Celia Martin de Leon, Gisela Marcelo Wirnitzer, Susan Petrilli, Christine Ji, Adriana Serban, Kelly Chan, Pamela Burnard and Valerie Ross.

I am grateful to Kingston University, UK, who supported my work, between two terms of Head of Department, by supporting a semester sabbatical, during which time I developed the proposal for this present volume. Special thanks to former managers Jason Piper and Alistair Payne. I am especially grateful to my colleagues also at Lulea Technical University in Sweden for allowing me to share much of my research work in draft in seminars and workshops: special warm thanks to Professor Stefan Östersjö and Carl Holmgren, and our PhD cohort who worked on Research Methods Online during the Covid19 Pandemic,

Mikael Backman, Georg Guylas, Jesper Nordin, Mattias Petersson, Robert Ek and Ann Elkjär. Many thanks go to my recent PhD students who have shared numerous conversations concerning with me concerning translation, musical meaning and artistic communication: Emma Haughton, Grace Gates, Debbie Moss, Major John Martin and Chamari Wedamulla. Finally, thanks to my research partners, co-editors, co-writers and friends for their constant support and to my sisters, Laura Hamer, Laura Watson and Manuella Blackburn for our weekly Friday evening conversations.

The editors and publisher gratefully acknowledge the permissions granted to reproduce the copyright material in this book. Every effort has been made to trace copyright holders and to obtain their permission for the use of copyright material. However, if any have been inadvertently overlooked, the publishers will be pleased, if notified of any omissions, to make the necessary arrangement at the first opportunity.

Note on the Text

All translations are the chapter author's own unless otherwise stated. Translations are presented in the text in parentheses, alongside the original source text where possible.

Musical references are a mixture of bar number and rehearsal figure as is appropriate to the example. Audio-visual or audio references are presented as time codes, for example 12 minutes and 30 seconds, 12:30.

Part One

Translation and Dance

1

Translation in Music and Dance Discourse

Helen Julia Minors

The concept of translation is highly poignant in contemporary society and within artistic practice for many reasons, not least the recognition that we communicate in multimodal ways all the time (Kress 2010), not only through language (both spoken and written) but also through memes, images, advertisements, television programmes, radio, films, dance, performances, physical gestures and more. Indeed as Kathleen Coessens has identified, 'communication exceeds verbal language' (2019: 70). The modes of communication are vast, and in an increasingly globalized and digital world, we communicate across cultures, across nations and across all forms of perceived and physical borders, as well as across languages. Many have written about the arts of music and dance in terms of language, and it is worth noting this needs to be done with caution, as Stephanie Jordan asserts when she alerted scholars to the problem of language in the field (2000).

The previous book, which I edited, *Music, Text and Translation* (Minors 2013) explored and expanded the notion of translation to show how there is a transference of sense between media, specifically between music and text. The book looked at songs, operas and musicals, painting, sculpture and biography. This current volume, *Music, Dance and Translation*, takes the premise that translation is crucial to all forms of artistic creativity, collaboration and performance by exploring the specific interrelationships between music and dance in various forms. It provides an exploration of the concept of translation as it relates to dance in particular. In exploring the role translation plays in dance-music works, which are inherently multimodal, this book questions the transference, exchange and dialogue between the arts and the artists, not only in performance, but during the collaborative process, during the archival process, and during the interpretation process, between music (musicians, directors, composers, among others) and dance (dancers, choreographers, designers, directors) and other 'texts' more broadly. The concept of translation is taken from language transfer, and rather used to model, question and chart how music and dance form meaningful relationships. If as Daniel Albright asserts, 'art is ascribed on the body' (2014: 281), then a focus on dance and translation is much needed for the field of translation studies to develop. As such the concept of translation refers to the process and dynamic act of trying to establish some form of meaning exchange and sensory transfer as part of the artistic collaborative aims. As Nicholas Cook has noted, meaning is constructed 'from dynamic interactions' (Cook 2013: 5). As a concept it is therefore central to all forms of artistic collaboration. Indeed, as I note elsewhere, all forms of collaboration rely on translation (Blain and Minors 2020), and as Pamela Burnard et al. confirm, 'intercultural translations are co-constructed through collaboration' (2018: 232). Translation as a process of communication across artistic media, between artists and across cultures, is explored.

The focus on the process of translation means that this volume speaks to different audiences. For a translation reader, much new information will be given about dance. For a dance scholar, or choreomusicologist, a new perspective on translation will be given. Susan Bassnett declares, translation always exists with 'multilingual and multicultural context[s]' (2014: 1). The source material is wide in that the focus on translation has to engage with people as well as the texts (e.g. scores, designs, letters, reviews, documents, photographs, videos, recordings) that are produced as part of the production process. The shared aim of the authors is to meet theory and practice-based research, linked to museums, libraries and theatre archives, from across this interdisciplinary field to ensure primary source materials are utilized in drawing out new readings of translation as a concept within this bespoke field of music and dance studies. It seeks to bring new perspectives, such as from theatre archives, a view of dance notation as an act of translation and other different perspectives. This means it deliberately does not cover well-trodden ground such as the excellent work done on Balanchine's choreographic inter-relationship with music, including work by Kara Yoo Leaman's volume, 'Analyzing Music and Dance: Balanchine's Choreography to Tchaikovsky and the Choreomusical Score' (2016) and Stephanie Jordan's seminal work on Balanchine, and others, in *Moving Music: Dialogues with Music in Twentieth-Century Ballet* (2000).

Many questions underpin this volume which explore the relevance of translation, as a concept, to dance and music, dance scholarship and history, dance practice and dance curation. How is music affected by its translation, interpretation and adaptation with, through and by dance? How might notation (of dance and music) act as a form of translation? How does music influence the creation of dance? How do creative collaborative artists communicate, interpret and translate each other's ideas in the process of creating a new production? How might dance and music be understood to exchange and transfer their content, sense and process during both the creative process and the interpretative process?

Bringing together chapters that explore theory and practice, this book questions the process and role translation has to play in the context of music and dance, and to do so, it provides a range of case studies across this interdisciplinary field. It is not restricted by genre, style or cultural location. As only the second volume to explore translation in relation to music and text, and the first to overtly tackle this topic in terms of dance, it moves the argument from a broad notion of text translation, to think critically about the sound and movement arts of music and dance using translation as a model to better understand the collaborative processes, potential and realization of these art forms. Jordan asked whether 'dance offer[s] us new insights into music?' (2018: 88). We can further develop this: does music and dance offer us further insights into translation, and can translation offer us further insights into the relationships between music and dance?

Translation and Music, and Beyond: Recent Developments in Multimodal Translation

Translation studies has opened up much since the publication of *Music, Text and Translation* in 2013. Since then, multimodal studies has become intersected with much translation literature, in terms of exploring meaning creation and transfer in the digital and globalized context. Research conferences and events since 2013 have increasingly looked to explore the intersectional relationships between the arts and the move in funding bodies has been to call for interdisciplinary projects. Indeed, following the first volume, my colleague Lucile Desblache and I led an Arts and Humanities Research Council funded network, Translating Music, through which we explored the ways in which musical texts were actively translated within the music industries (Desblache and Minors 2014). Conferences in dance, which have invited and actively explored translation include: *Musik als Experimentierfeld für Bewegung, Music as an Experimental Field for Movement*, Strobl am Wolfgangsee, held in Austria, on 16 September 2020, led by Professor Stephanie Schroedter (see Chapter 4). Two events have taken place at the University of Tartu in Estonia which opened the debate within an interdisciplinary context and the issues of the translational turn (defined by Bachmann-Medick 2009: 2) in relation to arts and humanities: the first, *4th International Conference on Itineraries in Translation History*, University of Tartu, Estonia, held on 13–15 December 2018, which was later refined to the conference topic for 2020, with a second conference entitled *Transmedial Turn? Potentials, Problems and Points to Consider*, University of Tartu, Estonia, held on 8–11 December 2020, led by Elin Sütiste. These were important events as they were the first to acknowledge that the translational turn had moved on toward the multimodal turn, and to a broad definition of translation spanning all art forms and art practices.

At the same time, a series of conferences have been held at the University of Cambridge in Translation Studies, in the Education Faculty and in the Humanities, all of which seek to explore the interrelationships of the arts and artists in looking to the meeting points and dialogues between the arts and artists. Each, in essence, questioned the meeting point of the arts with translation. First, *Beyond Words: Multimodal Encounters in Translation*, held on 5–6 July 2018, led by Monica Boria, Ángeles Carreres, Maria Noríega-Sánchez and Marcus Tomalin (see Minors 2019); second, *Building Interdisciplinary Bridges Across Cultures and Creativities*, October 2018, led by Pamela Burnard; and third, the *International Conference on 'Musical Intersections in Practice'* (MIP2019), 25–26 October 2019, led by Valerie Ross. I presented my work in the field of music and translation at all of these events and the starting discussion inviting authors to participate in the present volume began in Estonia in 2018. The above show a curiosity within translation studies and within the arts, as well as education, to further this field with a broad range of examples. This volume speaks to this spirit of inquiry and speaks across disciplines.

There are a number of publications within the fields of musicology, dance studies, theatre studies and choreomusical studies which underpin my thinking and research questions. There has been growth in literature related to the relationships between music and dance recently. Notable is the seminal work of Mariam Smith in establishing how dance reconstruction can function in relation to *Giselle*: her work develops a critical framework for how to approach and critically assess this exploratory and creative work situated in historical and cultural awareness (Smith 2000). Much has happened in the field of music theory to analyse the rhythmic, gestural and motivic relationships been the movement arts of music dance notably with the recently *Music Theory* journal volume (Jordan and Cohn 2021). This volume brings together new research which analyses the details of the relationships in terms of metre, and rhythm relation to cognitive science and multimodal analysis. The volume celebrates music and dance as dynamically interactive through a range of case studies. In choreomusical studies, Davinia Caddy and Maribeth Clark (2021) have presented a series of case studies concerning the historical and critical perspectives of how music and dance have functioned in a range of historical, largely European, examples of narrative ballet. The volume is unique as it shows the unque approach musicologist take toward dance.

Others, such as Sarah Gutsche-Miller, have looked at specific cultural-historical case studies to explore ballet, in this instance looking at the cultural relevance of Parisian Music-Hall Ballet (2015). In theatre and translation, Angela Tiziana Tarantini has explored the performative turn in translation studies by examining a specific practice research example situated in theatre practice (2021). More broadly in the arts and humanities, the book by the late Daniel Albright, *Panaesthetics* (2014), continues to engage with language and the mapping of the arts through the ways in which we think and perceive the different arts via our different senses. In the volume, he explores the notion of ekphrasis, whereby there is 'an intermedial translation – a pseudomorphosis' (ibid., 120). Significant to the concept of translation in the context of art, is that he identifies that something is lost in translation: 'a residue of the untranslatable if left [...] The translation is a falsification – but a falsification without which art could not exist' (ibid., 219). Albright's view of multimedia in the arts speaks alongside the multimodal semiotic work of the late Gunther Kress, who expanded the notion of translation to consider transformation and transmutation, discussed later. I am personally grateful to both Daniel and Gunther for their support over the years and for being able to share my ideas with them as my own work on translation and the arts has developed. Without them, this volume would not exist.

It is also significant to note that doctoral research is expanding in this field, often housed in music theory departments in the USA. Recent PhDs include Rachel Short, 'Musical Feet: The Interaction of Choreography and Music in Leonard Bernstein and Jerome Robbins' Ballet Fancy Free' (2016) and Jacob Fitzpatrick, 'Stravinsky, Balanchine, and Agon: An Intersection of Musical Movement and Dance' (2020). Both take well-known choreographers and composers to explore how these creative artists collaborate. Although their work is not specifically pitched in terms of translation, the processes of exchange and transfer are shared with the theories presented in this volume.

Many recent publications also actively engage with this translational turn, including most notably: *Translation and Multimodality: Beyond Words*, edited by Monica Boria et al. (2020), which redefines translation to chart multiple modes of communication at the same time; *Opera in Translation: Diversity and Unity*, edited by Adriana Serban and Kelly Chan (2020), which explores the wider reaches of translation from the libretto, to surtitles, to meaning, to movement, to set design, across sociocultural and historical periods; the third volume of *Tibon: Estudios Traductoloicos*, edited by Celia Martín de León and Gisela Marcelo Wirnitzer, which focuses specifically on the multimodal experience in the everyday (2021); and *Intersemiotic Perspectives on Emotions: Translating across Signs, Bodies and Values*, edited by Susan Petrilli and Meng Ji, which charts intersemiotic translation in music, film and other forms of artistic performance (2022). These volumes have brought together a wider network with dialogue reaching across translation studies, multimodal studies, cultural theory, music, dance, film studies, philosophy, psychology and literature studies. Working in this field of music and translation, it has been a personal interest to contribute to each of the above volumes (Minors 2019, 2021, 2022), and to bring together here a series of conversations which supplement this debate by focusing specifically on dance.

As the above recent activities evidence, translation in the context of music and the wider arts moves beyond the three well-established areas of translation (interlingual, intralingual and intersemiotic) (Jakobson 1959) and moves to advance the questions to different translation modes in an overtly multimodal context. This book celebrates that multimodal context. It projects translation across cultures (intercultural dialogue as projected through music-dance works), senses (recognizing and challenging the process of translation when the audio-visual divide impacts on the creative and receptive process of new works) and languages (referring not only to verbal language but also to bodily gestural language and musical language, by analogy). The multidimensional and multisensory requirement of translation is supported by Cronin, who states that: 'All the five senses can be pressed into the service of understanding' (2020: 76–7). In an age where translation studies is expanding to include adaptation studies, multimodal theory and intercultural research, research into translation in the context of the performing arts is pressing and necessary.

As the focus is unavoidably interdisciplinary, the volume draws on musicologists and musicians, dance scholars and choreographers, curators and museum/third-sector professionals, academics and linguists, deliberately to ensure a diverse range of voices from within this interdisciplinary field can speak collectively to the core questions, from their positions and experiences, to share the rich work in this field. In some instances, the authors here wear two hats, as musician and performer, as curator and dancer, as archivist and academic. This ensures that the experiential, somatic and lived experience of this field can be shared as an integral part of the research. The range of voices is therefore pluralistic, to demonstrate the impact of this field of study across music, dance, performing arts, translation, multimodal studies, media studies and cultural studies. Research originates from various cultures, countries and archives, from theatre archives in Canada, the USA, UK, Estonia and France, notably including collaboration with professional choreographers and designers. As such, this book speaks to a diverse disciplinary readership, including those in translation and multimodal studies, those in music and dance, as well as those within communication studies, cultural studies and beyond in the arts and humanities.

Aims and Chapter Outlines

In taking the next steps in the research of translation in the context of music and dance, this book is divided into four parts, enabling the volume to collectively represent a diverse range of perspectives which encompass, in Part One, 'Translation and Dance', the central aims and questions before a conversation piece which explores how translation is relevant to the dance reconstruction work of dance historians Millicent Hodson and Kenneth Archer. Chapter 2, 'The Role of Translation in the Practice of Dance Reconstruction', focuses on a conversation I had with Hodson and Archer, and explores the ways in which dance reconstruction is a process of translation in a multimodal, multidimensional project. Lived experience of archival work, interviews, dance reconstruction work to production, are shared to illustrate the processes Hodson and Archer take to establish each of their reconstruction works.

Part Two, 'Gestures Between Music and Dance', presents case studies from musicologists and choreomusicologists to shows the points of contact and negotiation between these arts forms. Chapter 3, 'Bases for Translations between Music and Dance', written by Lawrence M. Zbikowski, explores how music and movements are thoroughly connected and that these media utilize our inherent ability to interpret across modes through analogy. To illustrate this chapter, Zbikowski explores examples from choreographers Mark Morris and Twyla Tharp as illustrations of choreographers rediscovering and working with the resources offered by music. Chapter 4, 'Interactions and Correspondences between Music/Sound and Dance/Movement as Permanent Negotiations of Translation Processes' by Stephanie Schroedter, takes the specific example of the performance installation *Eadweard's Ear – Muybridge extended* (2017) under the artistic direction of Penelope Wehrli and musician/computer scientist Joa Glassteller. Schroedter explains translation as grounded by constraints, resistances and latencies, and asks whether the sound creations were initiated by the movement or vice versa, or whether the creative process was one of continual negotiation. In Chapter 5, 'Collaborative Ballet Dialogues in Translation and Creating *La Parade* (1917) in Paris', I explore the evidence of the collaborative creative process to chart how composer, choreographer, designer and librettist were constantly utilizing a process of translation to mediate and interpret each other's contributions to the production, to bring the work, through some troublesome issues, to fruition. Minors seeks to show how the artists are aware of this translation process and cites from letters, reflections and memories to show that the artists, a lot like Hodson and Archer (Chapter 2) were very much aware of the need for translation as a collaborative process.

Part Three, 'Translation through Music-Dance Performance', explores three case studies to illustrate translation in the production of the performance. Chapter 6, 'Maurice Béjart's Variations on Wilde's *Salome* and Kinetic Translation of Words and Music in *La Mort subite* (1991) and *Boléro* (1960)', by Juliette Loesch, explores how Béjart's choreographic practice is essentially musical, with reference to his memoire, and the chapter illustrates this through specific examples drawn from *Salome, Bolero* and *La Mort subite*. In Chapter 7, 'The Music has Movement in It', Lesley Main examines the role of translation in staging a work, specifically in reassessing the relationship between music and choreography. She uses two case studies, to explore the notion of intersemiotic translation between music and dance: *Passacaglia* (1938), Humphrey's landmark work set to J. S. Bach's *Passacaglia and Fugue in C minor*, alongside *With My Red Fires* (1936), set to a score by Humphrey's contemporary, Wallingford Reigger, which was notably composed after the choreography was complete. Chapter 8, 'Cranko's Reinvention of Pushkin's Text in his Ballet *Onegin* (1965)', by Anna Ponomareva, explores John Cranko's ballet *Onegin*. She treats it as a multimodal version of Pushkin's novel in verse *Eugene Onegin* (1830s) and Tchaikovsky's opera *Eugene Onegin* (1879). In so doing, Ponomareva frames the case study in relation to paratextual studies to analyse Tatiana's letter scene, referencing many critics and illustrating how the novel is reinvented through dance and music as an intersemiotic translation. Notably, she illustrates that the style of the author, from the source text, can be preserved in the performance of the target text.

Part Four, 'Institutional Representation: Notation, Archives and the Museum', shares three further case studies of work which relies on curation and archives to access and translate that work. Chapter 9, 'Two National Estonian Ballet

Translations of Theodor Amadeus Hofmann's *Coppélia* to Leo Délibes' Music by Mauro Bigonzetti (2002) and Ronald Hynd (2010)', by Heili Einasto, illustrates how Bigonzetti interprets this ballet in terms of the current century, bringing the production to a contemporary audience and setting. Einasto questions the artistic choices and suggests the approaches shown here are prophetic in terms of future artistic policy. Denise Merkle in Chapter 10, 'Fruitful Intersemiotic Transfers between Music and Choreography in the National Ballet of Canada's *Romeo and Juliet*', charts how the choreographer, in collaboration with ballet master and dancers, transforms music into narrative dance. She examines choreographical memory, choreology as ballet text and translation between texts, as well as the transference and dialogue between the modes of music and dance. Chapter 11, 'Dancing Symbols: Movement Notation as a Form of Translation', by Mary Wardle, tackles dance notation as a translation practice, and reassesses how dance notation sets about translating physical movement into written form by analysing the systems of Labanotation and Benesh Movement Notation.

A Theory of Translation for Music, Dance and the Arts

Translation is important to art, as it enables us to reassess how the sense and content of one mode can be transferred to another mode, to another art form. It enables us to relook at text set to music, to dance choreographed to pre-existing music, and more. As I noted in the first volume, *Music, Text and Translation* (2013b: 1), translation is no longer limited to the notion of language transfer, and is in fact vital to all forms of expression and artistic communication. If we speak through sound or movement, then we are speaking in gestures, and every connection and interpretation relies on a dynamic process of interpretation which is analogous to translation.

Translation could be a very broad concept as a result, but what we look at here in this volume is the process of translation, the move from the source text to the target text, across modes (Kress 2010). We look at the notion of translation as intersemiotic (Jakobson 1959) and multimodal (Kress 2010; Minors 2019). By considering the process of how meaning, an idea, the sense of something can be transferred between modes, we are asking ourselves as scholars, artists and practitioners to interrogate the connections between dance and translation, in a volume where all the dance works utilize music, and the underlining argument comes from the field of music and translation. When Albright questioned, 'can music aspire to more precise kinds of translation' (2014: 163), and interestingly, this is a question he also asked in a previous volume in 2009, he is looking at transference between modes (Minors 2020a and 2020b) but is also raising awareness that exactitude is not the aspiration, but rather the understanding of the processes of collaboration and multimodal communication which is of concern. In other words, there is always a dynamic interplay between artists, between audiences and the work, and between the modes. In order to reassess that dynamic interplay, the consideration of translation offers a new lens to dance scholars, and musicians, and offers a new perspective for translation scholars exploring multimodality.

Since the publication of the first book, theories of music and translation have advanced much. For my own work, I have looked at translation and opera, translation and dance, and translation and film. All the examples have music as one of the elemental features of the work. Following on from the Arts and Humanities Research Council Network, Translating Music, led by Lucile Desblache and Helen Julia Minors (2013–14), I developed research on how an intercultural dialogue was created, through a lens of translation, in a new version of *A Midsummer Night's Dream*, which utilized the original Shakespeare, Mendelsohn's musical setting and Britten's operatic setting, with modernized Italian translation and a multimedia wall, as part of the Macerata Opera Festival. By 'incorporating multiple attributes' (Minors 2016: 417), across multiple artistic modes, combined with sung English and German, sung and spoken Italian and surtitles in English and Italian, the work was actively 'speaking across cultures' (ibid., 426). The spectator had to be dynamic in meditating their experience of the multimodal, multilingual and multicultural elements. In this example, it was clear that '[t]he meaning of the text act[ed] as an intercultural catalyst for the composers [and other artistic collaborators]' (ibid., 428). The definition I have then of an intercultural performance is similar to that of the concept of artistic translation, in that the artistic work presents a combination of modes (and languages), 'operating across and through the characteristics of each other, in dialogue' (ibid., 428).

There are some very specific challenges in theatre translation, in opera and in dance, due to the multiple semiotic systems at play, existing side by side, in dialogue and in combination. This led me to expand the above case study to propose that opera itself is a mode of translation (Minors 2020a: 13). I described the opportunities for assessing this process as a transactional process (ibid., 14): this now seems like a limited view, as not everything is transferred, exchanged or retained, and as Albright notes, the art form needs this 'falsification' (Albright

2014) in order to leave room for creativity and for the attributes of each mode to speak for themselves (after Dayan, 2011, who asserted that each art needs to assert its own individuality). What this work revealed is that translation can operate in many directions, and that the 'directionality of translation is diverse' especially in multimodal contexts (Minors 2020a: 21). This directionality distinguishes opera and dance works from other modes of translation (ibid., 30–1).

The above ideas all develop from the translational turn within art and culture reception, and from the more recent performative turn in translation studies, and from the multimodal turn which has happened only in the last decade (Minors 2020a: 11–17). In exploring music and dance in translation, I proposed three lens of translation, those being languages, senses and cultures (ibid., 158). Dance exists across many of the modes identified by Kress in discussion of multimodal translation, not least including image, writing, music, gesture, speech, moving image, soundtrack and the body (Kress 2010: 79). As such, translation in this dance context 'invites us to explore the ways in which music and dance speak to each other, the ways they adopt each other's processes or contrast the other in a way that formulates an active dialogue across the arts' (Minors 2019: 163). In translating sense, one might be seeking coherence of experience between modes. In exploring language, one is looking at analogy and analogical thought. In considering culture and intercultural exchanges, there is a migration of content from one context to another, such as reimagining a setting. In many of these previous texts, I have asked where music and dance, or music and the other arts, meet. I do not mean physically of course but in terms of their creative intersection, their ability to exchange, to create friction, to combine, to separate and still remain part of the same cohesive work and artistic experience. In essence then, '[t]ranslation is a bringing together, not a separation' (ibid., 175) for the purposes of scholars, practitioners and so on.

If opera, dance and multimodal forms on stage are relevant to translation, then so too is film. If we have moved from the translational turn to a performative and multimodal turn in translation studies, then the fact that different art forms speak as one deserves more analysis (Minors 2023: 332–3). There is a place, between the arts, in the creative process, within the trace of the work, and within the reception of the work. That betweenness is of interest in a translation perspective. Bachmann-Medick's claim that we have had a translational turn (2009: 2) is reliant on the fact that we are now invited to interrogate the relational assertions of these multimodal attributes in a work (Minors 2023: 336). Translation not only happens within a mode, it also happens between those modes, in the gaps of what we see, hear, feel and sense in many ways (ibid., 338).

Or, as I concluded in analysing translation of emotions in a film music context, '[w]e translate what we see, hear and experience' (ibid., 432) in order for these multimodal attributes to make sense in a holist embodied manner.

Beyond the multimodal turn in translation studies, encouraging more scholars to explore translation beyond that of textual language, translation does offer artists and scholar new ways to interpret practice, performance and meaning. But that means we also need to consider the concept as a definition and its limitation and its myths. 'Translation ... refers to the process of how meanings, content and senses are transferred from one medium to another' (Minors 2022: 171). We must therefore recognize that 'there is a distinction between the language translation of inter and intralingual translation and that of translation as a concept, which in some ways is used as a metaphor of a process of exchange and transfer' (ibid., 171) throughout all existences of the art work, whether creative, exploratory, trace and printed, recorded, live, interpreted or remembered. To explore this, I have set out seven myths in my article on translation and multimodality. Those are: (1) music and other performance arts are not universal languages, they are contextually specific; (2) something is always lost in translation, and that is not a limitation but a necessary feature of these modes and what allows them to be art; (3) translation is not only language proper but is also a process we can use to foster analogical thinking; (4) music, dance, film, in some ways need no translation, we can appreciate it, but it can help us analyse, learn, explore and engage in a dynamic manner; (5) the translator is never invisible and silent, the person and people bring modes together to speak as one is in fact bringing their voice, their context, culture and identity to the work; (6) music does not only require hearing, it also requires feeling, sensing, and in a dance context, seeing – and vice versa; (7) knowledge comprehension is not only contained in words and should not only be considered knowledge if it is written or spoken in language. In fact, as I claim elsewhere, artistic research, and practice, can present new knowledge without words (Blain and Minors 2020). As such, the translation process in a collaborative multimodal work needs to acknowledge the position of each artist, their context, culture, ideas, recognizing meaning and gesture as combing together in a work which only achieves its full potential and creative glory once the multimodal elements are brought together in a single setting, such as a dance performance where there is also a venue, a scene, music, dancers, artistic, stage hands and so on. The list can be endless and not all elements are needed on each occasion.

Translation in this volume is used as a concept for us to consider the processes of those involved in the dance work, whether as a dance notator, a dancer, a choreographer, a researcher, an archivist, a historian and so on. Because there is some prior work on these issues in music and choreomusical studies, this volume starts with scholars in those fields before significantly moving to scholars from translation studies writing about dance works. Translation is therefore both intersemiotic, in the sense of Jakobson (1959), and multimodal (Kress 2010). It brings together the modes, and maps them through dynamic creative exchanges. The unique and distinctive artistic elements (features of each mode) are brought together (whether in consonance or dissonance). Together these modes move the message (the work, the aesthetic, the narrative, the idea) from the collective senders (the creative artists, those collaborating together) to the receivers (the audiences, the downloaders and spectators). At every level then, there is a mapping in questioning how these elements come together. Or, how they meet in space, in place, in time, in gesture, in a theatre, in a manuscript, in a recording and so on. In what follows then, each author sets out their own case study to illustrate the role of translation in their context. These contexts are deliberately diverse and deliberately bring dance scholars, music scholars and translation scholars together with archivists to show the diversity of the field and to speak to the same diverse audiences. The book does not repeat the musical content of the first volume though, and focuses on dance and translation.

2

The Role of Translation in the Practice of Dance Reconstruction

Helen Julia Minors, in conversation with Millicent Hodson
and Kenneth Archer

In exploring the concept of translation in relation to music and dance, it is necessary to explore a wider range of contexts throughout the book, from scholars and theorists analysing dance and music interrelations, to those exploring the performance element, to those working in the realms of notation, archives and museums. But there is also the vital part concerning the creative art of putting on the dance performance, and in particular, in reconstructing a historically significant performance of a balletic work. Dance reconstruction has been a vital area which has supported the revival of work in the theatre, such as *Le sacre du printemps* (originally staged by Sergei Diaghilev's Ballets Russes in 1913), to works such as *Skating Rink* (originally staged in 1922 by Rolf de Marie's Ballets Suédois). Both of these named examples were the results of long and hard creative work by two significant people, Millicent Hodson (who is a choreographer, a graphic artist and a dance historian) and Kenneth Archer (an art historian and scenic consultant). They have worked as a creative partnership for over three decades and had the results of their work performed across the globe. Together they have developed many publications, a series of bijoux books and five films, as well as videos of rehearsals and performances.

As a music and dance scholar, I had the privilege of seeing their work at Roehampton University, when working across music and dance, and since then have seen the results of their work and their education events, and had the opportunity to have many conversations over the last seventeen or so years. On starting this work, the second collection of essays related to the issues of translation and music, now with a focus on dance (previously with a focus on text, Minors 2013), it seems appropriate and exciting to speak with these two wonderful creative and supportive people. At first, we discussed a preface for the book, but following email correspondence, we mutually decided to meet for a structured conversation, which I would lead with a series of questions and prompts, that we audio-recorded. It was then transcribed, to enable me to put together this written version of the conversation.[1] The reason this is a dialogue chapter is not to blur voices, but to facilitate the voices of these two creative artists, in bringing out their experiences of working with dance and why they feel their work is analogous to translation.

The chapter deliberately takes their voices as a sole example (arguably narrowly, but arguably unique, in allowing the creative side of their work to be presented for consideration), rather than contextualizing the approach, as the other chapters do, to offer their voices as freely as possible. This is in recognition of the fact that we find much written about the reconstruction work of leading artists such as Alexei Ratmansky and Doug Fullington, but beyond short pieces in the press, many academic writings refer to their work but often little of their own voices are heard.

The personal tone here from Hodson and Archer is intended. In the structured conversation, I explored four key areas for discussion: redefining what reconstruction meant; exploring some of the problems and processes of the work; setting out the various source materials needed to be able to complete such reconstructions; and, of course, outlining the ways in which reconstruction not only might be seen as an act of translation, but also as the ways in which Hodson and Archer talk about their work in such terms. In what follows, I use italicized text to represent the words of Hodson and Archer. I reference the transcription (which consists of 80 pages) to give a sense of where the comments arose within what was a two-hour conversation in the outside gardens of Burgh House in North London. We met in person, after a delay, following the second lock-down of the Covid Pandemic in the UK, and remained socially distanced, having arrived masked. I note the context as the planned schedule for the book was delayed due to the closure of certain archives and the impact of Covid on the many authors in the volume. This was one of the first outings in a public setting, so our enthusiasm to be back in person discussing our love of dance works no doubt informed the tone of the conversation. But it must be noted that this conversation comes after years of discussions, within public events, education events and even within a few dance-focused garden parties at friends' houses. Thanks go here to Stephanie Jordan who first introduced me to Millicent and Kenneth in 2004, at an event as part of the Sound Moves conference hosted at Roehampton University, London. The conversation flowed easily and as anyone who has had the pleasure of meeting Hodson and Archer, they often complete each other's sentences and speak in enthusiastic and easy tones about the joy of their career.

Reconstruction, or Recreation, or Translation?

To reconstruct a historical ballet production is to work as *an anthropologist, an archaeologist, a dance historian, an art historian* (p. 48), as well as to look at the overall *architecture of the theatre and the production* (p. 36). To start the process of making a reconstruction one *starts with deconstruction* (p. 12). The process is slow and detailed, exploring the different modes, from another time and another culture. There is a clear goal, to stage the production as close to the original as possible, but to get to this final stage, it requires *us to become dance detectives* (p. 14), in questioning every possible source. As a partnership, Hodson and Archer are *problem driven* (p. 14). Of course, the aspirational aim to be *as close as possible* (p. 12) to the original is *impossible* (p. 12). But the aspiration is a driving force, and it encourages *a creative act* (p. 12) in finding solutions to problems where the answers cannot be found. *To me interpretation is a creative act, I never saw reconstruction as anything other than a creative act* (p. 12).

To formulate a reconstruction and stage it is to formulate *as close as possible* (p. 12) a version of the ballet which is *informed by* (p. 13) as much evidence as possible. *I mean what we do, we look at everything, music, design, the choreography, and everything around it, everything connected, all the contemporary magazines* (p. 8). There are multiple ways to capture evidence of a performance and *to express that memory* (p. 4), through drawings, interviews, archival work, looking at old costumes, programme notes, lists of names, rehearsal plans and so on. The key feature is to *speak with witnesses* of the original events, those *who experienced the performance* (p. 15). It is, as we discussed together, like peeling back an onion to *search for as much information as possible* (p. 14). Essentially the reconstruction becomes *the reasonable facsimile* (p. 12).

The Act of Translation

Translation as a process is *evidence based* (p. 18). As Alexei Ratmansky studied the score, and all evidence in reconstructing Petipa's 1890 production of *Sleeping Beauty*, by reading the notated score in detail and learning the content, they 'pored over old photographs and illustrations [...] they] were steeped in the dance culture of Petipa's time' (French et al. 2020: 79), so too is the process for Hodson and Archer. Considering reconstructions to be acts of translation is nothing new, indeed, Marian Smith cites a number of examples whereby emotions are, such as wit, are 'translated into pirouettes' and whereby the production was historically labelled as a 'choreographic translation' (Smith 2000: 77). In reconstructing a production, it is necessary *to look at everything* (p. 8), and to hear multiple voices. As such, in the process of reconstruction, Hodson and Archer *are enabling people to translate their experience, to share their memories, to share with us* (p. 16) details of the production we can use to make informed judgements about the detail of any reconstruction. Beyond the photographs, the letters, the notes, the rehearsal annotations, the score, the costumes, it is necessary to remember that these *people were there* (p. 16), they lived through this *experience* (p. 4) and could hold any small matrix not captured anywhere else. An example we discussed, which shows how *clues were found everywhere* (p. 10), was when Hodson and Archer got the opportunity to meet with the cor anglais orchestral player from the original premiere of *Le sacre du printemps* (1913). Despite at first the player noting that he could not see anything so could not comment on the dance, they requested that the musician describe his memory, to ensure they *heard his experience, and shared his memory as a witness to the event* (p. 61). The musician *described the noise* (p. 61) which *we first considered to be the shouting* and the orchestra, but on probing, he outlined the *pounding sound from the dancers*, not only their feet, *the pounding sound of their bodies* (p. 61). The realization was that the dancers were using body percussion. This *totally changes the understanding doesn't it?* (p. 62), it *reveals other possibilities* (p. 61).

The excitement in these reflections is clear in their tone but what is striking for the purposes of this book is that the language used, and the reflections speak to the process of translation, which seeks culturally informed contextual evidence to ensure any move from a source text to a target text, is as authentic as possible. In discussing authenticity as an aim and aspiration, it was clear that the reconstructed performance might even be *more authentic than the original* (p. 35). But how is this possible? Not every aspect of the original performance was always possible at the time due to budgets and technological limitations, so in documenting the premiere production, if something could not be done which now could be, *we realized it* in the reconstruction (p. 35). *We try to discover the original intention* (p. 35).

Something is always *gained as well as lost in translation* (p. 21) in the search for evidence and detail. Where something is *lost* it requires us to *intercede* (p. 33) which is why reconstruction is also a *creative translation* (p. 16). In enabling others to *translate their experience* (p. 16) the role of the reconstruction is to *ensure integration* (p. 16) of what all the *witnesses recall, integrating all this evidence* (p. 65). At every level of the journey, *two proofs of everything* (p. 12), *two pieces of evidence are required* (p. 9), especially due to the *time travel* (p. 9) that is necessary when looking at historical documents.

As part of the translation process, it is important for *us to be close to the texts, to use transcription, to draw, to reflect, to try to experience the work* (p. 4). In the *world of texts* (p. 65) that are collated in bringing together *multi-perspectives and voices* (p. 2) and as many *witnesses as possible* (p. 3), we must ensure that the *quotes given to us by those witnesses who survived* (p. 3) are transmitted through the production to the new audience. We discussed how sources can be hidden or lost. As such, the reconstruction will never be exactly the same as the original, so there is a process, that in accepting a *reasonable facsimilie* (p. 12), *we go back and put new material into the production to correct it* when new sources come along (p. 21). This happened with La Chatte, during a production in Montreal with Les Grandes Ballets Canadiens (p. 64). The company director found, just before the opening, an original stage photograph with proof of key choreography and special use of props. He presented it to us as a premiere gift. It is striking that they are never downtrodden, but accept that new information will come along and, rather than grumble, they were back in the studio the day after to ensure the second performance was as accurate as it could be. This is why they urge that they *have two pairs of eyes and ears on everything* (p. 64) to make sure that their different disciplinary perspectives help to inform the final production. They constantly check in with each other, sharing work as they go. *So originally it was lost in translation but then it was corrected* (p. 23). This continual process and openness to new material is commendable and necessary to realize their aim of as much authenticity as possible in reconstruction.

Translation, like dance reconstruction, is creative, but we *translate in a different way* (p. 35) *to ensure everything is dancer friendly* (p. 37). Because *what was intended but not originally realized* (p. 34) can be included in their reconstructions, the question of the *authenticity of the production* (p. 35) is significant. Experiencing the production through the voices of many witnesses, their role is like that of the *conductor with the dancers*, a *translation process* of *give and take* (p. 56). The orchestra relies on the eyes, not only the ears of the conductor within the balletic setting. *The maestro is the conduit, just as, in a broader sense, the instructors are* (p. 56).

There are always problems in translation, whether that is language translation across eras, cultures and nations, to ensure the target text can be understood in terms of the original, or whether translating across modes, to ensure the result is effective and can be produced in performance. In reference to the problems of creating a reconstruction, Hodson and Archer note that *it is a conundrum* especially as *each one, each performance, is an original* (p. 19), each relying on specific bodies, specific theatres, to bring the work together. This is why, in their bijoux book series and in their many publications they attempt to *show the chronology* of the evidence and the production, as that ordering can inform how things were *changed and developed* (p. 19). As such, their process of translation, as Hodson and Archer do name it, is *a creative translation* (p. 16), which produces *a reasonable facsimile* (p. 12), that is *as authentic as possible* (p. 35).

Source Materials: Finding Two Points of Evidence for Everything

The level of detail Hodson and Archer search for is commendable, not only from archives across the globe, but also in prioritizing the *witnesses* (p. 3) to these events, those who watched the events and performed in them. The *importance of the reviews* (p. 10) also cannot be underestimated. In *Skating Rink*, for example, because of its *extreme style* (p. 15), reviews had to *add detail* (p.14) beyond the usual description of traditional ballet in favour of commenting on the *spectator experience* (p. 10) of something so new. Hodson and Archer understand that such reviewers have added something to the evidence, not just repeated what was seen, and so have doubly informed the reconstruction. In this way, the reviews are looked at in the manner in which the *reviewers have to add something to the evidence, not only repeat it* (p. 14) to inform the reconstruction. In *sharing the memories* (p. 3), *witnesses are vital* (p. 3), transmitting their own embodied experience. In that way they are *a living archive* (p. 3).

Of course, in searching so many sources and voices, there will inevitably be multiple perspectives, which is why reconstruction requires much *checking, joining, verifying* (p. 10) across at least two sources of evidence. In working with Joffrey, staging *Le sacre du printemps two points of evidence* were not only found and integrated, but questioned: *how do they connect?* (p. 10). For Hodson and Archer, whenever viable in any reconstruction, speaking to the original dancers is critical: to understand muscle memory, to hear it *from the body* that danced it (p. 10). Likewise, they look at rehearsal photographs to see body gestures, which though stuck in time, often showed *completely different content* (p. 5), as in the case of reconstructing George Balanchine's *Le Chant du Rossignol* (originally staged by Massine in 1920, then staged by Balanchine in 1925). *A photograph of the Emperor, his prostrated court and stylized protectors revealed the transformation of the arch-antagonist into a key figure of the apotheosis. The Japanese Maestro, who brought the toxic mechanical nightingale that made the Emperor ill is now hidden behind him to make a sunburst halo of hands that bestow well-being* (ibid.).

A key source to the reconstruction process are also the letters: *what would I have done without Stravinsky's letters, Helen, they were vital* (p. 70). The letters of the composers, choreographers and those who performed give us eyewitness accounts of some of the rehearsals, framing how the production was developing: *that's how we know how the Old Women, the Witch, moves* (p. 70) in Le sacre du printemps. In using such sources though one first needs to establish a few things: the context of the letter, not only when it was sent but what is being discussed, and second one needs to understand the *style awareness* of the writer (p. 20), are they informed, an expert, are they a passing witness, are they a dancer embodying what is being written about. The letter can reveal *their processes* (p. 29) and reveal something *immediate* (p. 32) from the time which is different to the concrete evidence of costumes and photographs in archives.

Proof of how the body is used, though, is as crucial as the context the letters provide, especially when considering Nijinsky and Le sacre. It is necessary to ask of the choreographer and the dance how they are unique, for example: *What is so distinctive about Nijinsky?* (p. 13) And in considering his process of choreographing *you realize he's taking gestures from the individual body and translating those gestures into the small group; and translating those gestures into the whole ground pattern. There is this evolution of constricted design and that constriction breaks amazingly free by multiplication. So, the multiplication is really his goal* (p. 13). In searching for more evidence to this premise Hodson and Archer found a little-known journal called La Feu from 1913 which also discussed multiplication. *It is almost like Indiana Jones, the secret is there for you to find out where to find the secret* (p. 13).

This immediacy is a key concern for Hodson and Archer. They have had access to archives, museums and galleries across the globe, always *sending letters in advance* (p. 26), even when it meant they *started at the bottom* as they had done everywhere else, when in one particular setting, in Russia, they *should have started at the top* (p. 26). They speak warmly of all the archivists, librarians, theatre directors and performers they have had the opportunity to meet. They are keenly aware that each has a specific positionality in regard to the reconstruction, and hear the witness statement clearly and take note, but use each testament only when it is supported by a second piece of evidence, ensuring always that, as noted, *two pieces of evidence are required* (p. 9) for everything, to ensure authenticity. This has meant not including some items where only one piece of evidence has been shown. This is also a way to mitigate any bias or loss of detail *through memory* and *in history* (p. 9). The presence of the people involved is significant, unlike some archives where time is needed to collect one item and then another; instead, there is *immediacy of the people* when interviewing them (p. 32). It is full on and intense, it is impassioned and fast-paced, much as the recorded conversation I am drawing on here, with side comments, tangents and reflections across not only artwork but lived experiences.

The Reasonable Facsimile

In remembering a situation whereby a photograph was given to them after a premiere of a performance, they told me of a letter that was written with it, which outlined the world of reconstruction: *Reconstructing a ballet is rather like getting sardines out of a sardine tin, there is always a little bit left in the corner which you can't get* (p. 22).

In making the *reasonable facsimile* (p. 12), or rather in staging the reconstruction, there is much knowledge not only of the source material pertaining to the production, but also of the wider artistic journey of those involved, of the culture and the era. For example, it was vital to *look at the fashion model poses and the things that were being advertised. All these things are related to the cultural context of what we were doing* (p. 8). There *was a whole school of fashion drawing* which informed their understanding of the costume design changes and developments (p. 16). Going beyond only the archival material to the *living archive* of the people (p. 3) was balanced with printed material of the era: *the fashion magazines were really important to us for choreography* (p. 16). Such contextual awareness in the reconstruction process aligns with how translation studies encourage a culturally informed approach to translation. How Hodson and Archer work – seeking multiple points of evidence, incorporating multiple voices and checking each piece of evidence, cross-referencing it to another – is testament to a critical form of translation, in this sense an artistic and historical translation to resurrect a work from the past for current live performance. In a sense, the result is a way to understand a work from within, through performance. The emphasis is at every turn, on lived experience and on live performance practice.

In discussing examples of previous reconstructions and how they were formulated, it became clear how the method of Hodson and Archer parallels translation language and processes. In fact, translation itself was often mentioned, as shown above. Beyond seeing themselves as translators, Hodson and Archer observed – in the artists they researched and interviewed – translators as well. In discussing the relationship between Stravinsky and Diaghilev, it was important *to realise that Stravinsky was directed by Diaghilev and that Diaghilev had the knowledge to do so. How to do things. He understood ... Talk about translation in action* (p. 63).

Translation is important to reconsidering processes of artistic creation, as we spend so much time as scholars and creative artists' activity interpreting each other. *And translation just suggests a different kind of responsibility doesn't it?* (p. 18). We have discussed that responsibility at length over the years: the responsibility to be faithful to the source text in producing the target text, to keep something of the original sense of the work. The responsibility is to the original creators and to the next audiences, to ensure the sense, the messages, the aesthetic, of the original is carried forward to the new performance context. It is clear that Hodson and Archer feel this responsibility keenly in all they do, ensuring only to engage with something in practice when evidence has been found in at least two places/sources, and often in more. As a translator works for evidence in the source text (Jakobson 1959), so do these creative artists, the difference is the source text is not a single textual document, or a single performance, but remnants of many artefacts, including scores, photographs and so on. *So there you are, we have translated it* [a work] *but in a different way* (p. 35). This statement is not flippant. Rather, it represents the process they go by, which seeks out the source text (to use terms from translation studies), in all its details, before moving it from one mode (the various artefacts) into a live mode (that of the performance) for its target text (Kress 2010). Reconstruction is like translation due to the process it follows and to the aims of the result, to be faithful to the source text. It is *our responsibility* (p. 35) to be as authentic as possible, informed by evidence, in a culturally aware and sensitive approach, which is inclusive to a wide range of witnesses from the *living archive* (p. 3).

Note

1 I wish to thank Sarah Barnard for her hard work and assistance in making the transcription from the audio-recording.

Part Two

Gestures between Music and Dance

3

Points of Contact: Bases for Translations between Music and Dance

Lawrence M. Zbikowski

Let me begin with an example that will illustrate some important points about music, dance and translation: the 'Laudamus te' section of Mark Morris' *Gloria* (first performed in 1981 and revised in 1984). Morris' choreography is often marked by a close correlation between music and movement, with the result that the dance appears to be a visualization of the music. As others have observed, the choreography for 'Laudamus te' practices music visualization on a number of levels (Acocella 1993; Damsholt 2006; Jordan 2015). The most obvious of these is at the level of basic design: two dancers are paired with the music of the two sopranos who sing in this portion of Antonio Vivaldi's composition, and another two dancers are paired with the music of the orchestra that accompanies the singers. There is also music visualization on a much more local level. For instance, when the two dancers who are paired with the sopranos enter to the music shown in Example 3.1, they do so in canon just as do the singers, entering one after the other. More importantly, the dancers match their initial movements to the rhythmic design of the melody, taking a step with each successive note that sounds. As 'Laudamus te' continues, there are numerous instances in which the phrases of the dancers match the phrases of the singers, and in which the dancers describe movements that map smoothly onto the pitch contours sketched by the music. In the passage shown in Example 3.1, for instance, the dancers use sweeping gestures to capture the overall descent of the melody that sets 'Benedicimus de'.[1]

I would like to propose that both kinds of music visualization represent translations between music and dance, although the principles behind these translations are somewhat different. The sort of translation that occurs at the level of compositional design correlates important structural landmarks within the music (such as the return of a theme) with equally important landmarks

Example 3.1 Antonio Vivaldi, *Gloria* (RV 589), 'Laudamus te', bars 17–27, soprano 1 and 2. Text translation: 'We praise thee, we bless thee'.

within the choreography. This strategy can be seen in translations between music and other expressive media. For instance, Milan Kundera noted that his early novels *The Joke* and *Life is Elsewhere* replicate the overall structure of Beethoven's Opus 131 String Quartet (Kundera 1988: 91). The sort of translation that occurs with more specific music visualizations – when, for example, the movements of the dancers are closely correlated with the sequence of pitches sung by the sopranos – is subtly but importantly different. Here, translation relies on a close fit between the communicative resources exploited by each expressive medium: the fact that the events proper to both music and dance happen in time facilitates translating a sequence of events from one into the other.

As I shall explore further over the course of this chapter, both kinds of translation rely on humans' capacity for analogy. The capacity for analogy contributes much to the distinctiveness of human intelligence, and typically involves correlating structure from one domain – usually called the *source* – with another domain – the *target* – in order to structure the understanding of the second domain. This correlation can be thought of as mapping structure from the source onto the target. For example, translations between music and dance that involve basic design rely on mapping specific compositional strategies from music onto choreography. In 'Laudamus te', each time the orchestra plays the *ritornello* the dancers who are correlated with the orchestra enter and criss-cross the stage with a distinctive set of steps; each time the sopranos stop singing, the dancers who are paired with them momentarily halt their movements. As suggested by the design of Kundera's early novels, analogical mapping of this kind is relatively independent of medium and so could be thought of as comparatively abstract. Put more directly, mapping the basic design of a piece of music onto the basic design of a choreography, novel or painting does not involve a fine-grained correlation of temporal events. To be sure, mapping the design from one expressive medium onto another will often involve some sense of 'before' and 'after', but the phenomena that realize the design need not be otherwise constrained by temporal bounds. The translations between media that result will, in consequence, be quite approximate.

The analogical mapping that underpins the visualization of specific musical passages engages more directly with the temporal dimensions and thus the substance of music and dance. Let us return to Example 3.1 to explore this in more detail. As can be seen, the first soprano's melody for 'Lau-da-mus te' opens with a leap from G4 to B4 and then continues in a scalar fashion, arriving on D5 and spanning in total a perfect fifth. When, in Morris' choreography, the first dancer enters, she takes three backward steps, in time with B4 ('da'), C5 ('mus') and D5 ('te'). She then holds, the pause in her movement matching the note sustained by the soprano. The second soprano and the second dancer follow in a similar fashion. With each entrance, the sequence of musical pitches – their initiation, progression and (temporary) conclusion – is directly correlated with a sequence of dance steps. There is, however, one feature of the music that is *not* correlated with the dance: although the music of this short passage ascends to conclude on its highest pitch, each dancer concludes with a dip, momentarily lowering herself toward the floor. Although this might at first seem counterintuitive – surely an ascending movement should be matched with an ascending gesture – what is important here is less the sense of direction and more that of arrival. Within the G major tonality that dominates this section of 'Laudamus te', the arrival on D5 in bar 19 is a moment of temporary repose, one that presages the continuation of the melody in bars 21 and following. In a similar fashion, the dancer's dip toward the floor is a moment of temporary repose that serves as a point of departure for the continuation of her movements in the succeeding steps of the choreography. The translation of music into dance at this moment in Morris' 'Laudamus te' thus involves an incredibly close analogical mapping not simply between isolated events (like the D5 of bar 19 and the step that concludes the dancer's first step-unit) but between entire *sequences* of events.[2] Put another way, the translation relies on correlating the dynamic process proper to the musical phrase with the dynamic process proper to the sequence of dance steps.

The view of translation between music and dance that I would like to develop in this chapter relies in part on a fuller understanding of humans' capacity for analogy and the role this plays in our understanding of music and dance. I also aim to take the idea of translation seriously: as the music and movement for Example 3.1 shows, translations between music and dance have the potential to go beyond straightforward aspects of design and into the substance of each as communicative media.

While the resources for communication offered by music and dance are certainly different from those offered by language, they are no less important within human cultural interactions. To explore these resources, I will draw on my work on musical grammar, which sets out the principles for what cognitive linguistics call a construction grammar. According to this approach to grammar, the basic elements of a communicative medium – called constructions – combine features of both syntax and semantics. In at least some instances, the basic elements of musical grammar have correlates in the basic elements of dance, correlates that represent points of contact between the design features of music and dance, and that thus provide the basis for meaningful translations between the two.

Analogy will be key to this approach, and in the first section that follows I will offer a brief review of recent research on analogy, a description of analogical reference and a sketch of musical grammar that connects with dance practice. The whole will be illustrated with an analysis of a portion of an air and chorus from Georg Friedrich Handel's 1740 secular oratorio *L'Allegro, il Penseroso ed il Moderato*, a work choreographed by Morris in 1988. What emerges from this analysis is not so much translations between music and dance (although there are clear correlations between the two) but instead a more detailed understanding of the role analogy plays in the ways each medium constructs meaning. The second section that follows will turn to Morris' 2006 *Mozart Dances* to explore a moment in which music is translated into dance and to consider some of the consequences such translations have for the construction of meaning. The third, and concluding, section will summarize the overall approach I develop here and endeavour to draw further conclusions about music, dance and translation.

Analogy and Analogical Reference

Analogy

Most discussions of analogy begin with similarity, since it is the similarity of one thing to another that is the point of departure for any analogy. For instance, a pencil and a pen are similar to each other both in appearance and in function, although the kind of marks these tools make on a writing surface (permanent or impermanent; of relatively consistent colouration or subject to gradation) are different. Analogy takes as its point of departure similarity judgements of a more abstract sort. For instance, a finger is analogous to a pen in that it is an approximately cylindrical structure that ends in a point; unlike a pen or pencil, however, the finger leaves no discernible marks on the writing surface and its 'cylinder' is firmly attached to the larger structure of the hand. Making the analogy between a pen and a finger, then, involves drawing structural correlations between the two: the cylindrical shape of the pen maps on to the shape of the digits of the finger, and the point of the pen maps on to the tip of the finger. With the analogy in place, we can imagine using a finger to 'write', or a pen as an extension of our hand. More generally, analogies involve mapping systematic structural relationships between a source domain (such as that which includes writing instruments) and a target domain (such as that which includes bodily appendages) for the purpose of extending knowledge from the source to the target, and – in at least some instances – from the target back to the source (Gentner 1983: 155–70; Gentner and Kurtz 2006: 609–42; Holyoak and Thagard 1995: chapter 2; Holyoak 2005; 117–42).

It bears emphasis that analogy is not simply about correlating elements from one domain with elements in another domain but about mapping relationships between these domains as part of a process of inferential reasoning. It is thus often described as concerned with relations among relations (or 'second-order' relations): in the analogy between a pen and a finger, for instance, the relationship between *pen* and *finely tapered device for delivering ink* (that is, the business-end of the tool) is correlated with the relationship between *finger* and *tapered appendage for guiding communication.*[3] In the case of the brief passage from Morris' choreography for 'Laudamus te' discussed above, then, it is not simply that the steps of the dancers are similar to the progression of musical events. There is instead a close correlation of elements and relations between music and dance. Specific musical pitches are correlated with specific dance steps, and relationships among the pitches (which set out a purposive trajectory from G4 to D5) are correlated with the overall step-unit performed by the dancer (which brings her onto the stage and culminates in her brief downward dip).

Based on the knowledge we currently have humans are the only species that have such a robust capacity for analogical thought. Although other species are able to make some very sophisticated similarity judgments – there is research, for instance, suggesting that chimpanzees can understand the second-order relations basic to analogy (especially for spatial reasoning) and that bottlenose dolphins can perform rather involved body-mapping analogies – current evidence indicates that no other species comes close to making or using analogies with the facility and speed of humans (Call and Tomasello 2005; Herman 2002 275–83; Gentner 2003: 195–235). And this capacity is available from a very early age: children as young as ten months are able to solve problems by analogy (Chen, Sanchez and Campbell 1997: 790–801), and by the age of three years, analogical abilities are quite robust (Goswami 2001: 437–70; Gentner 2003: 195–235).

The ability to map systematic structural relationships between disparate domains bears witness to a capacity for abstract thought – for thinking about relations between relations – of enormous flexibility and wide application. Analogy has been recognized as a key factor in human creativity and has been linked to the conceptual flights of fancy and processes of meaning construction created through metaphor and metonymy (Fauconnier and Turner 2002: 14; Holyoak and Thagard 1995: 213–23). Given evidence of the capacity for analogy demonstrated by primates and pre-linguistic children, it also seems apparent that the conceptual domains involved in analogical mappings need not be restricted to those involving language. Perhaps more importantly, humans' capacity for analogy provides a resource for communication markedly different from that upon which language relies, a resource exploited in unique ways by music and dance: analogical reference.

Analogical reference

It is generally recognized that human language relies on a system of reference that employs what the late nineteenth-century semiotician C. S. Peirce called *symbols* (1955: 112–15). Symbolic reference involves various symbolic tokens – sounds, hand gestures, ink marks, or the like – that are systematically correlated with various referents. If I wish to refer to any one of the woody perennial plants with a single elongate main stem having few branches on its lower part that I see outside my window I could utter a sound, use the appropriate gesture from American Sign Language, or simply write 'tree'. None of these symbolic tokens need share any properties with the thing to which they refer: for example, there does not have to be any relationship between the token for 'tree' in American Sign Language and the shape of a tree. The fact that there *is* such a relationship in American Sign Language does not affect the way the token functions as a symbol, although it may help a user of the language to learn the connection between the token and its referent.

The inherent flexibility of symbolic reference makes it a powerful and versatile tool for communication. As the biologist Terry Deacon has observed in his work on language evolution, it is also a tool that is remarkably complex beneath its seemingly simple surface. Deacon, building on some of the key insights of Peirce's semiotic theory, shows that symbolic tokens can function only as part of a *system* of symbols. Within this system, symbols are connected not only to the things to which they refer but also to each other (Deacon 1997: chapter 3; Deacon 2003: 111–39; Deacon 2006: 21–53). The management of these manifold interconnections places considerable demands on cognitive resources, and Deacon argues that it is for this reason that no other species has been able to make use of symbolic reference with anything like the speed, flexibility, or sophistication typical of humans.

In contrast to this, music, dance and a variety of other non-linguistic communicative media make use of analogical reference. Analogical reference obtains when a token shares structural features with some other entity or phenomenon – this sort of token is what Peirce called an *icon* (Peirce 1955: 104–7). These shared features can then be exploited in the process of human communication, such that the token serves to refer to the other entity or phenomenon.[4] This is, of course, what happens in the brief moment from Morris' choreography for 'Laudamus te' discussed above: the steps made by each dancer refer – through analogical correspondences – to the pitches sung by each soprano.[5]

In most cases, the tokens of analogical reference do not connect with one another (although they may succeed or be juxtaposed with one another), and systems of analogical reference rarely achieve the sophistication and flexibility that typify systems of symbolic representation. When comparing these systems of reference, however, it is important to keep two things in mind. First, each system has its advantages and disadvantages. Because practically anything can serve as a symbolic token, such tokens are fairly easy to produce; the dense systems of reference of which such tokens are a part, however, require considerable effort to establish and learn. By comparison, analogical tokens require rather more effort to produce (to ensure that they have the structural features they share with their referents) but make far fewer demands on interpretation. There is also a contrast between the ways in which each system of reference tends to be used. Symbolic tokens are very useful for picking out objects and events, as well as for characterizing relationships between them. Analogical tokens are less useful in this regard, but they are very good at representing complex spatial relationships and summoning dynamic processes that unfold over time. The second thing that should be kept in mind about these systems of reference is that, while language most typically relies on symbolic reference and non-linguistic media rely on analogical reference, the employment of either system need not be exclusive. Language can quite readily make use of analogical reference (as onomatopoeia and, more generally, work on sound symbolism suggest (Hinton, Nickols and Ohala 1994: 1–12; Anderson 1998), and non-linguistic media can, in at least some cases, make use of the networks of interrelated tokens that underpin symbolic reference.

The communicative resources offered by analogical reference have been of central importance to the theory of musical construction grammar I have developed over the past few years. Again, this perspective supposes that grammatical units combine form and function. Musicians have long recognized that certain arrangements of musical materials – that is, musical materials with a particular *form* – are basic to the production of coherent musical utterances.[6] A straightforward example, ubiquitous in Western music of the sixteenth through nineteenth centuries, is the cadence, which is used to mark the temporary or final close of a musical utterance. On the account I have developed, the *function* of a cadence is to serve as a sonic analogue for the process of arrival. Put another way, the contrapuntal, harmonic and rhythmic features of a properly constituted cadence refer, analogically, to the embodied experience of reaching a goal. More generally, the function of musical constructions is to provide sonic analogues for dynamic processes that have been important for human cultures, including analogues for emotion processes, physical gestures and the steps of social dances (Zbikowski 2017: chapter 1). Before continuing, I should note that I am concerned here with the *basic* functions of music within human cultures. To be sure, the functions of music can be much more complex than those I have identified here (as much of the music created over the past hundred years might suggest). That said, I would like to propose that even the most abstract and cerebral music can still tap in to the more concrete and worldly functions I have outlined here.

I have previously described close relationships between music and dance in the dance practice of the *ancien régime* and the early nineteenth-century Viennese waltz, but the emphasis in those cases was, for the most part, on how music could analogically refer to the steps of dance (Zbikowski 2008: 283–309; ibid., 2012: 147–65; ibid., 2014: 143–63; ibid., 2017: chapter 5; ibid., 2018b: 57–75). With music visualization of the sort evident in Morris' choreography in *Gloria*, of course, it is the dance that is referring analogically to the music. As a preliminary first approximation of how music can be translated into dance or dance into music, I would like to suggest that the direction of the reference matters less than does the mechanism – namely, analogy – that is behind it. Relationships between music, dance and other media can, however, get rather complicated, and these complications are singularly instructive for understanding the role of analogical reference in music and dance. To explore such complications – and to illustrate more fully the notion of analogical reference – let me now turn to an air and chorus from Handel's *L'Allegro, il Penseroso ed il Moderato*, and to how music and dance can, independent of one another, visualize a text, and how each can make analogical reference to a separate, but related, dynamic process.

'Haste thee nymph'

In their adaptation of John Milton's youthful *L'Allegro* and *Il Penseroso*, Handel and his librettist Charles Jennens interleaved lines of the two poems to create a dialog between the contrasting personalities summoned by Milton. The text for 'Haste thee nymph' is taken from lines 25–32 of *L'Allegro* and expands on a pastoral scene inhabited by countless mythical personages, all disporting with mirthful abandon:

25 Haste thee nymph, and bring with thee
26 Jest and youthful Jollity,
27 Quips and Cranks, and wanton Wiles,
28 Nods, and Becks, and Wreathed Smiles,
29 Such as hang on *Hebe*'s cheek,
30 And love to live in dimple sleek;
31 Sport that wrincled care derides,
32 And Laughter holding both his sides.

Milton 2012: 28

Handel sets these lines once for the tenor's air, and then uses lines 25–26 and 31–32 for the chorus that follows; the tempo is a bright allegro and the key is F major, the latter regularly affirmed by cadences that punctuate the text setting.

During the eighteenth century (and in other periods as well), composers would often arrange their musical materials to evoke a particularly resonant image in a text they were setting. In German-speaking countries, this technique was called *Tonmalerei* – 'tone painting' – and was both celebrated and derided as a means to make more immediately evident the meaning of a text.[7] Handel often made recourse to tone painting, and in 'Haste thee nymph', his focus was on the image Milton summoned in line 32 of *L'Allegro*: 'Laughter holding both his sides.' The device Handel used to evoke this image is immediately evident from a quick survey of Example 3.2, which shows the relevant passage from the tenor's aria: there is a long melisma on 'holding' which, rendered staccato, creates a running series of 'ho-ho-ho's that provide a reasonable simulacrum of laughter. As with most cases of effective tone painting, however, there is more to the sonic imaged conjured by Handel than just this prolonged, idiosyncratic melisma. For instance, to support the first statement of 'Laughter holding both his sides' in bars 27–28 Handel introduces a novel rhythmic figure in the string accompaniment: two semiquavers followed by a quaver, a slightly unusual pattern that sounds somewhat like the start of a giggle. The figure, which invariably sets repeated pitches, first sounds only on beats 2 and 4 in bar 27 and then takes over almost all of bar 28, ending abruptly when the text repeats. The melisma that follows is framed by pedal points in the bass (first on F3 in bars 29–30, then on B-flat3 in

Example 3.2 Georg Friedrich Handel, *L'Allegro, il Penseroso ed il Moderato* (HWV 55): No. 6, 'Haste thee nymph', bars 25–35.

Example 3.2 continued.

bars 31–34) which join with canonic entries in the upper strings that redouble the running lines of the melisma. In addition to providing a simulacrum of the sound of laughing, then, Handel's setting creates a sonic analogue for the physical experience of laughing, with the high activation of the diaphragm and supporting musculature (the semiquaver figures and running quavers of the melisma) paired with overall immobility (harmonic progress having momentarily been suspended by the sustained pedal points).

In their commentaries on the choreography for this moment (which is replicated, in varied form, when these words are repeated by the chorus), both Stephanie Jordan and Rachel Duerden have noted Morris' use of the floor – the three male dancers, legs spread, roll on their bottoms in a slow circle while holding their thighs – as well as the heel-clicking step with arms waving wildly that follows (Duerden 2010: 205–9; Jordan 2015: 197–99).[8] The result creates an effective embodied analogue for the image summoned by the text: rolling on the floor in the throes of mirth, then momentarily losing physical control (as happens when one is consumed by paroxysms of laughter).

Although Handel's music offers a representation of the sound and physical activity of laughing, and Morris' choreography offers an enactment of unbounded high spirits, it is not the case that the choreography is a straightforward visualization of the music. Instead, both music and dance refer to the text. There is nonetheless a connection between the music and the dance, one that becomes quite evident in Morris' replication of this choreography in the choral section that follows. For this section of the dance the three men leave the stage, replaced by the twelve women of the troupe, who are initially arranged in four ranks. At the point when, in bars 66–76 of this number, Handel gives 'Laughter holding both his sides' its most extensive treatment, these ranks break down and the dancers, arrayed across the stage, perform the heel-clicking step in place, flinging their arms about with abandon as they do so. In consequence, there is now a clear connection between music and movement. The music, for its part, combines incredible activity – the choral voices cascade over one another, and the rhythmic figure of two semiquavers and a quaver (which I likened to the start of a giggle) has returned in force in the orchestral accompaniment – with pedal points that, as before, suspend harmonic motion. Similarly, the dance combines wildly gesticulating figures who nonetheless remain more or less in place. Both music and dance thus yield analogues – one in sound, the other in movement – for a process of active stasis, a compositional strategy that is often used by composers to focus the attention and increase tension immediately before an important musical arrival.

On the analysis I offer here, then, there are three different instances of analogical reference in play within 'Haste thee nymph'. The first involves tone painting, which Handel achieved by arranging his musical materials to create a sonic analogue for the sound and physical activity of laughing. The second involves Morris' choreography, which produces a physical analogue for behaviour and events associated with jollity, witty sayings, carefree jesting and laughter. The third, which appears toward the end of the number, involves a simultaneous reference by music and dance to a dynamic process not directly mentioned in or summoned by the text: active stasis.

Again, relationships between music, dance and other media can get rather complicated. That said, as the music and dance for 'Haste thee nymph' demonstrates, analogical reference can provide a significant resource for the construction of meaning that is immediate, temporally extended and thoroughly embodied.

Summary

The capacity for analogy is, on the best evidence we currently have, a truly unique aspect of human cognition – in the words of Douglas Hofstadter and Emmanuel Sander, analogy is the fuel and fire of thinking (Hofstadter and Sander 2013). I have proposed that one way in which humans exploit this capacity is through analogical reference, which obtains when a token used in communication shares structural features with some other entity or phenomenon. Although there is incredible power in communicative media that are based around symbolic reference – language being the example *par excellence* – through analogical reference spatial and temporal relationships can be summoned to mind with an immediacy of considerable force.

In my work on musical construction grammar (based on the idea that grammatical units are form-function pairs), analogical reference has provided the means to explain the basic function of music within human cultures, which is to provide sonic analogues for dynamic processes. I believe an argument can be made that the basic units of dance can similarly serve as analogues for dynamic processes. Having not worked on dance grammar to any extent, this is speculation on my part, but let me offer three examples of dance steps that might support such an approach. First, in the brief portion of the choreography for 'Laudamus te' that I discussed (and setting aside, for the moment, its connection to the music), the initial steps the dancer takes can serve as an analogue for setting up a frame for discourse: with these steps, she enters the stage in an orderly, directed fashion, and then pauses, poised to continue.[9] Second, within the practice of French noble dance specific step-units were often (although not invariably) used to mark cadences; as with musical cadences, such step units serve as analogues for the process of arrival (Zbikowski 2017: 143; Pharo 1997: 305–10). Third, as I noted in my analysis of the choreography for 'Haste thee nymph', the combination of the heel-clicking step (done in place) with the 'do-what-you-want' arms (following Jordan's description) serves as an analogue for a process of active stasis.

The potential for sequences of musical events and for dance steps to serve as analogues for dynamic processes is a point of contact between these two expressive media as well as a basis for translations between them. Through analogical correspondences, music can be translated into dance (as occurs in

'Laudamus te' and similar choreographies), dance steps can be translated into music (as occurs in French noble dance and the Viennese waltz), and each can translate a dynamic image prompted by words (as occurs in the music and the dance for 'Laughter holding both his sides').

Before proceeding, I should note that analogical reference is an approximate rather than an exact affair. For example, the combination of the heel-clicking step with the 'do-what-you-want' arms in the choreography for 'Haste thee nymph' *could* provide an analogue for the sort of active stasis that builds tension. Were it to follow even more frenetic movement, however, it could provide an analogue for a *release* of tension. As with any process of constructing meaning, context is important; equally important, in the case of analogical reference, are the structural mappings between source and target. Where these mappings are many, the analogy that is produced will be robust; where these mappings are few, the analogy may be difficult to appreciate. As an example of the latter, consider Morris' choreography for the very beginning of 'Haste thee nymph'. As the initial fanfare of Handel's music sounds, two male dancers stand on either side of the stage, their arms raised. At bar 4 the music arrives on the dominant and a new musical idea is introduced – a brisk sequence of repeated pitches that leads to a descending scale – and with this idea the dancers shift to a running-in-place step, vigorously swinging their arms back and forth. They continue this step until the conclusion of the introduction in bar 8, after which they leave the stage and two other dancers (quickly followed by a third) enter for the tenor's aria. Although there is an obvious structural mapping between the rushing lines that begin in bar 4 and the rapid steps of the dancers, there is no obvious mapping between the *progress* suggested by the music – those rushing lines are first presented by one set of orchestral voices and then quickly imitated by another set of orchestral voices, and the successive statements of these lines traverse a tonal span that ultimately comes back to tonic – and the lack of forward motion created by the dancers' vigorous actions. Put another way, the dancers' movements in this opening portion of the number present an analogue for a process of active stasis that has few correlates in the music.

While I do not find that there is a direct translation between music and dance in the musical and choreographic settings of 'Laughter holding both his sides,' it is nonetheless evident that both media make recourse to analogical reference to construct meaning. Let me now turn to an example of a more direct translation between music and dance from Morris' *Mozart Dances* that demonstrates the unique species of meaning such translations make possible.

Translations between Music and Dance in *Mozart Dances*

Mozart Dances is an extended and ambitious work that sets dance to three large-scale works for piano: Mozart's Piano Concerto No. 11 in F major (K. 413), Sonata in D major for Two Pianos (K. 448) and Piano Concerto No. 27 in B-flat major (K. 595). The connections between music and dance that I would like to focus on come from the choreography for the first movement of Piano Concerto No. 11 which, as Stephanie Jordan notes in her thorough analysis of *Mozart Dances*, is practically a textbook example of music visualization (Jordan 2015: 451). Although there are, in consequence, numerous opportunities to study translations between music and dance within this portion of 'Eleven' (as the dance set to the concerto was known), I would like to concentrate on one particular moment in which both music and dance bring forth new meanings.

The moment that is of interest occurs at the beginning of the development section. The orchestra has just closed the exposition with an arrival on C major (the dominant) and, as shown in Example 3.3, the piano immediately shifts the discourse to C minor. The piano's musical material at this point is drawn from the second principal theme, and to understand how it is transformed in the development we will first need to consider the initial occurrence of this material in the exposition. As shown in Example 3.4, the theme is introduced by the first violins and supported by the remainder of the strings, with the piano providing continuo accompaniment. Two features distinguish the theme: its neat two-bar construction, evocative of a minuet; and the trill-and-turn figure introduced in bar 26, which pulls the music from the third beat of one bar through to the second beat of the following bar.

Mozart changes this theme in several ways when he comes to use its material in the development. Perhaps most significantly, the trill-and-turn figure that pulls the music forward in the theme is extracted and used to drive forward motion. It is stated twice in quick succession in bars 172–174, a compression that disrupts the effortless elegance generated by the theme in the exposition and replaces it with a measure of intensity and urgency. The music then almost immediately gets stuck: beginning with the end of bar 174, the trill-and-turn figure is transformed into a bit of filigree, and there are two unsuccessful attempts (in bars 175–176 and 177–178) to move beyond the C5 reached by the melody in bar 174. The harmonies supporting the melody provide no help in all this, simply repeating the same succession of three chords again and again. Where the second theme had provided a sonic analogue for balance and easy grace, then, the return of its materials provides an analogue for darker emotions momentarily entrapped in a cycle of obsessive repetitions. The piano finally abandons these materials in bar 179 and, aided by new material and the entrance of the orchestra

Example 3.3 Wolfgang Amadeus Mozart, Piano Concerto No. 11 in F major (K. 413, first movement, bars 172–179.

Example 3.4 Wolfgang Amadeus Mozart, Piano Concerto No. 11 in F major (K. 413, first movement, bars 24–33.

in bars 180–183, moves on to G minor. This key having been confirmed, there is then a reprise of the material of bars 172–178, transposed down a fourth. The lower register together with the familiarity borne of the reprise of the material render the music somewhat less anxious, and yet forward motion is still impossible. For the transition that pulls away from this material Mozart transposes the music of bars 179–181 up a fifth, and it is this newly energized music that leads to a cadence on D minor and to the return of piano passagework that, in the exposition, provided a convincing analogue for forward motion.

As one might expect from Morris' close attention to musical organization, his choreography for the initial statement of the second principal theme is a model of poise and balance: while the seven women who will dance most of the movement stand with their backs to the audience, the seven men who dance the orchestra's opening material combine sweeping gestures with graceful turns, the steps conforming to the two-bar units that make up the theme. The situation is markedly different when the theme's materials return in the development: here, the principal dancer who has been associated with the piano part throughout this movement (Lauren Grant in the original production) enters with steps that bespeak effort and intensity.[10] Moving from the rear of the stage toward the front on a diagonal, she performs the same step-unit seven times (once each for bars 172–178): she steps forward into a plié on beat 2, pointing her right arm down, and then steps forward, bringing her left arm around in an arc to point upward, almost as though she were pulling herself up. This step-unit, comprised as it is of a series of short movements verging onto the abrupt that trace an effort-laden path across the stage, is not quite like anything else in her extensive choreography within the first movement of 'Eleven'. With the arrival on the repeated C5 of bar 179 she pauses, turns slightly to face the audience and then, with the shift to new melodic material that is supported by the orchestra's entrance, quickly performs three step-units, each of which has her lift her left leg on beat 1 to describe a quick circle and dip her head on beat 3. This sequence of step-units takes her toward the centre of the stage, where she pauses with the piano's arrival on G minor; the orchestra's confirmation of this arrival is emphasized by a quick return of the other women, who just as quickly leave. The principal dancer then performs those same effort-laden step-units to the piano's reprise of bars 172–178 (now in G minor), but this time in a large circle centre stage, and much more loosely correlated with the music. This is followed, finally, by the same head-dipping step-unit as before, and then the music and the choreography move on into the rest of the development section.

The sequence of step-units that opens the choreography for the development section of the first movement of 'Eleven' is, in many respects, a classic case of music visualization: each bar of music is rendered with a distinct step-unit. We can nonetheless add depth to our understanding of this passage by considering the multiple layers of analogical reference that are involved. The sequence of step-units, for instance, provides a *physical* analogue for the sequence of ephemeral *sounds* that make up the passage. As I suggested earlier, the music of this passage is itself an analogue for emotion processes caught in a cycle of obsessive repetition. Given this, the choreography could also be regarded as providing a physical analogue for these same or similar emotions. There is also an interesting tension between the analogues offered by music and dance: where the music of bars 172–179 appears to have gotten stuck, unable to move beyond C5, the dancer is able to make her way – albeit with effort – across a considerable expanse of stage. In some respects, the situation is the reverse of what happens in the opening choreography of 'Haste thee nymph': there it was the music that projected progressive movement and the dance that embodied active stasis. Where this passage from 'Eleven' is different is in what the dance brings to the music. The sense of physical effort projected by the dancer as she moves across the stage draws our attention to the different strategies employed by the melody as it tries to move beyond that pesky C5. First the melody tries a chromatically inflected ascending scale (in bar 175), then a chromatically inflected descending scale (in bar 177), yet each time it is thwarted, its efforts bootless. It is only after these strategies have been abandoned – much as the dancer abandons the step-unit that has taken her across the stage – that it becomes possible for the melody to move on.

It is in situations like this that the metaphor of translation between music and dance may break down. As conventionally understood, a successful translation preserves the meaning of the original utterance while restating it in a new expressive medium. In the case of this passage, however, the dance has imbued the music with new meaning. As a result, the music becomes more than an analogue for emotion processes caught in a cycle of repetition, for it now offers a sonic instantiation of the efforts taken to escape this cycle. When we hear the music in this way – when we hear it with listening practices shaped by Morris' dancer – its meaning both deepens and broadens, taking on a corporeal aspect that we might have missed when only attending to the sounds.[11]

Music, Dance and Translation

As the contributions to this volume demonstrate, there is a wide array of ways to look at the issues circulating around music, dance and translation. By approaching these issues from the perspective provided by research on analogy, I hope to offer a methodology grounded in cognitive capacities that appear to be uniquely human – as, in their fullest expressions, are music and dance. As I noted in my introduction, analogical correspondences between music and dance can be seen at the level of large-scale design as well as at the level of individual passages. For my part, the more fine-grained analogies that obtain in the latter case have the potential to tell us much about how music and dance generate meaning, and how translation between the two can be aided and limited by mapping between disparate domains.

One important element of this methodology is the notion of analogical reference, through which a sequence of musical events or a series of dance steps can refer to a dynamic process that may not have any obvious sonic or embodied dimension. Another important element is the notion that sonic or physical analogues can support communicative exchanges of fundamental importance within human cultures. This latter notion is behind the theory of musical grammar I have sketched here, which proposes that one of the basic functions of music in human cultures is to provide sonic analogues for emotion processes, communicative gestures and the patterned movements of dance. I should like to entertain the idea that dance can provide physical analogues in a similar way, but for the present this must remain speculative: my work on musical grammar is only at a beginning, and while there are hints that this approach could be extended (gleaned in part from the work of dance scholars) the evidence at present is at best fragmentary and inconclusive.

As I have endeavoured to show, a methodology that draws on analogical reference can show how dance can translate ideas presented in a text as well as in music; it also shows how music and dance can refer to a dynamic process not explicitly mentioned in a text. This methodology further encourages us to think carefully about what is meant by 'translation': while the metaphor of translation is certainly useful for thinking about how the communicative resources of one medium might be realized anew in another, to the extent that the notion is shaped by the kinds of meaning that typify language it may be limited in its application to music and dance. As demonstrated by the rich array of music and dance practices across human cultures, these non-linguistic modes of communication offer resources that are simply beyond the scope of language, resources that are also central to what it means to be human.

Notes

1 In association with and support of Jordan's *Mark Morris*, the Mark Morris Dance Group has kindly made video clips available for a number of the choreographies that are discussed in the book at: https://markmorrisdancegroup.org/jordanbookclips/ (accessed 18 February 2023), indexed to individual chapters. There are video clips available for all of Morris' dances that I discuss in the present chapter; that for 'Laudamus te' is indexed to chapter 5 (clip 5-5); the section of the dance upon which I focus begins at 00:19 on that clip.

2   As I shall want to give close consideration to the relationship between specific musical events (or sequences of events) and specific dance movements (or sequences of dance movements), I shall adopt distinctions Wendy Hilton developed for discussing French noble dance. Hilton distinguishes between a step (a passage of the foot forward, backward or to the side), a step-unit (which is made up of a number of steps) and a step-sequence (a sequence of step-units that reaches a conclusion) (Hilton 1997: 73).

3   The notion that fingers provide a 'tapered end for guiding communication' reflects work by Michael Tomasello and others on the role of pointing – most typically, with individual fingers – in human communication (Tomasello 2006: 506–24; Tomasello 2008). The interested reader may also want to refer to Jordan's discussion of Morris' use of a finger-pointing motif in *Mozart Dances* (Jordan 2015: 456–8).

4   As Michael Tomasello has noted, human communication relies on an infrastructure for cooperation and for sharing knowledge and attitudes; my invocation of a 'process of human communication' assumes that such a process relies on this sort of infrastructure. For a full account, see Tomasello (2008) chapter 1.

5   In this and similar examples analogical reference, as distinct from basic correlation, emerges quite clearly if the video is viewed with the sound turned off.

6   I use 'musical utterances' as a covering term for the sound sequences produced by musicians, both singly and in ensembles.

7   For discussions of both the benefits and liabilities of tone painting from the late eighteenth and early nineteenth centuries, see Engel (1998), 954–65; and Weber (1825), 125–72. Tone painting is also known as 'text painting' and 'word painting'; my preference for 'tone painting' reflects an interest in using the term current in the eighteenth and nineteenth centuries, and in broadening the perspective on music's analogical representations beyond the text to include phenomena that are both extra-musical and nonlinguistic.

8   The clip for this number at https://markmorrisdancegroup.org/jordanbookclips/ (accessed 18 February 2023) is indexed to chapter 6 of Jordan's book (clip 6-3), and the passage discussed here begins at 00:42.

9   The effect of these steps is not unlike the beginning of many fairy tales: 'Once upon a time . . .' Within the theory of mental spaces developed by the linguist Gilles Fauconnier, such constructions are known as space builders, in that they open up a mental space that serves as a frame for the ensuing discourse (see Fauconnier 1994: 16–18).

10 The clip for the first movement of 'Eleven' at https://markmorrisdancegroup.org/jordanbookclips/ (accessed 18 February 2023) is indexed to chapter 13 of Jordan's book (clip 13-1). The passages discussed here begin at 00:28 (the second principal theme) and 03:36 the development.

11 A fuller account of the meaning construction that happens in this moment can be developed with recourse to the notion of conceptual blending, discussed by Jordan as an analytical technique that can be applied to combinations of music and dance (Jordan 2015: 95–101). On conceptual blending more generally, see Zbikowski (2018a), 6–23.

4

Interactions and Correspondences between Music/Sound and Dance/Movement as Permanent Negotiations of Translation Processes

Stephanie Schroedter

The analysis of translation processes has implicitly and/or explicitly pervaded all arts disciplines, considering aspects of theory and (perception) aesthetic, but also building a bridge to more practical fields of application as, for example, artistic research.[1] Such analysis becomes more urgent when interactions, or even close interweaving between different art forms, occurs, as is often the case in the performing arts.[2] Provided that such inter- and transdisciplinary working groups are not reduced to a counterproductive trial of strength – that is, a power struggle fought with the means of the arts or sciences – translation analysis initially aims at understanding each other's 'language' in order to find a common 'language'. The latter is by no means limited to words, but also includes barely verbalized performative qualities and the perception of those based on our senses – that is, the sources decisively nourishing artistic-creative thinking and acting, as well as reflections on artistic processes (Minors 2019: 161).

In the following paragraphs, I would like to elaborate on translation processes between two arts disciplines, the interplay of which is as old as it is perpetually fascinating and disputable. Music and dance. Or, put more generally, sound and movement.[3] They have been closely connected from the very beginning, but since the turn of the twentieth century, they have been developing particularly diverse frictions between each other, characterized by an abundance of productive tensions. In this context, the first question to consider is: in what way can the 'language' of music be comparable with that of dance (and vice versa). This question enables the discovery of common ground, which could ease the communication between representatives of the respective arts. Furthermore, another urgent second question comes up: considering that music is substantially different from that of dance due to its 'materiality' or rather 'mediality', can the 'language' of music be 'translated' into dancing or rather choreographically designed movements (and vice versa)? If so, how can this be achieved? In this context, the question arises as to whether such interactions do show specific perception patterns, which again draw on cultural socializations, if not even conditionings. Or, to put it differently: in the end, do they actually tell us more about our perception than about different designs of the interplay between these art forms? As a prerequisite for this, the term 'translation', ought to be re-examined in more detail, including its capacities and limitations. The following rough analyses of several performances, which I consider revealing for this subject matter, are meant to selectively illuminate my theoretical considerations, in order to make them more concrete.

Music and Dance as Movements in Space and Time

The term 'choreography' is already based on a translation problem, or perhaps even on a first productive misunderstanding (of the ancient art of dance). The Greek *'choros'* does not only mean (circular) dance, but also refers to the performers that sing and move in this dance (choristers as an ensemble of singer/dancers). Second, it also refers to the place, or rather space, where this dance is performed. Particularly the latter aspect led to choreography (*gráphein*, Greek for writing or scratching) as the writing of dances – in a space and later on also on paper.[4]

Therefore, choreography can also be interpreted as (ephemeral) writing or drawing of movements (in the broadest sense) in a space, which does not only refer to dance (in the narrower sense of forms and styles of movement in specific cultures), but can also include music and sound compositions in particular. Music is closely connected with a space (no less than time), since it expands within it and constitutes the (sound) space as such (acoustically). Therefore, connections between music and architecture suggest themselves as much as those between dance and architecture. Music and dance are no less spatial arts than they are time-based arts, not only because they take place in time and space, but also because they create time as well as space. Spaces influence our perception of music/dance, as much as they are artistically constituted by music/dance (as spaces of perception) – contemporary choreographies and sound art in particular have increasingly made this a central aspect of their aesthetics.

But how can music, just like dance, be understood as movement? According to music theory studies based on cognitive sciences and often referring to metaphor theories, we process music 'as' movement (Zbikowski 2002; Larson 2012; Cox 2016). This does not mean that music actually is movement – although, from the physical point of view, oscillation and therefore movement forms its basis. The crucial point is that we perceive and understand it *as* movement. Our (long tradition of) linguistic descriptions of music are proof of that: melodic steps, runs and skips are just a few of the endless examples of movement-based musical terms. Or, to put it differently: music moves us (physically and also emotionally) because we understand it as (not visible but audible) movement – even without moving ourselves while listening to music.

The biggest commonality between music and dance is without doubt the time dimension; that is, their ability to arrange time artistically through rhythm. In this context, tempo, metre and rhythm is the decisive factor for perceiving both arts as corresponding temporally.

However, even if music and dance seem to be related as space-time-arts due to these prerequisites, do they inevitably share a common 'language'? Since the turn of the twentieth century, numerous attempts have aimed to compare the specific expressive qualities of music and dance, and to discover analogies between them, in order to 'harmonize' both arts. Therefore, the (anthropologically substantiated) endeavours to achieve an 'agreement' between both art forms remained. Émile Jaques-Dalcroze was very influential within this field, through his attempts to 'translate' music into movements. But even before him, there had been remarkable systematic and conceptual approaches aimed at achieving an equal interplay between these arts. The same occurred later on, when new approaches tried to establish an ever more sophisticated dialogue between music and dance, which finally fell back on comparable (language) structures (Jordan 2000: 15–25). In principle, I recognize two directions. The first aims to illustrate music through dance (and vice versa), that is, to underlay one art form with narratives of the other – for instance, to further support the (or at least 'a') 'meaning' of music through dance (and vice versa).[5] The object of the second direction is much more abstract. It aims to visualize the dynamics of one art through the other, to underline the movement qualities without semantically charged contexts (as far as this is possible) – a process sometimes, somewhat derogatorily, referred to as 'Mickey Mousing' (Jordan 2015: 75; White 2006). Both directions – implicitly or explicitly – know about the different 'materiality' and 'mediality' of music and dance. The most evident signal for this is that we perceive music as audible but not visual movements in space and time, whereas dance primarily interests us as visual but not necessarily audible movement through space and time. In the end, it is about 'translating' the audible into the visual – and vice versa. In order to define the possibilities and limitations of such a translation process in more detail, it is first necessary to summarize the current discussions around the concept of translation succeeding Walter Benjamin.[6]

Theories of Translations within the Arts

Early on, in his pioneering translation research in cultural and media studies, Walter Benjamin emphasized in his linguistic-philosophical essay, 'Die Aufgabe des Übersetzers' ('The Task of the Translator') (1923/1971: 9–21; Berman, Berman and Sommella 2018), that the original text and its translation will never achieve either congruence or the relationship between primary and secondary text. Instead, the original (source text) and the translation (target text) enter into a constant mode of interaction, at the end of which it is possible that the translation unearths passages which were only implicit in the original. Therefore, the task is not to achieve a word-for-word translation of the original into another language, but rather a 'semantic transparency' that aims at transforming the intention into another language (or rather into a different mode, see Minors 2020a and 2020b). However, who determines what is or was actually 'meant' in the original text – particularly when its author is no longer able to comment on it? Is this intention really definable and fixed – or is it subject to constant change?

This question becomes additionally explosive if something is translated from one 'media' to another – the term 'media' is used here in a general sense, as an intermediary that goes beyond verbal language, but is not reduced to a technically supported 'mediality', and also addresses 'sensorial' aspects. I use the term 'media' above all to build a bridge to cultural studies and media studies, but without equating arts with media (of any kind); that is, without declaring them as media (as done by Rajewsky 2002). Ludwig Jäger's explanations of his term 'transcriptivity', for instance, also applies to artistic-creative processes. Medial translations are subject to constant re-semantizations, since they always re- or overwrite the original (Jäger and Stanitzek 2002; Jäger 2004/2012; Jäger 2010).

According to Jäger, medial translations are multi-dimensional processes of relationization and correlating by the media between their respective (medial) sign systems (intermedial) as well as within their own sign system (intramedial). The term 'transcription' is used to draw attention to the transition from disruption to transparency, from de- to re-contextualizations. In this context, the interplay between disruption and transparency stands for that process during which the medium that has been initially in the foreground, and thus perceived primarily, gradually recedes into the background until it is hardly perceptible, because the medially transported 'content', its 'form' and 'meaning' have become the centre of attention. To put it differently: the interplay's final result or rather (aesthetic) event, which is something new and different from each original medium in itself, is central now: a so-called emergence effect takes place (for a general introduction to this phenomenon Holland 1998/2010). Thus. not only is the medium, or rather its interplay with other media, made the subject of discussion, but mediality itself as a specific (translation) phenomenon gains importance. This aspect is equally relevant for music-choreographic (or rather sound-performative) translation processes (or rather transcription procedures), if it is not only about the – unquestionably important – analysis of staging structures, but also including the intended effect and possible perception patterns of a performance.

For this approach, which increasingly expands the analysis of the production by including its reception, or rather the perception of an artistic event, there have been translation theories developed by cultural and media studies that offer further interesting starting points – especially those which emphasize that every translation (or rather transcription) is culturally framed (Benthien and Klein 2007: 11). In this context, following the approach of postcolonial studies, cultural developments are considered permanent translation processes and at the same time transformations of the cultural, which take place in a hybridized 'third space', a gap beyond the originating source culture and the target culture. Against this backdrop, the terms 'translations as performance' and 'translations in performance' come into play (Bigliazzi, Koffler and Ambrosi 2013: 1), which do not have a beginning nor an end beyond the connection with a supposed original but are still culturally influenced or rather permanently interpreted anew on stage and in everyday life.

'Translation' now comprises very far-reaching processes of a complex and multi-layered transfer of cultural practices, which are framed by conventions and continually re-framed by modulations which again can become firmly established conventions. By this, expectations of the audience/listener are fulfilled, but at the same time, surprises and disappointments are also created. Therefore, *what* we perceive it is not only crucial, but also *how* we perceive, due to the individual, social, cultural and media-technical circumstances. We are not always aware of the frames in which we perceive works of art, nor of how these frames are continually transforming. But such framing can be indicative of power-political practices of inclusion and exclusion, which merit critical examination.

Apart from working with music-and movement-analytical parameters in a narrow sense, my current research project also includes those far-reaching aspects following cultural and media studies in order to outline different modes of perception. With this, I want to show that translation processes (and our corresponding perception of them) are always culturally dependent and subject to permanent change. This will be explained in more detail in the following section.

Transferring Translation Theories into Practice

Since the historical avant-garde at the beginning of the twentieth century, the interplay between music and dance has become far more complex, with the challenging of their supposedly 'natural' connection. Music and dance entered a dialogue charged with tension, which could even result in an open rift between audible and visible occurrences, for instance by making the music appear unfamiliar to, or even alienated from, the dance movements, so that the audience might become confused, if not irritated. These procedures go back to Bertolt Brecht's concept of epic theatre and its demand for a so-called V-effect ('Verfremdungseffekt', alienation effect). Instead of allowing the viewer/listener to fully immerse himself/herself in the stage events, he/she was to be made permanently aware that there exists a gulf between the theatre and his/her everyday real-life experiences. This effect was later transferred to the level of music and dance to encourage the audience's skills in separating their watching and their listening. Music was no longer intended to evoke illusionary spaces for dance and thus support an escapist motivation for theatre consumption, to which ballets have always been particularly susceptible. Instead, this new approach aimed to develop critical listening and watching, through music and bodily movements, which were also intended to sharpen perceptions of circumstances outside the theatre.

Pina Bausch was an early exponent of this trend, especially with such early pieces as *Die sieben Todsünden* (1976, after Brecht and Kurt Weill) and *Blaubart. Beim Anhören einer Tonbandaufnahme von Béla Bartóks 'Oper Herzog Blaubarts Burg'* (1977). The latter seems to be a deconstruction of an opera, such as was also later made by William Forsythe in *Decreation* (2004) – albeit from completely different aesthetic preconditions. Based on her experiences with these early 'pieces' ('*Stücke*'), together with her musical dramaturge Matthias Burkert, Bausch developed her collage technique, which applied to the dance-choreographic level as well as the musical level. This resulted in putting two layers on top of each other, whereas the dance, i.e. the visible layer, was developed first, and the music, the audible layer, was 'intuitively' tuned to the dance (Pina Bausch in Klein 2019: 146). This overlaying generated utterly unexpected, new and very intense meanings of the music and ultimately opened up room for music-choreographic associations. It is striking, however, that particularly in the later 'pieces' of Bausch the music collages gradually mutated into synthesized musical montages through which the originally intended alienation effects increasingly gave way to immersion effects. This development was without a doubt caused by the digital cutting processes that emerged in the 1980s, introduced into her work by her younger musical dramaturge Andreas Eisenschneider.

Comparable processes of collage or rather montage of different musical models, which use intramedial recombinations (with other compositions) or intermedial confrontations (with dance) in order to cause new effects or rather break with usual perception patterns, are to be found also in the work of choreographers from the immediate sphere of the so-called German dance theatre (for example, Susanne Linke/Urs Dietrich, Reinhild Hoffmann and Raimund Hoghe). Whereas in the so-called contemporary dance scene (i.e. the dance performances of the younger generation), immersive sound spaces supported by electroacoustic music/sound design prevail (for example, the collaborations between Compagnie Marie Chouinard and Louis Dufort or between Ian Kaler and Aquarian Jugs).

A clash of extremely different visible and audible occurrences, which have been developed separately in order to avoid any accordances, can also result in emergence effects ('*Emergenzeffekte*'). Despite the intended discrepancy, these effects lead immediately to a fusion of very divergent impressions in our perception. This is a kind of survival strategy, which we develop quite early in life in order to survive in our media-saturated culture. An early and prominent example of such a music-choreographic or rather sound-performative experiment is *Variations V* from 1966, developed by David Tudor, John Cage and Merce Cunningham (Miller 2001; Cage 1965; Cage et al. 1966/2013). As a more recent example of comparable performances – particularly those in which the latest media technology was used as a further creative tool for choreographing dance movements – I would like to discuss the series of four 'editions' entitled *Eadweard's Ear. Muybridge extended* in more detail. Oscillating between installation and performance, these editions were staged under the artistic direction of Penelope Wehrli between February 2017 and October 2018 in four different locations. Those were the Uferstudios in Berlin (a centre for contemporary dance and performance), a sports hall during the Neue Musik

Festival Rümlingen/Switzerland, the Künstlerhaus Mousonturm in Frankfurt am Main and finally the closing show back in Berlin, this time at the Akademie der Künste. I listened to/watched all editions live and was rather baffled in view of how my perception kept changing during the continuous monitoring of this project for almost one and a half years.

As the subheading of this experimental series already suggests, it was inspired by chronophotography, and based on Eadweard Muybridge's work, in which the act of seeing was fragmented into single photographs (Frizot 2008). Penelope Wehrli and Joa Glasstetter, a media artist responsible for the programming, transferred the basic principle of these early experimental photographs by means of a digital notation system or rather an 'interface' onto the acoustic level to evoke a fragmentation of the listening process. The set-up of the experiment was as follows: in one corner of the hall, the musicians were positioned on a large rectangular field marked in dark blue. In the opposite corner stood a blue box, wherein the two dancers performed – Jutta Hell and Dieter Baumann of the Berlin duo *Rubato*. A divider separated these two corners so that the musicians and dancers were not able to see each other. On this enormous screen, snapshot-like movement sequences of the dancers were projected at increasingly greater intervals. A camera positioned before the blue box of the dancers recorded data for the projection of the movement sequences on the screen, which, unlike Muybridge's chronophotographic process, were digitally fragmented.

Since the Swiss edition (for the Neue Musik Festival in Rümlingen) was an exception[7] among the series of four due to an entirely new composition concept and instrumental ensemble, the following description focuses on the other three editions (two in Berlin, one in Frankfurt), which were staged with the same ensemble of artists. The ensemble consisting of an electric guitar (Alejandra Cardenas, who uses her instrument especially for an interactive and improvised 'live coding'), a bassoon (Stephanie Hupperich, who is trained in classical music and has focused recently on unusual playing techniques in the context of new music) and percussion instruments (Alexander Nickmann, who initially trained as a dancer) plays under the musical direction of the composer Gerriet K. Sharma, who specializes in electro-acoustic music. Along the walls, stands with loudspeakers mounted on top were positioned at regular distances, which served as an acoustic amplification as well as a visual frame of the sound space.

What was remarkable for the sound production of this ensemble was that they did not use the instruments as one might have expected: percussion was hardly used for rhythm, but instead mainly produced noise-like soundscapes by means of clappers and sticks, and also violin bows, sponges, tin foil and other pieces of equipment made of plastic, iron or wood. The sounds produced by the bassoon were mainly respiratory sounds and the moving of the valves, while the electric guitar was primarily lying on the musician's thighs without being connected to the amplifier, and was instead operated with the amplifier cable, various sponges and knives. Gerriet Sharma called his function at the display, which was similar to a conductor's stand, as 'thermostat', in other words, he seemed to subtly mix the sounds, which means he also directed and controlled – or, to put it in exaggerated terms, he manipulated the sound events.

The audience was able to move freely between the blue areas of the musicians and dancers, which were illuminated. Figure 4.1 shows the layout. They could sit down on the three-legged stools/camp chairs or position themselves with stools elsewhere. I noticed that I initially chose points of view (or rather points within hearing range) from which I was able to observe dancers and musicians simultaneously, despite the partition wall. This enabled me to reconcile the sounds, which initially were rather disconcerting but gradually became strangely familiar, with my observations of the dancers' movements. During this process, I kept asking myself: how is the relationship between the movements and the sounds structured? When are the sound creations initiated by the movements, and when vice versa? Could one actually speak of interactions between musicians and dancers, since the musicians couldn't see the dancers, instead 'interpreted' data generated by the movements of the dancers and 'translated' via a computer program in (for each musician individual) graphic scores on screens, which were positioned at their music stands – whereas on the other side the dancers could listen the musicians and could (but must not) react to what they heard? From my perspective (perhaps not from the perspective of the musicians and the dancers), it was a process of continually balancing out the relationships between the audible and the visible. Finally, I caught myself enjoying those moments with great delight whenever I had the amazing impression that sounds and movements were precisely coordinated – which was actually quite impossible, since the movement data of the dancers recorded by sensors were intentionally delayed (latency) and fragmented before they were transferred to the notation display of the musicians. The latter interpreted these instantly generated scores based on preset playing instructions (constraints), although they were allowed to take certain liberties in the arrangement. Therefore, they were not improvising, but constantly required to decide between various alternatives.

In no other production which I have attended did I notice a similar intensive oscillation between emergence effects and experiences of difference. This state

Figure 4.1 *Eadweard's Ear*. Instruments of the music ensemble (*from left to right*): conductor's desk, working place of the bassoon soloist (*above*), the electric guitar player and the drummer (*below*). (Copyright: Stephanie Schroedter).

required getting used to, and ultimately required more intensive attention, which thus led to a certain strain because of inner resistance. Each evening was subdivided into 7 or up to 9 sections, each of which was 15 to 20 minutes long. The audience had the opportunity to leave the hall in between and it was possible to re-join later. Therefore, it was not surprising that during the performance installations the audience thinned out noticeably, with only the 'hard-boiled' insiders staying until the very end.

Besides such extreme and exciting experiments, subtler interactions between music and dance can cause interferences: Small, at first hardly recognizable shifts at the choreomusical or sound-performative level, gradually increasing, so that the discrepancy between the audible and the visible movements can be noticed only over a longer stretch. For experiments with such perception phenomena, new music and especially minimal music of American provenance has proved particularly suitable. Anne Teresa De Keersmaeker has been giving illustrative examples for this choreomusical approach since the beginning of her career: In her solo *Violin Phase* (1981), based on the composition of the same title by Steve Reich (1967), she uses steps, turns, jumps and swinging legs to draw a big circle into sandy soil. These traces left by her footprints seem to have neither beginning nor end, and consist of detailed, thoroughly structured, virtually ornamental patterns. In the development of her movement motives, in other words, the building up of her body's rotations with accentuating arm swings, which correspond with the steps, at times contrapuntally, she orientated herself towards the compositional principles of Reich's music: first and foremost, the *repetition* of small motives with gradual, minimal changes or rather variations that lead to new motives. Furthermore, the *accumulation* achieved by a series of several motives resulting in complex structures as well as the *substitution* of motivic material and its *acceleration*.

De Keersmaeker also takes up movement impulses from the music – 'a very physical charge, carrying a kind of emotion' (De Keersmaeker and Cvejić 2012: 13) – which she transfers into dance movements (despite or perhaps of her apparently prevailing orientation towards clear structures). However, Reich's music and De Keersmaeker's choreography (or rather her respective phase-building) do not coincide; the transfer of principles of the composition to the level of the choreography is no literal translation, just as the four violins in Reich's composition subtly oscillate between playing in unison and *phase shifting*, which might be an example of an intramedial transcription (Jäger and Stanitzek 2002; Jäger 2004/2012; Jäger 2010).

De Keersmaeker applies this compositional principle of phase-shifting to her choreography by directing the arm and leg movements against each other in subtle, changing nuances. As a result, music and dance compete with each other in constant shifts between synchronization and de-synchronization. This artistic decision is all the more consequent since the audible and visible movements can never be in accordance with each other due to their respective *materiality* and *mediality*. The impression of a coincidence between music and dance is mainly the result of our brain's capacity for quick syntheses of divergent impressions and is thus due to neuronal resp. cognitive processes.

The play with interferences and *entrainement*, that is, the refined oscillation between synchronizations and desynchronizations of movements, which cause irritations of perception, are essential for *minimal music*, which developed during the late 1950s. De Keersmaeker meticulously transforms these musical achievements into her dance aesthetics – in spite of her affinity for US postmodern dance and its refusal to work with music. For example, the principle of phase-shifting in dance, which De Keersmaeker developed in *Violin Phase*, was expanded shortly afterwards in her *Piano Phase* (1982), a choreography structured as a duo this time – again based on a composition of the same title by Steve Reich (1967), but now with two pianos. In this piece, the interferences do not only occur between the phases but also between different qualities of movement. Three choreographic phases are based on different arrangements of three movement motives, each of them danced in one line that is shifted forwards twice, to the front of the stage. Thus, it is performed on three different levels in space – comparable to the effect of zooming in. At the same time, the quality of the movements with which the motives are performed shifts within each level – from 'fluent' (as the basic quality) to 'suspended' (with reduced speed) and 'attacked' (fast and coming to an abrupt halt, comparable to the musical staccato).

There is only one brief moment when the movements drift apart, because of a female dancer increasing her speed, which again is duplicated by special lighting or rather by the shadows cast onto the stage's background (see the photo by Herman Sorgeloos in De Keersmaeker and Cvejić 2012: 52). Otherwise, the two female dancers stay in unison, whereas the choreography as a whole stays comparatively independent from the music, or strictly speaking interdependent, since the compositional and choreographic processes match each other on an aesthetic meta-level. Against this backdrop, the *materiality* and *mediality* of the (bodily) movement and sounds are not intended to supposedly achieve a congruence of audible and visible movements: instead, they emphasize their own *materiality* and *mediality* – despite their inner ties as (audible and/or visible) movements in space and time. And whereas in *Violin Phase* the bird's-eye view is crucial for comprehending the movement traces, it is the frontal view in *Piano Phase* that is decisive for recognizing the phase-shifting resulting from the movements (including their reflection in the shadows).

In *Drumming* (1998) and *Rain* (2001), the next two choreographies by Anna Teresa De Keersmaeker based on compositions by Steve Reich (the first on a composition of the same title from 1971, the latter on his *Music for 18 Musicians* from 1976), the spatial dimensions become even more complex, since the floor paths as well as the vertical evolving movement motives are based on spiral movements as elementary path forms. Furthermore, the comparably simple conception of the movement motives encourages an even more complex processing through (what she calls) 'canonical', 'contrapuntal' or 'declining' composition techniques (the last one is comparable with the crab movement in musical counterpoint). In *Drumming* these spiral movements are executed within a square or rather a structure consisting of several squares, the proportions of which are based on the Fibonacci sequence. At the same time, they are mirror-symmetrically shifted into each other with a slight rotation (thus spiral-shaped on the horizontal level). In *Rain*, these spiral movements are performed within a big circle, which again is subdivided into the very square structures that De Keersmaeker had developed for *Drumming* (De Keersmaeker and Cvejić 2014: 20–6 and 113). However, *Drumming* is based on just one unisex *phase*, whereas in *Rain* there are two gender-specific *phases*. Finally, *Drumming* is asymmetric in its macrostructure, with two unequal parts that are based on the Golden Section, whereas *Rain* is designed symmetrically and can be traced back to an extended ternary form (ABA). Nonetheless, in principle, the choreographic proceedings in *Drumming* and *Rain* are comparable, and based on general characteristics of De Keersmaeker's work: *phase-shifting*, *mirroring* (with *videoscratching* as special form that shortens it abruptly), *accumulation*, which is a condensation of movement motives, increasing or rather decreasing speed ('kinoking'), a gradual construction of phases ('stacking'), partner work in the style of contact improvisations ('manipulations') and fabric-like, almost woven arrangements of dancers with continuous changes of place ('tresses') (De Keersmaeker and Cvejić 2014: 118–22).

Against this backdrop, not only the rhythmic dimensions of music but also those of the (structural) architecture of music gain choreographic importance – or at least, such an effect emerges in the perception: the sounds inscribe themselves into space by the movements of the dancers. Thus, the dance points far beyond the visible events and opens up a listening space which invites experiences of *interference* or rather of *différances* as defined by Derrida, which, in this case, might be seen as a very complex process of translation.

Notes

1 As a recent example of this approach by analysing Pina Bausch's Tanztheater (Klein 2019, English translation 2020).

2. The following observations are part of my research project, 'Körper und Klänge in Bewegung' ('Bodies and Sounds in Motion', 2017–2021), which was subsidized by the Deutsche Forschungsgemeinschaft (DFG German Society for Academic Research). In this project, I develop models of a choreomusical respiratory sound-performance analysis.
3. In the following text, I define music and dance as generic terms, which naturally also include sound and movement phenomena. At the same time, I am very much aware that sound and movement can be interpreted as generic terms in their own right, including music and dance as specific forms. It is undisputed that this is not only about a mere definition of terms but also about a fundamental hypothesis, which indicates a specific cultural imprinting.
4. The ability to note down movements on paper was also called '*Choregraphie*' (in German) in the eighteenth century. It has turned into an art or science in its own right, or, rather, into a profession, which is called 'choreology'.
5. One of the earliest examples of this procedure is a dramatized choreography of Beethoven's Symphony No. 6, the *Pastoral*, which André Jean-Jacques Deshayes created for the London King's Theatre in 1829. Back then, the audience considered it a rather strange experiment, although it reflected general aesthetic tendencies in the context of the newly developing concept of programme music (Davies 2003). It might be considered as an early approach to a phenomenon, which we call dance/ballet symphonies today.
6. In this discourse, I follow Benthien and Klein (2017: 9–23).
7. The accordionists, Olivia Steimel and Sergej Tchirkov, played under the direction of the composers, So Jeong Ahn and Thomas Kesser.

5

Collaborative Ballet Dialogues in Translation and Creating *La Parade* (1917) in Paris

Helen Julia Minors

In creating the new production known as *La Parade* for the Ballets Russes, Jean Cocteau attempted to lead a troupe of hand-selected collaborative artists through a quagmire of disagreements, power struggles, misunderstandings and, sometimes, in-house manipulated confusion. Ballet requires the bringing together of various artists working within and across music and dance. In 1917, *La Parade* premiered, bringing together a playwright (Jean Cocteau, 1889–1963), a choreographer (Leonide Massine, 1896–1979), a painter (Pablo Picasso, 1881–1973) and a composer (Erik Satie, 1866–1925), working with the impresario Serge Diaghilev (1872–1929) and his company the Ballets Russes. In discussing an inter-art aesthetic and the importance of being aware of the differences between the arts and in fact to assert them, Peter Dayan has cautioned, there is 'no unproblematic collaboration' (Dayan 2011: 3). In this context, the problems were multiplied not least due to the wartime environment of the work's creation, the complex interrelationships of characters involved and the aim, at least on Cocteau's part, to respond to Diaghilev's request to 'astound me' (Steegmuller 1970: 179). In setting Cocteau this challenge, Diaghilev had given Cocteau not only the instigation to formulate a new work, which was different to what had gone before in ballet, but he also gave him license to seek new collaborators, to break any well-established moulds, and to assert his authority and agency within the team he would ultimately bring together. Cocteau would later describe the collaborative dialogue between the core group of this ballet production, shockingly, as 'the dog fights of great art' (Steegmuller 1970: 162).

Satie's ideas about collaborative art have informed my own ways of researching collaborative ballets and other collaborative ideas for some time. As I noted in the preceding book, *Music, Text and Translation* (Minors 2013c: 107), Satie referred to his compositional procedures in terms of translation, in terms of borrowing processes from one art form and applying them to another. He strove to 'traduire musicalement' ('translate musically') (Satie 1924: 2). The letters, postcards and notes he (and others) wrote during the creative act refer to the process of translation, or to its related processes of adaptation, transformation and issues of language as a vehicle for creative agreement and disagreement. Although the words 'translate' and 'translation' are used sparingly, the interest resides in the processes discussed concerning how ideas are moved across modes, e.g. from design to movement, or from dance to music. The descriptions in the letters reveal a dialogue which gives a detailed insight into their creative dialogue. This chapter focusses not on the work, per say, but on these creative dialogues.

In reference to another ballet, *Mercure* (1924), Satie claimed to 'translate musically' the ideas of one of his collaborative partners, Picasso (Satie 1924: 2, in Volta, 1989: 79). This is significant for a few reasons: first, Satie's first collaboration with Picasso was within the work done for *La Parade* during 1916–17, and second, it shows he was critically aware of the processes of the other artists and that he was interested in integrating the arts to metaphorically speak together in the production. That does not imply speaking the same content, but rather speaking through a shared aim and collaborative process. Or, as Satie articulated: 'J'ai essayé de traduire musicalement. J'ai voulu que la musique fasse corps' (Satie 1924: 2, in Volta, 1989: 79) ('I have attempted to translate musically. My aim has been to make the music an integral part' (Orledge 1990: 232)).

Focusing on the extant writing of the collaborative team, including letters, memoirs, creative notes and varied correspondence, this chapter seeks to explore how the dialogue between the collaborators and organizers of this ballet shared their ideas, concerns and wishes. It explores therefore the transference and exchange of ideas in these written documents and the ways in which these artists were 'translating' each other's understandings of the work in order to bring the production together. Such interpretation of each other's ideas comes from a place of bias and personal artistic perspective. Notable, is the reference to translation and language among the artists which informs their miscommunications, misunderstandings, debates and disagreements.

The central questions underpinning this exploration are as follows: How do the collaborative artists refer to processes of translation and artistic transfer in what they write to each other? In referring to this concept, what can we learn from the documented evidence regarding how this production came together? How might this transfer of sense, in terms of the collaborative aim and then the narrative content of the work, be understood as translation and what can we learn from using this concept of artistic translation in exploring the creative journey of this ballet?

These written communications illustrate points of contact between the artists which occurred prior to the rehearsal stage while creative developments and changes were happening. As such, each artist is required to interpret the main aims of the production, as originally set out by Cocteau, and then to create their individual artistic contribution which would be original and yet work in a unified manner to produce the final ballet. What the letters and other documents show therefore is a continual process of negotiation and perhaps most importantly to my reading, a persistent attempt to interpret and to 'translate' each other's intended meanings. The focus on translation then, is to understand not only your own interpretation and creative goal, but to see the aims and creative possibilities of your collaborative partners from their perspective, to ensure the art forms come together as a unified collaborative work.

La Parade, Programme

The programme note for the premiere was commissioned from Guillaume Apollinaire and published a week before the premiere in *Excelsior* on 11 May 1917: his dual role as a poet and an art critic is captured in the way in which he offers a prophecy of a new artistic era born from this new production. He places much credit on Erik Satie as the 'innovating composer' and Leonide Massine, who is labelled 'the most daring of choreographers', surmising that their collaboration 'heralds the arrival of a more complete art' (Apollinaire 1917: 19–20, reproduced in English translation in Steegmuller 1970: 513–14). Apollinaire makes a great deal out of the national context of the work, marking the music as projecting 'the wonderfully lucid spirit of France itself' (Steegmuller 1970: 513–14). As is well known and referred to in almost all literature about this work, Cocteau subtitled the work, *Ballet réaliste*, referring to the fact that it is almost more real than reality, in that it merges high and low art for the stage, it brings together mime and expressive gesture, and so on. But Apollinaire picks up on this idea and mentions little else of Cocteau's involvement: far less credit goes to the instigator of the work, its librettist, Jean Cocteau, than to the other artists. The programme note serves at least four functions: it offers something of an overview of the story; it highlights the names of the key collaborators and outlines what they have contributed; it sets out a theory for the future genre which could grow from this work; and, if the audience members had time to read it, it would have managed their expectations (or perhaps warn them) as to what to expect: 'Parade will upset a few people in the audience. They will be surprised, assuredly, but in the pleasantest way' (ibid).

In responding to the performance and writing the preface to the published score, Georges Auric (one of the group of composers known as Les Six) waxes lyrical about Satie's contribution to La Parade, but he also asserts the notion of realism alluded to by both Cocteau's subtitle and Apollinaire's programme note:

> The terrible mysteries of China, the sadness of a bar at night of the little American girl, the astonishing gymnastics of the acrobats: all the poignancy of the trestle tables is there – nostalgia for the barrel organ which will never play Bach fugues. / Satie's score is conceived to serve as a musical background to a foreground of the stage noises and percussion. / In this way it submits humbly to that 'reality' which stifles the nightingale's song beneath the wheels of a tram.

Along with the programme note, the original programme booklet also includes the full scenario by Cocteau:

> Les mystères terribles de la Chine, la tristesse de bar nocturne de la petite américaine, les gymnastiques étonnantes des acrobates: c'est là toute la douleur des trétaux, – notalgie de l'orgue de barbarie qui jamais ne jouera de fugues de Bach. / La partition de Satie est conçue pour servir de fond musical à un premier plan de batterie et de bruits scèniques. / Ainsi elle se soumet très humblement à la réalité qui étouffe le chant du rossignol sous le roulement des tramways.
>
> (The stage set represents Paris houses on a Sunday. Fairground theatre. Three music hall numbers serve as a promotional Parade. / Chinese conjuror / American girl / Acrobats. / Three managers organise the publicity. They communicate with each other in such terrifying language that the crowd takes the promotional Parade to be the spectacle inside; the managers try vulgarly to make the crowd convinced. / Nobody is convinced. / /After the final music hall turn, the managers make a supreme effort. / The Chinese [conjuror], acrobats and [American] girl leave the empty theatre. / Seeing the managers' failure, they try one last time to demonstrate their virtues. / But is it too late.)

> Potter 2016: 79

The scenario itself reveals that communication is a core dramatic thread to La Parade. In a way, the 'terrifying language' of this production is an analogue to the miscommunications and misunderstandings of the creative process I will outline below. Qualifying the production as language is an analogy, which articulates that music, dance, design and unspoken narrative do indeed communicate something to the spectator without need for words. As such, the creative artist must be active in the collaborative interpretative process when the communication is nonverbal and verbal (written).

The Concept of Artistic Translation

Multimodal translation is increasingly of importance today in ensuring that we, as scholars and artists, continually strive to learn, to adapt ourselves to new perspectives, and to ultimately engage with diversity in a mutually positive manner (Minors 2019). Of its era, *La Parade* attempts to integrate a wide range of cultural and national symbols, which ultimately might form a character from a stereotype, but in some ways, it is forward thinking for its time by attempting to bring these cultural references into an intercultural dialogue as a commentary of the era.

As Susan Bassnett has shown in translation studies, all acts of translation exist, and must exist, in a 'multilingual and multicultural contexts' (Bassnett 2014: 1). Such a context is represented by the collaborative team for *La Parade*. If translation can be creative, in forming the ways in which a dialogue occurs between these artists, it is not a limiting concept. It does not seek word for word, media for media, equivalence. Rather, it offers creative problem-solving, changing each artist's perspective, and as we can see in the written communication, this changes how they make their artistic contribution. Indeed, Venuti is aware that translation as a process is not a singular model, with a single result, but rather, that 'no act of interpretation can be definitive' (Venuti 1998: 46). Gestures of one art form can be transferred to another by using equivalences, but this also requires some form of adaptation (Jordan 2000: 9). As Jordan explores, music can change the way we see and experience dance, for example, a jump might feel higher, lighter, longer.

The importance is to value the differences between these artistic modes. What is transferred is not the same, it cannot be literally 'translated into the medium of another' (Dayan 2011: 21), but rather an exchange of the idea, the way of doing something, the process, is what is translated. The key thing Dayan identifies of relevance here is that translation is a continual process when artists work together, but that exact transfer of content between the arts is not the main aim. Working with difference is important to allow the arts to each assert their own value and identity (ibid.). As such, if one subscribes to this view, translation becomes hugely significant to all forms of collaborative work in understanding how artists communicate during the creative process. Collaboration is reliant on the communication during the creative process, and during that process each artist can inform each other's creative process and therefore impact change and development (Blain and Minors 2020). As such, Kress' approach to multimodal translation is highly relevant here, as he places 'transformation' (Kress 2010: 129) as a subcategory of translation. For Kress, translation is 'a process in which meaning is moved' (ibid., 124). He has two subcategories: transduction, referring to 'moving meaning-material from one mode to another' (ibid., 125); and transformation, which is a 're-ordering of the elements in a text [...] within the same culture and the same mode' (ibid., 129). As such, Kress recognizes the importance of the different modes, different cultures beyond that of lingual language.

The written creative evidence shows a constant transformation of ideas and outcomes. It demonstrates a semiotic shift: how a sign can be reassigned meaning (Kress 2000). In fact, the multiple voices informing this production feed into the characterization of each role, through costume, make-up, choreographic movement and musical depiction. It is no surprise then that Davies notes that the 'variety of references and allusions ... intensified the characterisation of *Parade's* Little American Girl' (Davis 2006: 125). Indeed, transduction (to borrow from Kress) occurs, as Massine implies, when contemporary artforms are fused and adopted into the balletic setting, including 'ragtime music, jazz, the cinema, billboard advertising, circus and music-hall techniques' (Massine 1968: 105). This *mélange* is ripe for a discussion of translation across the art forms.

Dialogues and Analogical Thinking

The translation potential of moving gestures from one art form to another have been discussed before. In fact, in relation to dance, Paul Hodgins considers that there was an exchange of gestural content between music and dance in particular, when he constructed the concept of the *choreomusical*. Hodgins noted that: 'the degree of music visualization in dance depends to a large extent upon both the choreographer's own predilections and the translatability into movement gesture of the musical topology involved' (1992: 13). His choice of vocabulary is of particular interest here: in referring to the translatability of movement and music, he is asserting the transfer of sense, of idea, of process, of content, between media (in the creative process), across the senses (in the interpretative process) and therefore intersemiotically (to borrow Jakobson's famous term of the translation across modes) (Jacobson 1959 and 2004: 138–43). Dance scholar Bannerman notes that 'dance shares commonalities with language and like language it communicates according to cultural codes' (Bannerman 2014: 66). Recognizing the analogies to language in that artistic modes communicate via their own semiotic codes is so important. It means difference is vital and not to be ignored. So, how do these creative artists communicate across those artistic, media and cultural dimensions? Zbikowski suggests a way to communicate and to exchange sense across artistic roles is to develop 'analogical thinking' (Zbikowski 2018b: 60). Thinking in terms of each art form, each mode, as is implied in analogical thinking, is itself a translation act. It encourages us to think through the lens of another mode. As such, an artist seeks to be able to think in terms of the other artist, to then communicate effectively with each other, to develop a coherent work together.

Cocteau's 'Dog-fights' with Satie and Picasso

Massine recalled how there were torments between the collaborative group. In particular: 'Cocteau, whose outrageous suggested amused and sometimes irritated Diaghilev' (Massine 1968: 101). The problematic dialogue is summed up by Cocteau's biographers, Sprigge and Kihm: 'Cocteau wanted to-and indeed did-write dialogue for [Parade], whereupon Satie refused to write the music, insisting that the ballet was to be *parade* without words, such as is presented before a booth at a fair' (Sprigge and Kihm 1968: 63).

The so-called 'dog-fight' was not only between the collaborative artists. Some of them communicated with and via friends of the leading creative artists, which no doubt added fuel to any fires under way. The importance of Valentine Gross and Misia Sert within the letters cannot be underestimated, but who were they to this production? Misia Sert (1872–1950) was a good friend and business colleague of Diaghilev, who often funded his projects for the Ballets Russes as well as hosting her own Salon, including saving him, financially, on many occasions. A pianist herself, she often informed the Ballets Russes in terms of ideas for costumes and other things. As such, she had a strong influence on Diaghilev, and it seems as though some of the collaborators in *Parade* were trying to manipulate this relationship. It was Sert who introduced Satie to Diaghilev, in fact, as she noted (28 June 1914): 'Diaghilev was in Paris at that moment, and for some time I had been reproaching him with never having taken an interest in Erik Satie. [...] I brought them together at my home' (Sert, 28 June 1914, in Volta 1989: 102).

Valentine Gross (1887–1968) was an artist and writer, she often collaborated with Cocteau and formed a close friendship with him, and in fact she met her husband, the painter, theatre designer and author, Victor Hugo (1894–1984), through Cocteau. As such, Satie's letters to her must be read with the knowledge that Cocteau would likely become aware of their content.

It is significant that Valentine Gross remarks on Satie's letters in reflecting on her friendship with him. She remarks that the letters show his '"medusan" side', before continuing that: 'His letters made us laugh a lot. [...] The interchanges between the collaborators, sometimes harmonious, sometimes catastrophic, prevented me from thinking of anything else' (Gross 1952: 139–44, translated in Orledge 1995: 166). The reference to 'us' confirms that she discussed the letters with the other artists. Satie often wrote to Gross and she clearly liked him, referring to him as 'Poor dear Satie', but the letters were taxing for her: 'I did my best to calm his rages and resentments [...] Sometimes I had to invent extraordinary methods of restoring social edifices that he'd demolished' (ibid., 163). Satie's letters do move from compliment, to frustration, to uncertainty. In writing to Cocteau (2 May 1916), he declares Cocteau's *Parade* to be, 'Stunning! I'm sorting out my ideas. You'll write to me, won't you?' (Volta 1989: 111). The question here seems to be someone requiring attention and contact as a collaborative artist. Is it insecurity? Or is it his collaborative need, to be kept informed at every stage? Cocteau does inform Gross of Satie's letter the day after, and asks her to follow up with Satie – clearly using Gross as a contact to find out more information. In early May 1916, Satie refers of *Parade*, to Gross, as 'a dream' (ibid.), but by 8 June 1916 he is reassuring Cocteau: 'Don't worry, don't be nervous; I'm working' (ibid., 113). Not surprisingly Cocteau did then panic, and he wrote to Sert (June 1916) to express his disquiet, while making sure Sert is aware that Gross started the relationship for this production, and that he is in charge (ibid.: 114).

Cocteau drew on Gross a lot, asking her to speak with Sert, specifically to 'use her influence with Diaghilev' (Sprigge and Kihm 1968: 63). But he also wrote to her with his ideas concerning his new productions and we can see here why Satie might have felt threatened, or at least the need to assert his musical agency: 'I believe *Parade* to be a kind of renewal of the theatre and not a mere opportunity for music' (Reynolds 2013: 141). Cocteau had wanted Satie to include more sounds of the context, such as sirens, typewriters and so on, but this resulted in a series of letters from Satie asking questions, demanding answers and searching for what was being asked of him. Satie is trying to understand Cocteau's artistic aims. The questions reveal his analogical thinking in that he is trying to view the work from Cocteau's perspective. Notable are those letters to Cocteau dated between 24 and 29 March 1917, when he asks for more details of what is wanted. While we also see in the written reflections Cocteau's willingness to adapt his wishes on working with Satie and others, for example, he had wanted the managers to speak, or to shout from megaphones, but he reflected on this: 'je constatai qu'une seule voix, même amplifiée, au service d'un des managers de Picasso, choquait [...]' (Cocteau 1917a: 29–31) ('I realised that one voice alone, even amplified, for one of Picasso's managers was inappropriate' (Reynolds 2013: 142). The idea of a single voice being removed is again analogous to the collaborative process, as the production is a collective voice.

Cocteau explained that: 'Peindre un décor, surtout au Ballet Russes ... c'était un crime' (Cooper 1967: 16) ('to paint a stage set, especially for the Ballets Russes, was a crime ... the worst thing was, we were due to meet Serge Diaghilev in Rome'). Expectations of the Ballets Russes and the other artists prior achievements inevitably informed how each artist approached this production. When Cocteau and Picasso went to Rome, Satie remained home. At this time, you can see in the letters and notes the impression both Satie and Cocteau have of Picasso. Cocteau wrote to Sert that, 'Picasso amazes me more and more every day' (Sprigge and Kihm 1968: 64). While at the same time, Satie also writes to Sert about his progress. Sert's influence on Diaghilev is important in reading the remaining letters as the collaborators seem to keep her informed, to keep her on side, in case of future disagreements. In a way, she acts as both a negotiator and translator of the ideas being put forth. Or, to put it another way, she encourages them to think analogically.

In essence, *Parade* was born in Gross' apartment, not that of Sert, as Steegmuller has shown in his biography of Cocteau (Steegmuller 1970: 162). Her connection to all the artists and her support and input was clear across letters where Cocteau and Satie send her updates. She became the middle woman of the two artists. Satie grew a rage, questioning her. While Cocteau was asking her to intervene. For example, on 30 July 1916, Cocteau writes to Gross, asking: 'exorcise the devil, see Satie, learn what is going on' (ibid., 163). The problematic nature of collaboration seems to fall down here to miscommunication or even selective communication. The to-and-fro nature of the letters must have been exhausting for Gross. But despite Cocteau's complaints and repeats that Satie was causing him issues (that he was 'frightfully depressed and confused' (5 August) and that Satie was complaining that Cocteau was 'a bitch!' (8 August)), by 9 August all seemed to have gone ok, with Cocteau informing Gross of the: 'Very good day's work with Satie' (ibid).

The turmoil continued that month, as Cocteau recalled to Gross in a letter (13 August), noting that Satie was 'composing *marvels* for me and refuses to see Tante Brutus [Diaghilev] [...] To tell you the truth, Diaghilev [...] finds it clever to attribute to me all the blunders' (ibid., 164). This shows two things: that Satie is producing music and seems to work well in person and when in regular contact but he shows stress via letters when he is left alone; and that Diaghilev is devolving responsibility for this collaborative process to Cocteau during this time. Interestingly though, Satie's anxieties, shown in the letter, are also reflected by Cocteau who seems worried that 'Picasso and Satie get on like Misia and Serge' (31 August 1916) (ibid., 165). In others words, he sees a trusted close bond between Sert and Diaghilev. The letters therefore show a tussle for power and control – and a fear of being left out. Cocteau was initially positive about Picasso's inclusion then becomes negative and self-congratulatory, noting that: 'What concerns me is Picasso the theatrical designer. He became one thanks to me' (ibid.). Cocteau was clearly aware of the letters Satie had sent to Gross and what he had said of Picasso, as seen when Cocteau writes (4 September): 'It hurts me when he dances around Picasso screaming "It's you I'm following!"' (ibid., 167). Cocteau did have something to be worried about though, as Satie makes clear in a letter to Gross (14 September), noting that: '*Parade* is changing for the better, behind Cocteau's back!' (ibid.). Satie must either have been deluded to think that Gross and Cocteau were not talking, or he was saying the following to give himself some sense of authority: 'I am all for Picasso! And Cocteau doesn't know it' (ibid.). The sense is that Satie was insecure, concerned about his status in the production and seemed to need constant reassurance. The letters from Satie are beautifully dramatic and make the collaborative process sound even more traumatic than it probably was, notable when he says (20 September) that: 'He [Cocteau] and Picasso have come to terms' (Ibid.). Satie is crafting his own PR choreography here. Cocteau aware of this, seems to thrive on the power struggle when noting to Gross (22 September) that Satie was: 'Caught between Picasso and me, our good Socrates from Arcueil has lost his bearings' (ibid., 168).

This threesome of creative power was a tool for Cocteau. In writing to Gross, he outlined the situation as it was on 22 September 1916: 'Our good Socrates [Satie] is creating confusion between Picasso and me – and imagines one is saying white and the other black because of differences of vocabulary. We've decided with Picasso to lie so that he goes along without getting everything confused' (Volta 1989: 122). Two things are pertinent here: the first, is that the creative confusion is being used as a device to ensure that the work progresses with Cocteau in control, knowing what is happening where, but by doing this, he is effectively trying to manipulate Satie. Second, though, the reference to vocabulary and language is significant as it shows that the translation of ideas and the communication across media is not smooth or easy, and in fact requires effort and misunderstanding to develop this new reality of this new ballet. In many ways, the problematic nature of the language helps the creative discussion explore new options. The problems encourage transduction and develop a need to think analogically.

With playwright and composer seemingly at war, placing the theatre designer between them, the rest of the production team must have been aware of the unease. So, when Massine is brought in by Diaghilev not only to choreograph but to dance one of the key roles, that of the Chinese Conjurer, the melting pot for collaborative disagreements, misunderstandings and arguments might have become unbearable.

Grigoriev explained the position of the dancers in relation to Picasso's costumes: 'The dancers detested these costumes, which were a torture to move about in ... they, too, had to do a lot of stamping, which was intended to suggest conversations between them ... a relic of the fascination exercised over Diaghilev by pure rhythm divorced from music' (Grigoriev 1953/1960, cited in Richardson 2007: 34). Every element of the production is an analogue to communication, here communicating via rhythmic footwork. Picasso's designs were described by another reviewer in terms of the Vaudeville theatre he had visited during the Rome trip: 'A skilful parody of popular scene painting' (Barr 1946/1980: 98). The aim to transpose popular theatre into ballet seems at least successful in terms of the design elements. Likewise, Massine saw Satie's score to be 'witty, satirical [...] with its subtle synthesis of jazz and ragtime, offered me excellent material on which to base a number of new dance patterns' (Massine 1968: 102). Those outside the creative 'dog-fight' were critically seeing the aims of the production fulfilled via a transference of stylistic process and elemental features between genres and arts forms.

Despite the difficulties between these artists, it is clear that Massine at least could see the processes Picasso was using to 'transpose and simplify' the symbols, styles and features he was fusing into his designs (Massine 1968: 106). Seemingly this simplification was an aim for Cocteau who had declared Satie the master of such an approach. Cocteau noted that: 'A poet has too many words in his vocabulary, a painter too many colours on his palette, a musicians too many notes on his keyboard' (Sprigge and Kihm 1968: 66). In referring to the communication modes, he is showing analogical thinking and a keen awareness that individuality of the arts is vital in the production process.

The leader of the disagreement may have come from Diaghilev, who encouraged everyone to offer their new ideas. This would have impacted Cocteau's agency, but it also ensured creative debate to explore new ways of doing things. When Cocteau wrote to Gross in 1914 noting that, 'Every collaboration is a more or less successful misunderstanding' (Steegmuller 1970: 176), he seems to be prophetic in seeing the potential disagreements.

Massine's Inclusion: Choreographic Embodiment of Mime and Gesture

Massine was brought in by Diaghilev, and Diaghilev had given Cocteau the challenge to 'Astound' him, so it is no surprise that Cocteau's notebooks show a similar aim with approaching the dance for *Parade* when he writes: 'Make the dancing realistic like cubism, which is realistic [...]' (ibid., 179). In aiming to make the ballet 'truer than true' (ibid.), in line with cubism, it is no surprise that he began positive work with Massine on feeding him ideas and discussing the choreography. But did not Massine have a hard position to fill? Employed by Diaghilev, to work for, or with Cocteau? To produce dance for Picasso's massive cubist costumes, to dance to music which was angular and sometimes late arriving was no easy task.

Picasso was aware of the visual importance of the movement, which his costumes clothed. Cocteau documented some of Picasso's remarks in his notebook, citing Picasso saying: 'Don't be afraid to glue a piece of newspaper to the canvas – i.e., to use a movement whose meaning cannot be misunderstood, and which, remaining untransposed, give full value to the other movements' (ibid., 180). Movement is at the fore of his analogical thinking, aware that his designs become embodied gestural objects.

Massine took on board, it seems from Cocteau's words, various ideas of mime from Cocteau in developing his choreography. Massine was also dancing the role of the Chinese Conjuror which is significant to understanding how he might have approached appeasing Cocteau to ensure he won the overall creative battle rather than each incursion of a new idea. I play with language here myself by saying incursion, but the warlike language Cocteau has used in referring to 'dog-fight' conveys the sense that he was struggling to keep authority and to bring everyone onto the same page.

There is potential for dance to utilize bodily gestures to carry forward specific images and ideas into dance from the narrative concept: 'dance movement functions as a translation from one medium to another – from the musical movement impulse into flesh and blood movements' (Carroll and Moore 2008: 16). Carroll and Moore detail here a process of translation, moving from the source text and source mode to the target text and new mode. The translation referred to is intersemiotic. Moving from one thing to another implies there is scope for creative transduction. As such, Carroll and Moore's argument aligns to the multimodal understanding of Kress (2010 and 2000) that modes can take on the content and significance from other modes. The resulting dance movements may have come from the musical impetus but they are not restricted by then and they are not a direct copy either. The importance of their interpretation is that the translation, the process of interpretation of idea to creative outcome, music be an 'embodied translation' (ibid., 17). This is significant to the role Massine played as both choreographer and dancer, living and feeling his choreography, creating on his own body. He may have been the last to participate actively in the collaborative process, first needing the musical score, the costumes and the story, but he was in the end the only visible person within the premiere performance offering to some extent a greater capacity to articulate his role and therefore his creative choices. Although this meant he was also a very visible translator, if you will, in that he transformed the costumes through his bodily movements. As he puts it: 'I learned the value of concentrating on detail, and giving full significance to even the most minute gesture' (Massine 1968: 95).

The translation from text to dance is noted by Lifar when he states that Massine's style 'derive[s] directly from Cocteau, as does its literariness and circus stylisation' (Sprigge and Kihm 1968: 64). Lifar goes further with accrediting Cocteau with reinventing ballet, that 'literature too [has] its say in the ballet, since painting and music had each had their turn' (ibid.). Cocteau seems to have had a smooth working relationship with Massine, as recounted in a letter to his mother (22 February 1917): 'Massine désire que je lui montre chose et j'invente les rôles qu'il transform séance tenante en chorégraphie' (Cocteau 1989: 296) ('Massine wants me to show him the smallest detail and I'm inventing the roles which he transforms there and then into choreography' (Reynolds 2013: 159)). Such detail of an idea ensures Massine can think analogically, moving Cocteau's idea from a textual mode to his mode of dance. He was self-critical and self-aware though:

> I allowed my imagination to run away with me and created such a variety of simultaneous movements [...] that each group overshadowed the next [...] The scene was so lacking in artistic coherence that instead of an exciting conclusion

it was nothing but a frenzy of disconnected activity. When I saw the finished ballet I realised that I had still not grasped the basic principles of choreographic counterpoint.

Massine 1968: 101

This disconnected, frenzied activity, sounds again like an analogy to the wider creative process, but it also speaks to bringing a new manner to ballet which is less focused on smoothness of line.

We have an insight from Massine's memoir of his choreographic and embodied decisions regarding the movements of his character, the Chinese Conjuror. He explains Cocteau's prompts, as he initially could not 'decide what sort of tricks this type of performer would do' (ibid., 103). But the 'artistic [in-]coherence' he notes above, seems highly structured for this gestural moment. The mime movements which followed were metaphoric of the birth and growth of an idea:

With an elaborate flourish I pretended to produce an egg from my sleeve and put it in my mouth. When I had mimed the action of swallowing it, I stretched out my arms, slid my left leg sidewards till I was almost sitting down, and with my left hand pretended to pull the egg from the toe of my shoe. [...] it had to be done with the most clearly defined movements and broad mime.

ibid.

It seems clear from Massine's extended description in his memoir that the whole scene was a physical translation of a narrative, of a magician and of a popular fairground scene, embodied and encapsulated in a single character. The play with the egg, or with 'pretend[ing] to breathe out fire' (ibid.), was an embodied way to 'intrigue the fairground public' (ibid.) as they question the meaning of the gesture; he ensures that the audience of *La Parade* had to try to interpret the meaning of these movements. Other gestures Massine integrated would have been more readily accessible for a contemporaneous audience, such as 'the imitation of the shuffling walk of Charlie Chaplin' (ibid., 104). Importantly through, Massine separates the realistic representation shown via mime in comparison to the music-hall non-realistic but mimetic attempt of 'two men wearing a horse's head with a cloth draped over them' to display the horse (ibid.).

Conclusions: Attributions, Authorship and Power

Cocteau and his troupe were ahead of their time, seeking to change the nature of ballet, fusing the low and high art concepts into one work. The narrative play on the audience, who experience a performance outside the 'real' performance which is not seen, challenges the notion of performance but also brings into question the role of the audience who need to be active in many ways to interpret the work. Stephanie Jordan has noted that contemporary audiences are invited to 'one whole experience' (Jordan 2012: 226), where the arts of dance, music, set design, costume and libretto are brought together in one work: the Ballets Russes were very much aware of this, as shown in the dialogues between the creative artists for *La Parade*. The confusion of their communication is also an analogue of the audience, who may see this pre-show event as the main event.

Jean d'Udine seems frustrated with the premiere, noting in this review that there was 'nothing' but a 'bad joke' (1917: 239). Davis describes Cocteau's book *Le Coq et l'arlequin* (1918) as a 'collection of aphorisms designed as a defence of Parade' (Davis 2007: 115). Perhaps it is a way for Cocteau to communicate his artistic intensions. The *Carnet de la Semaine* responded on 10 June 1917 with a different overview:

> Un rideau soi-disant passéiste, en réalité laborieusement primitif, sur lequel des artistes forains sont représentés dans l'attitude contorsionnée du torticolis; un décor dont la prétendue originalité réside en ce qu'il est pose tout de travers...; de hideuses constructions géométriques à plusieurs plans, encageant le manager en frac et la manager de New York.
>
> Spies 2008: 123

> (An apparently regressive but in fact laboriously primitive curtain on which showmen ae shown looking as if they'd cricked their necks; a set who supposed originality consists in being exactly the opposite ..., ghastly geometrical structures on several levels, pinning down the theatre manager in evening dress and the manager from New York.)

These powerful reviews show interest certainly in this production. Diaghilev wanted to spark interest and attention in the work of the Ballets Russes, and to that effect this production was successful. The event was a spectacle that even made it into the art world in concrete form. Diaghilev had invited audience members specifically to see *La Parade*, including Apollinaire, Valentine Gross, E. E. Cummings, and composers such as Auric, Francis Poulenc and Germaine Tailleferre. The box in which Diaghilev sat was that of Sert, and was later drawn by Michel Georges-Michel (1917: Fine Art Museum, San Francisco) and shows he was sat with Picasso, Cocteau and Marie Laurencin (a painter and member of the Cubist Section d'Or). However, this takes artistic license as Laurencin was in Spain and Picasso had this own box for the occasion (Richardson 2007: 39).

As Richardson remarks, though: 'The first performance left Cocteau consumed with envy. Picasso and Satie were perceived as the stars; Cocteau had been eclipsed' (ibid., 40). This of course was largely down to Apollinaire's review, in which he refers to the 'astonishingly expressive music' of Satie, going as far as declaring that it conveys 'marvellously the lucid spirit of France' (ibid). Perhaps worse for Cocteau was the pairing of Massine with Picasso in declaring that Massine had adapted and followed 'the discipline of Picasso's art' (ibid.) – implying then that the intersemiotic translation from costume to dance and back was a success. Massine, for one, thought the review was appropriate, noting that, 'Apollinaire had clearly understood what we were trying to do' (Massine 1968: 112). Cocteau clearly strove for attention, in his later accounts he exaggerated the audience response in referring to scenes where the 'audience wanted to kill us' (Steegmuller 1970: 52). It hit the press though and this was good for Diaghilev who loved a good scandal. Diaghilev referred to *Parade* as: 'my best bottle of wine. I do not open it too often' (in Richardson 2007: 43).

In particular to the claim of the power of words, though, is Massine's assertive statement that: '*Parade* was not so much a satire on popular art as an attempt to translate it into a totally new form' (Massine 1968: 105). The transition between genres and styles, bringing together new approaches to each art form, was asserted as translation – in other words, it was a deliberate attempt to move elements of one art into another, from a source text to a target text. It goes beyond a creative response to a deliberate transduction from one mode to another. The aspirations to make ballet transition into a new artistic style meant that the resulting work was in some ways a mystery to all until the final production was realized. Indeed, Cocteau likewise recognized this translational process, when he reflected on *Parade* as a 'transposition of music-hall' (Rothschild 1991: 41). Here the source text of music-hall style was taken and inserted into the target text, that of a ballet production, transposing elements between genre contexts. In line with this idea of taking something from a source text and adapting it to a new media, Cocteau wrote of Picasso that he had created 'a new way of copying' (ibid.). Translation at its core takes a source text, a meaning, and copies the meaning and sense into a new context, that of the target text. Their use of language is important then to revealing how they were thinking and processing the challenges of such a collaborative act. At every level, translation processes, in moving elements from one mode to another, were persistently active.

Part Three

Translation through Music-Dance Performance

6

Maurice Béjart's Variations on Wilde's *Salome* and Kinetic Translation of Words and Music in *La Mort Subite* (1991) and *Boléro* (1961)

Juliette Loesch

Introduction: Translation from the Page to the Stage[1]

Maurice Béjart's choreographic oeuvre is intimately linked to music. In his memoirs, the French dancer and choreographer (1927–2007) argues that human beings have a vital and organic connection with music that is most fully expressed and materialized through dance: 'c'est la rencontre de nos rythmes vitaux avec ce son étranger à notre organisme, mais pourtant accepté, aimé, intégré qui provoque ce phénomène qu'on nomme la danse' ('the encounter of our vital rhythms with this sound, external to our body and yet accepted, loved, integrated, provokes the phenomenon called dance') (Béjart 1996: 211). Béjart's ballets explore this sensuous and rhythmical encounter that lies at the heart of dance, and he used music as an essential impetus to his creative practice. His musical interests were wide-ranging, from classical music to raga, from pop-rock to opera.

Igor Stravinsky, Pierre Henry, Richard Wagner and Wolfgang Amadeus Mozart were constant sources of inspiration and many of his ballets transpose or rather translate into movements whole pieces, such as Stravinsky's *Firebird* and *The Rite of Spring*, Gustav Mahler's *Songs of a Wayfarer*, Mozart's *Magic Flute* and Ludwig van Beethoven's *9th Symphony*. In an interview, the choreographer stressed the 'magical' influence of great musical scores on his creativity, noting for instance that he was forced to surpass himself when working with these masterpieces (Béjart 1998, interview with Pastori). He conceived of the relation between music and dance in translational terms, as he expected his dancers to absorb and respond to the music through bodily language. The mediation is effected by the dancer who 'avale la musique, nous empêche de l'écouter avec les oreilles pour nous la faire entendre avec ses gestes, gestes nourris de musique, gestes qui jouent pour la musique le rôle d'interprète et la rendent visible et *traduite*, c'est-à-dire compréhensible' ('swallows the music, prevents us from listening to it with our ears to make us hear it through his/her gestures, which are fed with music, which play the role of interpreter for the music and make it visible and *translated*, i.e. understandable') (Béjart 1979: 152, my emphasis). The dancer becomes an embodiment of the score as s/he translates music into kinetic, visual and visible language for the audience. The synesthetic aspect of Béjart's description foregrounds the central role played by the body in this sensory experience, as the medium through which the translation is produced. In this translational relation from music to dance, music becomes fully intelligible to the spectator as it is materialized through the dancer's body. In this chapter, I will examine three modalities of the body in relation to music, namely the dancer's body as the mediator and translator of music, Béjart's revisiting of his own body of work, and finally the ensemble's body, the corps de ballet, as yet another body created by Béjart.

Besides music, Béjart kept exploring some favourite literary works (Béjart 1996: 123), such as Oscar Wilde's play *Salome* (1893).[2] Present in no less than nine choreographies, Wilde's dancing heroine centrally nurtured Béjart's creativity almost to the point of obsession. By returning to his muse repeatedly, Béjart worked under the constraint of a set script which paradoxically freed up his imagination in order to experiment further each time he restaged the princess' tragic story for ballet. He first choreographed Salome's dance for two films by François Weyergans (*Salomé 70* in 1969) and Pierre Koralnik (*Salomé* in 1969). Then, Béjart created ballets centred on Wilde's play (*Comme la princesse Salomé est belle ce soir* (How Beautiful is the Princess Salome Tonight) in 1970, *Salomé* in 1986 and *Iokanaan* in 2003), or where Salome makes an apparition (*Casta Diva* in 1980, *La Mort subite* (Sudden Death) in 1991 and *Opéra* in 1992). Marc Bochet (2007), Alain Montandon (2017: 187–207) and Jean-Pierre Pastori (2017) have noted Salome's central role in Béjart's career, but Fanny Pawyza (1996: 151–65) is the only one who studied the significance of this figure in the choreographer's repertoire in an article where she analyses two of his ballets, *Comme la princesse Salomé est belle ce soir* and *Salomé*.

Furthermore, Béjart also staged a version of Richard Strauss' opera with Julia Migenes Johnson at the Grand Théâtre de Genève (1983). Strauss' *Salome* (1905), whose libretto is based on Hedwig Lachmann's translation of Wilde's play, is also closely linked to Béjart's life-long fascination with Salome. In the programme of his opera staging, he observes: 'J'ai depuis très longtemps vécu avec la figure de

Salomé dans le cercle de mes désirs; j'ai toujours beaucoup *écouté* la Danse des sept voiles, j'ai toujours été fasciné par la terrible scène finale, et j'ai en fait plusieurs fois eu l'envie d'embrasser Salomé, sans jamais oser vraiment' ('The Salome figure has long been part of the circle of my desires; I have always *listened* to the Dance of the seven veils, I have always been fascinated with the terrible final scene, and I have actually wished I could kiss Salome many times, without ever really daring to') (Béjart 1983: 31; my emphasis). Strauss' music is thus central to Béjart's representation of Wilde's princess, and this intimate, even erotic, relation epitomizes the role played by both music and literature in his choreographies. Indeed, it is telling that Béjart's obsession for Salome, mediated by Strauss and Wilde, is congruent with his own creative practice which combines and transposes various art forms on stage. As Ariane Dollfus observes, Béjart can be considered a contemporary dance precursor because of his transversal pursuit of a 'total art' which challenges traditional boundaries to strengthen productive exchanges between the arts (2017: 233). He deliberately mixed high and popular cultures, and his unconstrained approach contributed to bringing dance to wider audiences around the world.

Moreover, the productive interplay between Strauss' opera and Wilde's play underlines the intrinsically transmedial nature of Salome as a cultural myth. The biblical story of the dancing princess who asks for the head of John the Baptist on a platter as a prize has a particularly rich intertextual and intermedial history. After dancing in front of the Tetrarch Herod in the Gospels of Mark and Matthew, Salome's performance has been re-enacted by countless artists and writers throughout the centuries, from biblical text to pictorial representations, from poetry and prose to opera, theatre and ballet adaptations. These many reworkings of the myth have made Salome a transmedial figure *par excellence* who keeps dancing between languages, art forms and media.

Wilde's own *Salome* already foregrounds the figure's transmediality. In *De Profundis*, the letter he wrote to his lover Lord Alfred Douglas from prison, he refers to 'the refrains whose recurring *motifs* make *Salomé* so like a piece of music and bind it together as a ballad' (Wilde 2003: 1026). His play, originally written in French, is set in motion by rhythmical refrains emulating the musicality of ballads. This rhythm also turns the text into a dance of sorts, even though Salome's 'dance of the seven veils' is famously left undescribed and open to interpretation in the stage directions.[3] Besides these intermedial connections within the play, Wilde was inspired by visual renderings of the enigmatic figure, most notably by Gustave Moreau's paintings of Salome: *Salomé dansant devant Hérode* (Salome Dancing before Herod) (1876) and *L'Apparition* (The Apparition)

(1876). He also culled rather openly from various textual sources, such as Stéphane Mallarmé's 'Hérodiade' (1871), Gustave Flaubert's *Hérodias* (1877) or Joris-Karl Huysmans's *Against Nature* (1884). With *Salome*, Wilde thus created a polyphony of voices, texts, art forms and media[4] that is in turn echoed and pursued in Béjart's choreographic work.

In this sense, Béjart's Salome ballets can be analysed through Roman Jakobson's linguistic concept of intersemiotic translation from verbal to non-verbal sign systems (2004: 139). Jakobson contributed to opening translation to non-verbal arts and media, and his seminal article has paved the way for more elaborate theorizations on interartistic and intermedial dynamics (see Louvel 2002). In the last decades of the twentieth century, translation studies shifted their focus from a linguistic model of equivalence between languages to foreground the cultural and creative dimension of translation instead (Bassnett 1993; Lefevere 1992).

Since the 'creative turn' in translation studies, translation is viewed as a form of creative rewriting, shaped by a set of sociopolitical, economic, formal and poetic constraints (Boase-Beier and Holman 1999: 6), and which implies the recreation of a text in a different linguistic and cultural system (Bassnett 2014: 10; Loffredo and Perteghella 2006). This paradigm shift has also awakened an interest in articulating translation studies and adaptation studies, with scholars noting striking similarities between the two recreative processes and fields.[5] Among these critics, Julie Sanders points out the need for 'a kinetic vocabulary' that departs from the linear and hierarchical relation between source and target artwork to foreground instead the creativity entailed by productive dynamics of adapting (Sanders 2016: 50). To this end, she suggests the musical term of variation, whereby a theme is reworked to create new musical phrases (ibid., 51–2).

This notion offers a metaphorical view of adaptation and translation as mobile and multimedial processes, and it captures Salome's potential for repetition with variation across different media and art forms, especially in the case of Béjart's own variations on the theme. Not only does Béjart refer to this musical concept when commenting on his creative practice, but the term is also used in choreography to describe a segment danced by one or several soloists and which can be extracted from the ballet to be performed on its own. As such, the variation is a moment that foregrounds the interpreter's creativity, because it 'constitue la pierre de touche, le joyau chorégraphique, où le chorégraphe peut déployer ses talents de composition tout comme le danseur démontrer son art' ('constitutes the touchstone, the choreographic gem, where the choreographer can deploy his/her composition skills and the dancer display his/her art') (Launay 2017: 81).

Therefore, I refer to this multilayered concept to shed light on the (re-)creative dynamics that give rise to new interpretations of the Salome theme. I also conceive of translation as an enlightening concept to study Wilde's and Béjart's creative movements between arts and media, especially when focusing on Béjart's use of music to adapt Wilde's *Salome* for ballet. To account for the dynamic process of translation and transmediation at work when Béjart translates both music and text into movements, I expand on Jakobson's concept of intersemiotic translation to describe Béjart's approach as kinetic translation. Béjart's variations on Salome are not simply a direct transposition of words or music into dance; rather, his work is enhanced by the productive interplay between his sources of inspiration and the ballet in the making. His creations are also nourished by a self-reflexive approach that calls back previous choreographies on stage in order to rethink and reconsider his own art. His interest does not simply lie in offering a choreographic version of a musical piece or a text, but he plays with the interaction of these various arts to create interartistic ballets and to stage the art of dance.

Indeed, Béjart underlines the transversal nature of dance by bringing together various art forms on stage, such as cinema, theatre and opera, and drawing on their rules of composition to shape his choreographies. In this chapter, I study the evolution of the Salome figure in two ballets by Béjart which translate music into their composition, structure, and choreographic syntax. *La Mort subite* (Béjart 1991),[6] starring the music-hall artist Ute Lemper, uses opera leitmotivs and musical variations to build an episodic ballet. Among the seven women embodied by Lemper, her Salome variation restages Béjart's previous versions of the dancing princess, along with one of his masterpieces, *Boléro* (1961: online). As Salome, Lemper reproduces gestures performed by the soloist who dances on Béjart's red table to the famous tune by Maurice Ravel (1928). The ballet recapitulates Béjart's past works in a musical mode that recalls Wilde's own vision of *Salome* as a ballad with recurring refrains. Although *Boléro* does not explicitly relate to Wilde's play, its reworking in *La Mort subite* helps reread it in light of *Salome*.

I am especially indebted to Pawyza who was the first scholar to draw a parallel between Béjart's *Boléro* and his obsession for Salome (Pawyza 1996: 153), even if she does not mention its restaging in *La Mort subite*. My analysis strengthens her claims and develops further the study of Béjart's variations on *Salome* by looking at the evolution of the myth in his work and in his self-reflexive approach to dance. For this reason, I start with *La Mort subite* and then reconsider *Boléro* as part of the series of variations on Wilde's text. Moreover, *Boléro* blurs artistic boundaries by dramatizing the encounter of dance and music in allegorical fashion through the soloist's representation of the Melody who is eventually swallowed by the Rhythm, embodied by the forty dancers around the table.[7] The choreography illustrates how music is translated into gestures and movements, and becomes ballet's driving force. Using the transmedial theme of Salome as a red thread for my analysis foregrounds the productive interplay between music and dance in Béjart's work and how the choreographer contributed to the open-ended sequence of variations on the emblematic dancer.

La Mort subite: A Ballet Built around Leitmotivs and Variations

La Mort Subite – Journal Intime (Sudden Death – A Diary) is a ballet that blurs generic boundaries. It doubles up as an autobiographical book (Béjart and Berger 1991) about the choreographer's relationship with his father, the philosopher Gaston Berger, whom Béjart last saw in the Brussels bar also named *La Mort subite* after the Belgian beer. From the start, *La Mort subite* moves between media and art forms. In the diary interspersed with his father's notes, Béjart muses about 'un ballet qui s'intitulerait "La mort subite", un ballet labyrinthe composite (la matière en transformation), dynamique, drôle même, variations sur un thème de ... mais qui serait la mort de tous mes ballets!' ('a ballet called "La mort subite", a composite (transforming matter) labyrinthine ballet, dynamic, even funny, variations on a theme by ... but which would be the death of all my ballets!') (Béjart and Berger 1991: 185). This composite labyrinth, shaped as musical variations which constantly transform and evolve, came into existence a few months after the publication of Béjart and Berger's diary.

Nevertheless, contrary to what the title suggests, the ballet is not so much about death as about punny variations on 'passing away/on'. As Béjart and the dramaturge François Regnault (who co-signed the texts for the performance) explain, 'c'est un ballet autour du passage, du passé, de la passation, de la passe, de l'impasse et surtout des pas' ('it is a ballet around the passage, the past, transfer, the pass, the impasse and more specifically steps [*pas*]') (Regnault and Béjart 1991: 1). It reads in French as a playfully alliterative and transformative sequence on passing that echoes themes central to Béjart's oeuvre: death, but also transmission, filiation, and dance as the favourite art form to thematize and enact them. The ballet is centred on seven female iconic figures representing cultural memory, all played by the music-hall star Ute Lemper: La Salute,[8] Salome, Faust's Gretchen, Penthesilea, Lulu, the Virgin Mary and Mother

Courage. This fatal woman kills seven times throughout the ballet under different guises, thereby sequencing the ballet in seven episodes, a possible hint at Salome's dance of the seven veils.

Béjart does not only memorialize his life and his relation with his father, but he also seeks to move on from his past works, and 'donner leur congé à quelques ballets du XXe siècle' ('dismiss some ballets of the 20th century') (Regnault and Béjart 1991: 1).[9] This nod to Béjart's previous company in Brussels, the Ballet du XXe siècle,[10] highlights the sense of continuous interplay between Béjart's ballets, while marking a need to turn the past, and death, into something dynamic that can also be joked about. Steps or even whole passages from previous works, such as *Le Chant du Compagnon errant* (Songs of a Wayfarer) (1971), *Gaîté parisienne* (Parisian Gaiety) (1978) or two major successes, *Le Sacre du printemps* (The Rite of Spring) (1959) and *Boléro* (1961), are thus revised and integrated to *La Mort subite*. In short, this performance emerges from a double movement: Béjart pays homage to his previous ballets while also staging his need to leave them behind and move on, in a self-parody of his work and role as choreographer.

Music appears as an essential structuring device in Béjart's farewell ballet to his previous pieces. In their explanatory note, Béjart and Regnault observe that, 'les thèmes s'enchevêtrent comme les leitmotivs d'un opéra sans que la citation ne soit jamais un "numéro" ou une suite de concert. Métamorphose perpétuelle, comme la variation musicale, de certains éléments originels de pas – reconnus' ('themes are entangled like opera leitmotivs, but the citation is never associated to a "number" or a concert sequence. Perpetual metamorphosis, like the musical variation, of some existing – and recognized – steps') (Regnault and Béjart 1991: 1).[11] The ballets of the twentieth century are represented as musical themes that dancers reshape like a variation, different but still recognizable. Instead of simply quoting from previous ballets, Béjart compares those references to a more subtle musical work where the melody would still be present although barely audible (Béjart 1990: 1, interview with Pastori). The repetition with variation mode is inspired here by opera where different leitmotivs interact to form a coherent whole.

Not only does *La Mort subite* dramatize music, but it also interrogates the art of dance and the ballet form in a kinetic translation of Béjart's previous works that stages and parodies the power of the choreographer over his dancers. This can be seen as a variation on the shifting power relations at the core of the Salome myth in the confrontation between the all-powerful Tetrarch Herod and the young dancer. Béjart's voice is heard repeatedly throughout the ballet as if he were rehearsing with his dancers and directing their steps. He keeps interrupting the narrative flow of the performance, thereby breaking the fourth wall and involving the audience in the creative process of choreographing.

As a kind of outsider from a different and more popular art form, Lemper plays a central role in challenging Béjart's authority over the ballet. When she enters, the meta-choreographic dimension is first highlighted by the dancers who clap and cheer to welcome the star on stage. Béjart underlines this mise en abyme as he then observes 'Comme vous êtes belle ce soir!' ('How beautiful you are tonight!') (Béjart 1991: 13:22–13:23). This echo from Wilde's *Salome*, which opens with the line 'Comme la princesse Salomé est belle ce soir!' ('How beautiful is the princess Salome tonight!') (Wilde 2006: 44–5), is a first hint at Lemper's future transformation into the dancing princess. However, Lemper interrupts Béjart's fantasy by asking him, 'Pourquoi ... ce soir?' ('Why ... tonight?') (ibid., 13:24–13:27). When Béjart persists and repeats, 'Comme vous êtes belle!' ('How beautiful you are!') (ibid., 13:27–13:28), she observes that, 'les hommes font toujours des compliments aux femmes dont ils n'ont pas envie' ('men always pay compliments to women they don't want') (ibid., 13:31–13:35). With this joking repartee to her director, the singer ironically points out the staged dimension of their exchange and performance, while accepting to play her part in his work of art. Despite Lemper's sarcastic attitude towards him, Béjart still remains in control over the sequence of episodes in the ballet. He orders for instance her transformation into Salome when he calls the princess on stage by quoting 'Comme, la princesse, Salomé, est belle ce soir' ('How, beautiful, is the princess, Salome tonight.') (ibid., 30:08–30:16). The quotation is followed by an extract from Strauss' opera, the 'Dance of the Seven Veils', where Salome stops singing to dance for her stepfather Herod. Lemper reappears then, perched on high platform shoes used in Kabuki theatre.

The entrance of Lemper as Salome references several of Béjart's past variations on the theme. In his pas-de-deux about Wilde's play, *Comme la princesse Salomé est belle ce soir*, the choreographer prompts his dancers' transformation into Salome and Iokanaan, John's archaic name in *Salome*, with the same direct quotation from the text. At first, Josiane Consoli and Michaël Denard are two dancers warming up on stage, but Denard interrupts their exercise session and utters in a very slow and articulate manner this line which will reveal the two protagonists to one another and to the audience. Lemper's outfit also hints at two other versions of Salome from Béjart's series of variations, namely *Casta Diva* and the *Salomé* solo for Patrick Dupond. In these two versions, a male Salome, played by Béjart and Dupond respectively, is dressed in Kabuki costume and shoes. Another object has been carried across these two ballets to reappear in *La*

Mort subite: the playball that symbolizes the severed head of the Baptist. It is first represented as a white rugby ball in *Casta Diva* when a masked Béjart recites Salome's final monologue to the head. The choreographer develops this motif further in Dupond's solo, where a rugby player slowly metamorphoses into a ballerina as he parodies academic ballet in a dance with the same white ball. The latter also transforms throughout the solo, and it is eventually replaced by a reproduction of Dupond's own head which he kisses when the curtain falls. In *La Mort subite*, the head has become a red basketball that dancers throw at each other during Lemper's Salome variation, thereby highlighting the playfulness behind any scenic performance, be they comedies or tragedies. The moment Lemper catches it signals the death of the dancer playing Iokanaan, who falls down simultaneously. These different playballs also relate dancers to sportspersons, which draws attention to the athletics of ballet and the efforts of the dancers' physical body. These recurring motifs create a sequence of Salome that evolves towards parody and where each new ballet echoes previous variations to stage the myth anew in the interplay of repetition and difference.

Salome becomes an occasion for Béjart to interrogate further the relation between the choreographer, the dancer and the spectator in *La Mort subite*. After Lemper has taken off the platform shoes, Béjart's voice can be heard again, asking in German 'Tanz für mich, Salomé' ('Dance for me, Salome') (ibid., 31:11–31:13). In addition to reinforcing the link with Strauss' opera, this intervention foregrounds the meta-choreographic reflexions of the ballet. Lemper replies indeed, 'Je ne danse pas pour mon metteur en scène. Je danse pour le public' ('I don't dance for my director. I dance for the audience.') (ibid., 31:24–31:29). The singer rejects Béjart's Herod-like fantasy and authority to proclaim the audience as the real target of her seductive dance. Nevertheless, it is Béjart who gives her the beat for the next dance. In response, Salome, accompanied by several dancers, starts a sequence of movements from the *Boléro* choreography. Not only is Lemper's Salome associated to previous adaptations of Wilde's play, but she also evokes Béjart's well-known ballet. Béjart thus activates his audience's memory and invites them to identify the different extracts that constitute his composite ballet, thereby involving them in the process of creation. Nevertheless, he plays with the public's expectations by modifying the music of his previous work. The choreography that is so strongly attached to Ravel's score is performed here to a repetitive speech uttered by Gil Roman, one of the soloists, and then to a Chaconne by Christoph Willibald Gluck, thereby freeing the dance from its musical origins. Only the movements mark the link with the initial choreography here. This variation, that Béjart himself coordinates in his dialogue with the dancers, blurs the lines between original performance and restaging, rehearsal and live production, to shed light on the instability of dance as an art form that constantly evolves with each new performance, interpreter and audience, thereby moving away from the choreographer's initial idea.

The figure of Salome is also released from Strauss' opera, which announced her entrance, thanks to this other score and choreography that reinvent her dance of the seven veils. In the manuscript notes written by Regnault in preparation for *La Mort subite*, the Salome episode is described as follows: 'la belle inconnue meurtrière est revenue, mais nul ne la reconnaît. Sur une *Chaconne* de Gluck, elle danse le Ballet du *Boléro*. À la fin, elle est engloutie dans l'ensemble des Danseurs compact' ('the beautiful and murderous stranger has come back, but no one recognizes her. She dances the *Boléro* ballet to a Chaconne by Gluck. In the end, she is engulfed by the compact group of dancers') (Regnault 1990: 2). Salome hides by blurring the lines between the different musical and choreographic references. Although the ballet has evolved since this initial idea and Lemper is not engulfed by the dancers at the end, Regnault's staging spells out the link between Wilde's *Salome*, *La Mort subite* and *Boléro*. Wilde's play ends with a similar scene, as the Tetrarch Herod orders Salome's death who is then 'crush[ed] beneath [the soldiers'] shields' (Wilde 2006: 164). Through *La Mort subite*, Salome's death is related to the ending of Béjart's *Boléro* where the Melody is absorbed by the forty dancers symbolizing the Rhythm. Moreover, the composite ballet with Lemper helps reread Salome as the *Boléro*'s Melody, a moving representation of music that translates visually and kinetically Wilde's conception of his play as a 'piece of music' (Wilde 2003: 1026). Echoing the repetitive structure of Ravel's piece and of Béjart's homonymous choreography, the theme of Salome is thus revisited with variation throughout the choreographer's oeuvre. His reworking process in *La Mort subite* sheds light on the creative potential of variation, whereby a known theme or ballet can be read anew in light of their intertexts or of previous variations.

Rereading *Boléro* Backwards: The Melody as Salome

Although Béjart never explicitly acknowledged it, *La Mort subite* thus underlines how *Boléro* relates to the choreographer's life-long obsession with Salome. He explains that the dynamics of his ballet are centred on the interplay between melody and rhythm, which is based on Ravel's famously repetitive ostinato:

Une mélodie (d'origine orientale et non espagnole) s'enroule inlassablement sur elle-même. Symbole féminin, souple et chaud, d'une inévitable unicité. Un rythme mâle, qui tout en restant le même, va en augmentant de volume et d'intensité, dévorant l'espace sonore et engloutissant à la fin la mélodie.

Béjart 1988

(A melody (originally Oriental and not Spanish) winds around itself ceaselessly. A feminine symbol, flexible and warm, inevitably unique. A male rhythm, which remains the same, increases in volume and intensity, devouring the sound space and engulfing the melody in the end.)

The ballet translates his vision of the musical piece into shape and movement, with one main dancer in the role of the Melody and forty dancers representing the Rhythm. The Melody dances on a red table, surrounded by the forty dancers who gradually get up from their chairs to join in the dance and finally engulf the lonely soloist. This kinetic translation follows the principle of *replication* that Susan Leigh Foster develops as one of the four modes of representation in dance (Foster 1986: 65). She explains that replication represents the events 'as a dynamic system, an organic whole made up of functionally distinct parts' and that 'the movement replicates the relationship of these parts' (ibid., 66). Béjart thus chooses to replicate the musical relationship between the Melody and the Rhythm through gestures.

Boléro was first performed in 1961 in Brussels with Duška Sifnios in the lead role of the Melody surrounded by forty male dancers lusting after her.[12] Pawyza analyses the link between Salome and the Melody, explaining that:

la Salomé du *Boléro* inscrit dans l'air toute la jubilation qu'éprouve l'être dansant à penser, sentir, regarder et posséder autrui par sa seule présence mouvante. C'est précisément parce qu'elle ne se fixe ni ne se fige jamais que la danseuse séduit et inspire la convoitise tout en s'en délivrant cependant.

Pawyza 1996: 154

(*Boléro*'s Salome inscribes in the air the dancing being's jubilation as she thinks, feels, looks at and possesses the other thanks to her sole moving presence. It is precisely because she never stops or freezes that the dancer seduces and provokes desire while remaining free.)

The figure in continuous motion on the table highlights the power of dance and of the dancer over her audience: much like the hypnotic melodic themes repeated throughout Ravel's score, the ongoing movements of the dancer trap the public in a voyeuristic trance emulating Salome's dance in Wilde's play.

Nevertheless, like Wilde's Salome, killed under the soldiers' shields at the end of the play, Béjart's melodic Salome is absorbed by the male Rhythm. The choreographer underlines how desire underpins the interplay between the Melody and the Rhythm, and he describes how the Rhythm is seduced and lured by the Melody, until everything is 'consummated' when the Rhythm 'devours' the latter (Béjart 1979: 151). Other elements relate Béjart's Melody to his vision of Salome. In his memoirs, he explains that he used elements from striptease in the erotic version with Sifnios (ibid.). This element coupled with his focus on the Oriental dimension of the score, instead of the more obvious Spanishness of *Boléro*, links the Melody's dance with Wilde's Oriental princess and her dance of the seven veils. Moreover, Béjart describes his first interpreter as 'superbe et fastueuse, faisant impudemment étalage d'un narcissisme d'enfant' ('superb and sumptuous, displaying child-like narcissism') (ibid., 152), which echoes his vision of Salome as 'une femme-enfant, une ingénue perverse mais où l'ingénuité doit être très forte' ('a woman-child, a pervert ingénue whose naivety must be very strong') (Mannoni and Béjart 1985: 26). Therefore, Wilde's princess had already started her obsessive dance in Béjart's work as of 1961, dancing her way through the choreographer's kinetic translation of Ravel's score.

A Kinetic Translation of Music

In his version of *Boléro*, Béjart offers a personal reading of the intimate relation between dance and music. Not unlike the structure of *La Mort subite*, which draws its inspiration from the episodic construction of opera, music is central to Béjart's *Boléro*, as his choreography closely follows the structure of Ravel's piece. The latter is organized in eighteen sections – preceded by a two-bar ritornello – where a theme A (one section of sixteen bars of melody) alternates with a counter-theme B (another section of sixteen bars of melody) (Gut 1990: 35). The theme A and its counter-theme B are played twice before alternating, except in the last two sections before the final modulation, where they are played once only (ibid.). Deborah Mawer, a specialist in Ravel's music, explains that the piece 'is not strictly a crescendo but a series of terraced steps from *pp* to *ff*' and that 'its basic plan comprises two related, repeated melodic materials (AABB), of thirty-four bars' duration' (Mawer 2000: 156). Only the last section does not feature the ritornello, the two bars where the famous ostinato rhythm is usually in the foreground. Mawer describes the last six bars as 'the breaking-point: melody is destroyed, reiterated movement is merely impotent stasis' (ibid., 160).

Béjart reproduces a similar pattern as his ballet is also structured around eighteen sections. This construction principle follows the syntactic choice of *mimesis* theorized by Foster and which 'functions whenever the choreography reproduces the structure of the music,' (Foster 1986: 93).

In order to remember the sequence of these different sections, Béjart named them according to the kind of movement prevalent in each part.[13] From the end of the second section onward, the ritornello is depicted by the 'Camel' move, where the dancer bends with a flat back, arms extended down and hands facing the floor, her pelvis going up and down in rhythm with the ostinato. At the end of *Boléro*, the Melody is similarly destroyed by the forty dancers who climb on her table to bring her down. Maurice Fleuret has underlined how Béjart's choreography reworks the usual relation between music and dance in ballet and observed that 'the choreographic work, instead of being a puerile compromise between the storyline-as-pretext and the music-as-filler, becomes a reading through movement, an exploration and exaltation of the musical sense' (in Mawer 2006: 243–4). Unlike ballets using music as a simple score to accompany movements, Béjart's choreography becomes a gestural staging of the musical dynamics at stake in Ravel's *Boléro*.

Much like the music which grows from *pianissimo* to *fortissimo*, bringing in ever more instruments, the dance starts with simple movements that mobilize only specific body parts before gradually involving the dancer's whole body. The arms are the first limbs to embrace the melody, by tracing half-circles around Sifnios' body, first one after the other, then both together. Even if she does not focus on the relation between music and movements in her study of Béjart's *Boléro* as a 'site of memory', Stéphanie Gonçalves offers a convincing analysis of the central and precise role of the arms in the choreography, noting how '[ils] ne cessent de "chanter" la mélodie et de donner les accents, comme un chef d'orchestre' ('[they] never stop "singing" the melody and indicating accents, like a conductor') (Gonçalves 2019: para 11). Although the dancer on the table represents the Melody, the ostinato rhythm still circulates through her body and influences her movements from the beginning.[14] Ravel's melody starts only after four bars where the snare drums play the famous ostinato motif twice. Nevertheless, Sifnios' body is already in motion before the flute starts playing the first notes of the melody. Her pelvis follows the beat of *Boléro* and the change of weight instilled by this rhythm has repercussions throughout her body and activates her feet which then maintain the cadence throughout the ballet. In her extensive study of *The Ballets of Maurice Ravel*, Mawer analyses Jorge Donn's performance and she observes that this 'repeated footwork also constitutes a compelling dance ostinato, analogous to Ravel's one-bar units' (Mawer 2006: 244–5). In the first sequence, the dancer's arms, aligned with the melody, seem distinct from the body which follows the impulse of the rhythm. The latter serves as the canvas upon which the melody rewrites the dancer's body. More precisely, the rhythm allows the soloist to create the weight transfer that proves essential to the dancer's space-time, as Laurence Louppe argues:

> l'espace-temps du danseur doit, lui, se trouver à travers un travail de corps, et ne peut faire, pour exister dans la danse, l'économie du transfert de poids, seul capable de transformer et même de susciter une figure ou un lieu.
>
> Louppe 2004: 206

> (the dancer's space-time is to be found in the body and cannot exist in dance without weight transfer, the sole dynamics that can transform and even create a figure or a location.)

It is only through weight transfer that the dancer is able to shape space and create moving forms. In this case, *Boléro*'s repetitive rhythm creates this essential movement that then gives birth to the Melody and its kinetic translation through the dancer's body and space-time.

As more instruments join in and the dynamics slowly move from the initial *pianissimo* to the final *fortissimo*, her body is more and more mobilized. In the second sequence, where the clarinet takes over from the flute, both arms move together to encircle the dancer's body. This second sequence repeats the theme A in Ravel's composition, and the dancer's doubling of her previous arm movements echoes this repetition. As the music progresses, the movements of the Melody dancing on the table become more complex and operate in different planes in space. For instance, she arches her torso in different directions and changes the orientation of her moves, exploring diagonal lines or circles. Moreover, the dancers representing the Rhythm enter gradually as of the ninth sequence, first two by two and then four by four until the whole remaining group joins in for the final modulation that eventually destroys the Melody.

The choreography for both the Melody and the Rhythm thus reproduces the intensification of the dynamics. Gut observes that three secondary parameters of composition vary in Ravel's *Boléro* – namely the dynamics, the tone and what he terms the 'thickness' of the melody – whereas the three main parameters – i.e. the rhythm, the melody and the harmony – remain stable in 'repetitive immobility' (Gut 1990: 37–8). The choreography follows a similar principle as the dancers' movements are contained within one clearly delineated space (either on or around the table). The 'Camel' move that translates Ravel's ritornello into a reiterated gesture keeps calling the Melody back to this 'repetitive immobility' in the centre of the table.

The final modulation in E major abruptly puts an end to the 'incantatory enchantment' (ibid., 44). The melody departs from its previous organization around the theme and the counter-theme and the rhythm gradually takes on the central role as more and more instruments embrace it and abandon the melody. The dance reflects this power imbalance and disrupts the clear-cut spatial boundaries between Melody and Rhythm when the latter assaults the table. In this last sequence, the men do not simply admire the Melody from afar but surround and climb on her table to trap her and eventually swallow her up under their extended arms. Gut reads Ravel's ending not as 'une explosion libératrice, mais plutôt [un] hurlement de désespoir provoqué par l'éternel retour de la même ritournelle dont on se demande si elle ne va pas nous annihiler' ('a liberating explosion, but rather a cry of despair provoked by the eternal return of the same ritornello which threatens to annihilate us') (ibid., 44). His interpretation underlines the need to destroy the Melody to escape its nerve-racking repetitiveness, which finds echo in Herod's order to kill Salome, the dangerous woman who could destroy him and his realm. Therefore, Béjart's choreography and continuous relation to Wilde's *Salome* unveils hidden similarities between the play and Ravel's music.

Going Full Circle: History of *Boléro* and Salome

Béjart's ballet was not the first to bring Ravel's music and Salome's dance together. In fact, Ravel's piece was created for a dancer who played an important role in the *Salomania* that shook modern dance at the beginning of the twentieth century, namely Ida Rubinstein. In 1908, the Russian dancer performed *Wilde's Salome*, thereby joining the many female dancers who embodied Salome to experiment with a freer dance form that moved away from the rigid codes of classical ballet and from the ambivalent fantasy of the fatal woman. As Toni Bentley observes, Salome could not express herself in the fixed world of ballet; 'she did, however, uncannily incorporate the prerequisites of early modern dancers – barefoot, uncorseted, half-naked, uncompromising, and ruled by her need for self-expression. Hers was a solo act' (Bentley 2002: 43–4). Rubinstein thus joined Loie Fuller, Ruth St Denis and Maud Allan in creating her own version of the dance of the seven veils, in a performance choreographed by Michel Fokine from the Ballets Russes and whose costumes were designed by

Léon Bakst. Twenty years later, she commissioned Ravel to create a Spanish ballet that became *Boléro*. The 1928 programme note describes her performance, choreographed by Bronislava Nijinska, as such: 'Inside a tavern in Spain, people dance beneath the brass lamp hung from the ceiling. [In response] to the cheers to join in, the female dancer has leapt onto the long table and her steps become more and more animated' (Mawer 2006: 227). Gonçalves also underlines 'la dimension sexuelle et sensuelle' ('the sexual and sensual dimension') of this first version, where a woman becomes the centre of attention (Gonçalves 2019: para 5). The tavern table thus symbolizes the filiation between Rubinstein's performance and Béjart's choreography, which both stage dynamics of desire and seduction.

To conclude, *Boléro* captures the ongoing translational movement between Wilde's *Salome*, Béjart's choreographies and Ravel's music. Like the score's repetitive rhythm and the melody that constantly winds around itself (Béjart 1988), these different works are set in an ongoing motion. Wilde's text contained *in potentia* the lyrical and kinetic qualities that continued to inspire musicians and choreographers as they transposed the play into other art forms, referencing and combining more and more variations. Even though Ravel's piece was not inspired by Salome, it has become a variation on this theme via both Rubinstein and Béjart, up to *La Mort subite*. Béjart's ballets, with their strong focus on music, are meant as total works of art, bringing various media and art forms together on stage. More specifically, the choreographer's vision of the dancing body as an instrument capable of translating music and literature, and of mediating cultural history for a contemporary audience, has made his work an essential link in the chain of variations that has kept Salome dancing for centuries.

Notes

1   I am very grateful to Martine Hennard Dutheil de la Rochère for her careful reading and her insightful comments on this chapter. I would also like to thank the SAPA Foundation (Swiss Archive of the Performing Arts) for giving me access to their rich archival fonds, the Maurice Béjart Foundation and François Regnault who kindly gave me permission to quote from these archives, as well as Kathryn Bradney for the stimulating conversation about her work with Maurice Béjart.

2   The play was originally written in French and titled *Salomé*. Lord Alfred Douglas' English translation, *Salome*, was published a year later, in 1894. Since this chapter is written in English, I will use the English spelling to refer to Wilde's play throughout.

3 The elliptical stage direction only indicates that '*Salome dances the dance of the seven veils*' (Wilde 2006: 140).
4 In 'Decadent Senses: The Dissemination of Oscar Wilde's *Salomé* Across the Arts', Polina Dimova analyses how Wilde's *Salome* and its transformations into Aubrey Beardsley's illustrations and Richard Strauss' opera are related to translation and intermediality and argues for the recognition of interartistic and 'intermedial translation as a creative act securing the artwork's "afterlife" in Walter Benjamin's terms' (Dimova 2013: 15).
5 Katja Krebs notes, for instance, that 'both translation studies and adaptation studies are interdisciplinary by their very nature; both discuss the phenomena of constructing cultures through acts of rewriting and both are concerned with the collaborative nature of such acts and the subsequent and necessary critique of notions of authorship' (Krebs 2012: 43). Manuela Perteghella explains that: '[t]he diversity between [translation and adaptation], I have maintained, is not so much "in the "process" of writing, always an act of reworking material, and not so much in the final product, always an interpretation, but rather in the ways this product is subsequently perceived by its receivers"' (2013: 205).
6 The performance is first presented in Paris on 6 February 1991, and then reworked and performed with texts in German in Recklinghausen in May 1991 (Béjart and Pastori 1992: 19).
7 As *Boléro*'s Rhythm, Béjart's dancers embody what Stephanie Jordan defines as the 'point of contact' between music and dance. Jordan has theorized the relation between these two art forms as 'choreomusical' and she identifies rhythm 'as the main component for the comparison of music and dance' and 'an immediate point of contact between the two art forms' (Jordan 2011: 52).
8 The French masculine noun *salut* (salvation) is here used as a proper name in a feminized form.
9 Reprinted by kind permission of François Regnault and the Maurice Béjart Foundation.
10 Béjart and his company left Brussels in 1987 to settle in Lausanne, where the company was renamed Béjart Ballet Lausanne.
11 Reprinted by kind permission of François Regnault and the Maurice Béjart Foundation.
12 Béjart realized that this pattern could be reverted in a *Boléro II*, and in 1979 he gave the role of the Melody to one of his greatest dancers, Jorge Donn, who danced in the middle of forty female dancers. This gender shift also changes the dynamics of the ballet to transform it into a ceremonial, as Béjart explains in his memoirs (Béjart 1979: 53). The ritualistic dimension of *Boléro* is emphasized in the third version where a male dancer is surrounded by forty other male dancers. A *Boléro IV* was also created in 2004 with a female and a male dancer dancing simultaneously. In this

chapter, I will focus on *Boléro I* because its dynamics are more closely related to Salome's story.

13 The complete sequence is: Arms (1 and 2), Hands, Pincers, Shoulders, Folded arms, Samba, Développé, Pincers, Jeté arabesque, Belly, B.B., Mill, Cat, Folklore, Greek, Big jumps, Jambe à la main. These steps are listed, illustrated and explained on a written document by Angela Albrecht, one of the *Boléro* soloists, which I could consult at the SAPA Foundation. For more details on this document (see Gonçalves 2019: para 21).

14 This is especially visible in the recording of Sifnios' performance, as it starts with a wide shot in full light. Ensuing recordings and performances emphasize first the dancer's embodiment of the Melody by casting a spotlight on the arm moving up and down, and leaving the body in complete darkness.

7

The Music has Movement in It

Lesley Main

This essay examines the place of 'translation' in relation to the staging of a dance work, with particular reference to the relationship/s between music and choreography, and the consequential impact of one on the other through the process of staging. Taking as a starting premise the idea of translation as a means of communication, the discussion will consider what such a premise brings to a staging process, and the resultant impact on a work from the perspectives of director, performers and audience. The title for the essay is taken from a letter written in 1943 by Doris Humphrey, the American modern dance pioneer, to John Martin, dance critic at the *New York Times*. The letter was essentially a defence of the choreographer's use of J. S. Bach's music for a number of her dances from 1928 on, a practice that did not find favour, with the critics at least, over a period of years (Main 2012: 83).

Within the discussion, the notion of 'intersemiotic translation', as highlighted by Minors (2013), is explored through two case studies that provide contrasting yet connecting musical/dance investigatory examples – *Passacaglia*, Humphrey's landmark work from 1938 set to J. S. Bach's work of equal stature, *Passacaglia and Fugue in C minor*, and *With My Red Fires* (1936), with music by Humphrey's contemporary, Wallingford Riegger and composed *after* the choreography was complete. Labanotation and music scores are considered in terms of what these parallel languages can add to a staging process. In the case of *Passacaglia*, a further layer is added through the various recordings and arrangements on offer, including Leopold Stokowski's 1922 orchestral arrangement.

The discussion draws on established positions such as Stephanie Jordan's argument, that 'one role of dance *is* to illuminate music, to provide a new experience of music that is already known to the audience member/listener/observer' (Jordan 2015: 85). Here, Jordan is referencing the work of Mark Morris, including his extended use of the Baroque canon throughout his career, which provides an apt reference point for the case study of choreomusical relationships in Humphrey's *Passacaglia*. More broadly, ideas including the translation of sound, dynamic and structure; the embodiment of sound; the significance of structure and rhythm, patterns, impulses will be interrogated through the case studies.

Translation as a Means of Communication

Having written previously about staging dance works from the interconnecting perspectives of 'transmission, translation, transformation' (Main 2017: 89), new questions arise when shifting the starting premise to just one of these positions. What does a translation-based approach bring to a staging process? What is it that is being translated – scores, choreography, movement, interpretation, recordings? What could the notion of intersemiotic translation mean in relation to dance? In relation to the latter, Minors offers a useful definition – 'a transmutation, or transference, of sense from one art form, or sign system, to another' (2013b: 2), and further, '(t)hrough the process of translation, this sense is transferred into a new language system' (ibid., 5). 'Sense' could be further defined as meaning, understanding, identity, signifier, as but a few examples. What interests me is the idea of process (as also explored in Chapters 2, 3, 4 and 5) and the activity of transference which, together, provide a channel for communicating meaning into a new and/or different context.

To explore these questions and others that will undoubtedly arise along the way, I offer a model generated from the idea of 'a score being a map', as observed by composer Matteo Fargion (Perazzo Domm 2008: 133) in relation to *Both Sitting Duet* (2002), a dance work he co-created with choreographer Jonathan Burrows. Fargion was discussing their instinctive responses to Morton Feldman's score, *For John Cage* (1982), 'We translated note for note this very long piece for violin and piano into movement – and then discarded it completely – so you don't hear the music when we perform the dance' (Cripps 2004: 18). To give this example some further context, Feldman's composition is described as:

> a 70-minute work for violin and piano that invites the performers to traverse a myriad of inflections, intonations and asymmetric patterning. Notes are rendered repetitively in variable constellations of duration and shading, making for a measured musical construction that is deceptively static.
>
> Cruttwell-Reade 2012: October

One can detect a rich complexity within this musical piece that Fargion and Burrows worked through to arrive at their own creative response – I use the word 'through' particularly here rather than 'on' or 'over', to distinguish the deep and careful relationship with the source material. The idea of the 'map' invokes the presence of navigation, of an active participation in the discovery of direction or, equally, the direction of discovery as the Fargion/Burrows example illustrates.

If the premise of 'score as map' is accepted as the vehicle through which a work is to be staged/translated/communicated, an early step in that process is determining 'what' constitutes the score. In relation to the approach to dance staging that I take, and have previously documented in some detail (Main 2012 and 2017), the score of a work can have multiple components including but not restricted to the following: Labanotation score; music score; known and embodied choreography/movement from previous stagings; pre-existing recordings or arrangements of the music; text, including poetry, or visual images drawn on by the choreographer during the original creative process. This group of components exist as material entities that can be studied, considered, analysed independently, in relation to each other and as connecting parts of a whole. Approaching the defining of component parts of a score in this way places the focus on that which already exists and, further, of using these fixed entities to communicate meaning, or 'sense' (Minors 2013b: 2), in a different sphere.

The Score as a Map

Whilst the aforementioned entities themselves may be fixed, their inclusion as components of a score will likely alter from one production process to another depending on directorial choice. As one example, there may not always be a Labanotation score of the version of a work being staged. Equally, a director may choose not to involve a Labanotation score at all because the work is staged from embodied memory, a longstanding staging practice in dance. Having identified the component parts, the score/map then acts as a conduit to an interpretation of a work, a process in which the reading of the map involves the translation of its signs/components. To give an illustration using Humphrey's *Passacaglia*, the entities/components/signs that could be identified as forming 'maps' to previous productions of the dance include, as one set, the Labanotation score written by Lucy Venable,[1] an organ recording of the music performed by Lionel Rogg and a filmed version of the dance directed by Venable; another set comprised the embodied choreography, Leopold Stokowski's orchestral arrangement of the

Bach and written observations on the music by Humphrey. These two sets of components indicate the range of possibility that can be available to a director in relation to a single work.[2] Once the director is at the point of having a confirmed set of components, such as a map, the task of translation can commence and the processes of navigation and discovery, as referred to earlier, can come into play.

To explore these ideas in more depth, the discussion will now focus specifically on potential 'maps' for staging two Humphrey works, *Passacaglia* and *With My Red Fires*. For *Passacaglia*, the components are the director's embodied knowledge of the choreography from previous stagings; the Stokowski arrangement and a recording he conducted with the Philadelphia Symphony Orchestra in 1973 (see Johnson 1973: sleeve notes); and this following extract from Humphrey's letter to John Martin written in 1943:

> I picked Bach for music because I still think he has the greatest of all genius for these very qualities of variety held in unity, of grandeur of the human spirit, of grace for fallen man; not only this, but I sincerely believe the music has movement in it, based on dances of forgotten men and women who are the authors of much of the music of this or any other age.
>
> Cohen 1995: 256[3]

For *With My Red Fires*, the map comprises a Labanotation score, the musical score by Wallingford Riegger, an unattributed photograph of Humphrey in the leading role of 'The Matriarch' and an extract from William Blake's epic poem *Jerusalem*, 'For the Divine Appearance is Brotherhood, but I am Love; Elevate into the Region of Brotherhood with my red fires' (Blake *Jerusalem* 1804: lines 53–4). When considering these components from a translation-based perspective, my observation is that there is a shared equitability, with each component signifying a layer of knowledge intrinsic to communicating the work, as opposed to one or other element being dominant and more influential on directorial interpretation. The act of translating each layer creates a composite set of meanings that, when considered together, produces a navigational route to conveying the meaning of a work.

For *Passacaglia*, the components/layers lie in the domains of movement, sound and text; for *With My Red Fires*, two distinct notation (language) systems, visual imagery and text. I would argue that making 'sense' of these components is a process of intersemiotic translation in respect of Minors' definition that 'sense is transferred into a new language system' (2013b: 2). The transference is twofold, first from each component's primary state to the composite map, and thence, through the map to the work as manifested in (the new language system of) performance.

Navigating *Passacaglia*

To give some brief context, *Passacaglia* is cast for a group of eighteen including two 'leaders', originally danced by Humphrey and Charles Weidman, her artistic partner. Humphrey layered her choreographic structure over Bach's musical structure. The work is in 3/4 meter, with the *Passacaglia* section musically arranged in twenty-one 8-measure phrases. The *Fugue* form, following musical convention, is more asymmetric. Bach adopted a structure comprising twelve phrases of differing length and a coda. The opening tableau shows the entire group arrayed on a configuration of rising platforms positioned centre stage, facing away from the audience with arms held aloft in a striking pose. As the lighting builds and Bach's music seeps into the gathering, a collective stillness pervades the arena until one figure then a second turn toward the audience. They emerge into the space and trace a circular pathway from one side of the group to the other, their arrival causing the whole group to turn as one in a slow, dignified manner. A second pair of dancers joins the first as they open up the space further, this time on diagonal pathways, until the 'leaders' take over, addressing the audience head on in a series of rising, expansive gestures that reach out invitingly. There follows an exposition of ensemble choreography that takes the audience through all manner of small groupings and configurations that constantly move in and out of the main ensemble, on and off the platforms. The 'leaders' lead without domination, the ensemble dancers all have individual significance within the 'whole'. The movement vocabulary encapsulates the ever-changing dynamics of Bach's music, at one moment, intricate rhythmic gestures followed by expansive off-balance swinging turns. The group wends its way together through a dynamic procession in which each individual member participates in trios, quartets and quintets and in the magnificent ensemble displays that climax both parts of the dance. The mood is never introspective and maintains an open, engaging tone to the end (see Main 2012: 79).

Humphrey's choreographic process for *Passacaglia* was influenced by Stokowski's orchestral arrangement of the music, although performances of the dance were routinely accompanied by piano.[4] The significance of the presence of the Stokowski orchestration during the period of creation in 1937–8 relates to Humphrey being exposed to the 'sound' produced by the orchestration, and how that in turn correlates with her 'Fall and Recovery' movement style which is inherently full-bodied (see Figure 7.1) and expansive (see Main 2012: 17).[5] There is indication, therefore, that a sound/embodiment connection existed from the work's conception in addition to Humphrey being interested in exploring other musical elements, including Bach's phrase structure and rhythmic patterning.

Figure 7.1 *Passacaglia 14* MOMENTA Dance Company 2007: Stephen Green Photography.[6]

Add to this her observations on Bach's composition cited above – 'variety held in unity', 'grandeur of the human spirit', 'dances of forgotten men and women', with the overarching statement that 'the music has movement in it' (Cohen 1995: 256) – and the interconnection between component layers begins to reveal itself alongside the potential for translatable meaning.

Stokowski was well known for his transcriptions of Bach's music, having tackled almost forty compositions over his career. At one time, musicologists discredited his approach because of the idiosyncratic nature of the arrangements. Debates in musicology on the interpretation and performance of Bach subsequently broadened beyond the traditionally acceptable 'geometric' style to encompass the performer-centred 'vitalist style'. Stokowski's approach, representative of the latter position, became less controversial over time (Main 2012: 83). Having previously staged Humphrey's *Passacaglia* solely to organ recordings, encountering the Stokowski orchestration was a major discovery in directorial terms, with the most distinctive element being the sound because it offered a scale or magnitude that, in my view, was less present in alternative arrangements. In defining what I mean by 'the sound', in broad terms it is about expanse, resonance, drama, colour, nuance, variation, all terms that could equally be applied to the sound produced by an organ. The distinction for me relates to instrumentation, and the range of musical voices and lines that exist within an orchestration and, concurrent with that, the presence of these voices alongside other contributing factors such as variance in phrasing, dynamic and tempi. One could argue, therefore, that the properties created by orchestral playing are different from those created by an organ, thus the musical layer of the map will be different and, following on, the response by the translator/director would likely shift depending on which musical 'sound' was employed.

An example that illustrates the distinction between orchestra and organ comes early in the work. The orchestration becomes more luminous and layered throughout the opening four variations of the Passacaglia section, in direct contrast to the ponderous chordal sounds produced by the organ (to the ear of the author). The opening bar of Passacaglia 4 creates a unified optimism through the dual aspect of the strings picking up the theme and a purposeful increase in tempo, at the very moment, choreographically, that the group moves as one for the first time. The movement, a unison pivot-turn from up-stage to down-stage, is a powerful moment for the ensemble because the combination of the movement with resulting colour change (as the two-sided costumes reverse) conveys the start of something significant (see Figure 7.2). Stokowski's orchestration gives this moment a greater resonance than the organ in two specific contexts. From the dancer's perspective, the pivot-turn feels more uplifted and energized by adopting the dynamics produced by the sound of the strings. This heightened sense of suspension is manifested both aurally and visually, and also increases the impact of the first sighting of the ensemble and the possibilities of who or what this group might be?[7] To answer that question, the director can incorporate elements from the third layer, the text, say the idea of 'forgotten men and women' alluded to in Humphrey's letter. Each layer, therefore, has the capacity to contribute meaning from its primary state to be explored conjointly within the framework of the interconnecting layers of the map. An audience may never know who the forgotten men and women were or why they were forgotten and, indeed, that does not necessarily matter for the reception of the dance work to be successful. The significance of incorporating such a phrase is because the word 'forgotten' implies something happened and thus creates the possibility for dramatic response.

Figure 7.2 *Fugue 7* MOMENTA Dance Company 2007: Stephen Green Photography.

A further example can be found in the final two bars of Passacaglia 8. Choreographically, the two soloists execute a forward lunge to respective downstage corners then pivot around and upward in an expansive suspension before releasing into a falling run which brings them back together centre stage. The climactic moment here is the suspension on measure 7/beat 3, as Stokowski pauses for some time at this 'high point'. His pause on that particular note and beat is ideally matched with Humphrey's suspension. It is an exhilarating passage to dance because of this synthesis, and because of what precedes and follows. The dancer is both musically and choreographically drawn up to a climactic point through a deceleration in tempo, and then allowed to fall out of the suspension in a corresponding acceleration which creates a seamless flow into the next suspension. When this same movement is danced to the organ, the suspension does not have the time to breathe and fully expand as it could because the tempo remains constant throughout the variation. This constancy has implications for the rest of the phrase as the steps into the lunge do not have the *decelerando* Stokowski provides, but retain the tempo of the preceding movement. The run out of the suspension, likewise, maintains the tempo. The constancy in tempo and lack of dynamic contrast, in comparison with the orchestration, produces a quite different movement experience, to dance and to view, an observation that is reflective of the complete work. Overall, the organ version produces a feeling of gradual progression in contrast with the dramatic and unexpected surges created throughout by Stokowski (Main 2012).

The Passacaglia 4 and 8 examples illustrate the navigational choices that can exist for a director. Layering the 'sound' of the music with the full-bodied, expansive choreography and the idea of 'forgotten men and women' creates a platform for exploration that is derived from three distinct language systems. The translation that will ultimately be conveyed through the sphere of performance (a fourth language system) will not show these individual layers side by side but will instead be the transference of a composite meaning. This new meaning, or sense, can only exist because of the interconnection between the three components/layers, and thus, can only make sense once it is 'transferred into its new language system' of performance by way of intersemiotic translation.

To examine the music/dance relationship further, I would like to turn to Jordan's observation that 'one role of dance *is* to illuminate music' (2015, 85), a comment made in relation to Mark Morris' use of baroque music throughout his career. Notable Morris works that draw parallels with Humphrey's *Passacaglia* are *Gloria* (1981) to Vivaldi's Gloria in D and *L'Allegro, il Penseroso ed il Moderato* (1988) set to Handel's piece of the same name. Morris returned to the baroque canon throughout his career, but I refer to these two earlier dances having seen them in performance on a number of occasions, and because Humphrey's 'the music has movement in it' statement is equally applicable, certainly to my ear. Jordan refers to the notion of multiple voices operating, and of 'separate musical voices being taken over by dance' (ibid., 101), two distinct but connected ideas. Regarding the latter, Jordan is referring to Morris mirroring the musical roles/voices in *Gloria* (for example, soprano, alto, tenor, bass, chorus) in the casting, a practice he also uses in *L'Allegro* (see Jordan 2015: 135–45 and 183–218). I would stop short of defining Morris' approach as a music visualization of the kind that are familiar in dance history through the work of Ruth St. Denis and others, and including some of Humphrey's early works from 1918–20. In *Gloria*, and again in *L'Allegro*, I would suggest that Morris is pursuing a more sophisticated engagement with the music that involves a careful interrogation of the musical work before he embarks on the choreography. Through this informed approach he is then able to convey embodied renderings/responses that first establishes a relationship between the choreography and music, (for example, elements such as rhythm, phrasing, dynamic, structure), that in turn, through performance, can add new meaning and dimension to the musical work.

The musical works referred to in this section can all be defined as grand of scale with myriad lines running through the respective compositions. In her monograph, *Mark Morris, Musician-Choreographer* (2015), Jordan provides rich and detailed analyses of Morris' opus, including discussion on the presence and impact of multiple voices in *Gloria* and *L'Allegro*. Morris and Humphrey use their musical acumen to draw out musical lines that may be secondary or underlying within the composition but can have greater prominence within the choreography and thus have a new 'meaning' created for the audience/listener. An example from *Passacaglia* occurs in Fugue 9, where a 9/8 phrase is repeated three times and is set against the regular 'four bars of 3/4' structure. Here, Humphrey sets the 9/8 phrase for a trio whilst the ensemble movement remains within the 'four threes' structure. The ensemble dancers are seated on the floor and arranged in a wide semi-circle around the stage. The trio travels on a circular spatial pathway, tracing the inside line of the main group by way of falling, swooping and expansive turning around the body's axis. By positioning the ensemble on the ground and the trio upright and 'flying', Humphrey lifts the 9/8 phrase-line to greater prominence visually and, in my view, aurally because of the spatial perspectives and suspended high points that are created by the movement, thus 'illuminating the music' in ways the listener may not previously have encountered.

The examples above indicate that there is a transference of sense going on from the music to the choreography and thence to the audience. However, I would argue that an intersemiotic translation-based approach involves aspects beyond the processes Morris employs, not least because he does not intentionally set out to take such an approach. My argument is that an intersemiotic approach is intentional and is about a process of discovery rather than, first and foremost, a process of creation, and further, is a navigational process informed by the 'discovery of direction/direction of discovery' idea cited earlier in relation to the Fargion/Burrows example. The Morris example is useful, however, because it illustrates the respective capacities of music and dance to operate concurrently.

Discovering *With My Red Fires*

With My Red Fires, structured in two parts, is an exploration of the destructive elements of possessive love.[8] The central theme is depicted through the inter-relationships between three symbolic characters – 'The Matriarch', the 'Young Woman' and the 'Young Man', who entices the Young Woman away from home. A large ensemble of men and women represents a fourth 'character'. This ensemble at first celebrates the young couple finding each other in Part One, but subsequently turns against them in Part Two through increasing coercion by the Matriarch (see Figure 7.3). The choreographic ideas intersperse rigid power and conformity with gloriously uplifting, if fleeting, moments. The dance is an exhibition of opposition, of contrasts in movement dynamic, in emotion, in confrontation and resolution. Wallingford Riegger's dissonant score for two pianos and percussion was added after the choreography was set, and one can hear how his composition was influenced by the percussive angularity in Humphrey's choreographic vocabulary (Main 2012: 106).

The component layers here comprise a quite different set of materials for the director in comparison with those for *Passacaglia* and literally do constitute 'maps' of the music and choreography through the presence of the respective scores. Add to this the floor plans and director's breakdown of phrase structure for each role/group and there are four sets of documents to spread out on the table, or more likely the floor. Whilst only one part of a directorial process, the translation of these documents offers an important opportunity to investigate the framework of the work and the relationship between music and choreography. To examine this relationship in more detail, the discussion will focus on the

Figure 7.3 Doris Humphrey as 'The Matriarch'. Photographer unknown. Image reprinted with permission of Charles H. Woodford.

opening section (A) of Part One which is preceded by a 23-bar overture and marks the first entrance from stage right of the ensemble, here arranged into three groupings. Table 7.1 loosely captures the structure of section A, indicating a musical phrase of 11 bars with varying time signatures alongside three sets of choreographic phrases.

Group 1 and Group 2 take the form of clusters with Group 3 in a processional line. Groups 1 and 3 enter on count 1 of the musical bar, with Group 2 entering after 4 counts. Group 3 proceeds straight across the stage on a forward path, with Groups 1 and 2 in a more advancing and retreating pattern. Humphrey offers further intricacies by giving Groups 1 and 2 the same movement vocabulary but varying the number of steps, length of pauses, and rhythms employed. An

Table 7.1. Structure of Section A

Music	5/4 2/4	5/4	2/4	2/4	3/4	4/4	4/4	4/4	4/4	4/4
Group 3 (up-stage)	4	4	4	4	4	4	2 2	2 2	2 2	3
Group 2 (mid-stage)		6		6	7		6	7		3
Group 1 (down-stage)	7		7		7	7	8			3

example is the first 7-count phrase for Group 1 and 6-count phrase for Group 2 in which there are two particular differences. The movement comprises three low skimming walks forward in triplet time (1&a); a step/strike and hold (2); hold (345); three low walks back, triplet time (6&a); step and backwards pitch (7&). The first difference is that Group 1 has a 3-count hold and Group 2 only a 2-count hold whilst the choreography is the same; the second is Group 2 beginning after 4 counts which in turn creates an overlap in the advancing/retreating pattern of the two groups and in the points of stillness. This first section proceeds with further variation in the number of walks, from three to six, shorter holds, and added jumps and tilts at the end of each phrase in place of the opening backwards pitch.

To counterbalance the intricate motion of Groups 1 and 2, Group 3 provides a ground bass effect, first over four counts (x 6) and then over two (x 6), through a repeated movement phrase that consists of a series of lunge/poses struck on the first beat of each bar. This group most closely matches the chordal musical line although the down beat of the dance and music bars never coincide after the opening count of bar 1. Humphrey lifts up this ground bass by setting the movement along a raised platform that runs across the back of the stage, thus giving greater visual prominence to the group, to the sustained dynamic created by both movement and the bar-long chords for Piano 1 (whilst Piano 2 and the timpani maintain a crotchet pulse), and to the asymmetric relationship between choreography and musical phrasing.

A further example comes in Section B, from bar 8. Set in six bars of 4/4, the crotchet pulse for Piano 2 (left hand)/timpani from Section A continues, with the addition of an anacrusis/crotchet pulse for Piano 1 (left hand). The right handwriting for both pianos becomes more elaborate, conversational in places and maintains a sense of asymmetry through extensive use of dotted crotchets, triplets, notes tied over bars. The added complexity in the music is accompanied by slow sustained movement for two of the three groups throughout this section, with Group 2 providing contrast through a repeated triplet (1&a), quaver/hold (2) rhythm. This group is seated, side-on to the audience, in a high back lift (see Figure 7.4). The movement takes the form of a chopping, alternating action for the arms held above the head, with the feet tapping out the rhythm on alternate legs. The choreographic rhythm does not match anything within the music, thus continuing the asynchrony of Section A.

If Sections A and B are considered as a microcosm of the full work, and a 'score as map'/intersemiotic approach is applied, the fact that Riegger composed the music after the choreography was complete takes on a different context within the directorial process through the idea of 'equitable layers'. Other forms of staging practice that place significance on a choreographer's intention may take a more hierarchical approach with documentary evidence, and give less emphasis to what the musical score can offer because it post-dates the initial creative process. In taking an intersemiotic approach to *With My Red Fires*, the musical score, when considered alongside the Labanotation score, can add fresh insight in terms of structure, dynamic and, potentially, abstracted narrative. Section A provides one illustration and, from a structural perspective, the 'busy-ness' of the choreography is matched not by the sound of the music but by

Figure 7.4 Groups 1, 2, 3 in Section B, Middlesex University dancers, May 2015. Photographer Andrew Lang.

the structure of the musical phrasing. The 5/4 2/4 5/4 2/4 3/4 4/4 4/4 4/4 4/4 4/4 set against a 7 7 7 7 8 3 (Group 1), a 6 6 7 6 7 3 (Group 2) and a 4 4 4 4 4 4 2 2 2 2 2 3 (Group 3) is exhilarating as a set of patterns to explore in terms of what they could convey. There is no single point where all four collide, with Group 2 starting 4 counts after the musical phrase and Groups 1/3, and in the final bar, when all three Groups do finally converge on a bar of 3, the musical phrase is a beat ahead. This asynchronous structure is not only indicative of the entire work but of the jagged dramatic line that runs through the narrative.

The introduction to this essay made reference to the significance of structure and patterns. The examples cited here from *With My Red Fires* illustrate that, through a translation-based intersemiotic approach, both structure and patterns can impact on a directorial process to the point of creating new insights. Here, I am thinking of patterns of beats in the first instance, as in the phrase structure of Section A, and then the rhythmic patterns that exist within phrases. Mapping these sets of patterns creates a foundational/structural layer of the work. The discovery aspect comes about through considering the interplay between structure and rhythm and how that, in turn, is manifested in the 'distinct language systems' of sound and movement. In Sections A and B, there is an overt sense of energy that can be discerned through studying the various sets of asynchronous patterns outlined above. This sense of energy can be translated through the 'language' of movement as the sensation of a force surging idiosyncratically through space. How such an approach differs from past encounters is that meaning is derived from an abstract entity such as structure rather than formed from thematic narrative. Previous stagings of mine, for example, have focused on evidence drawn from Humphrey's stated intentions, her writing about the work and her secondary, underlying themes including intolerance and bigotry placed into a contemporary context. If one had to define the approach, a thematic interpretation would be an appropriate descriptor. For Sections A and B, the dramatic intent was conveyed through an emphasis on 'the gaze', with the impetus for movement through space driven from the front surface of the body. By shifting to an intersemiotic approach, the idea would not be to 'become' or depict an energy force, but to embody the sensation/sense of what that might be. The thrust of the movement through space, for example, could be driven from behind, from the back surface of the individual and collective bodies in each Group which, in turn, can create a different intention behind who the Group are and where they are going. In similar vein, the dynamic of the movement changes because the initiation point has changed, meaning that different connections are taking place within the body in the execution of the same movement vocabulary.

The examples above illustrate what could emerge and be discovered by interrogating the structure and patterns offered by the respective scores. It would also be important to consider what dance and music are contributing to each other beyond the patterns. In fact, one could consider *With My Red Fires*, or at least the ensemble sections, as a 'visual orchestra' because of the sheer volume of rhythms, dynamic colour, variation, drama, that are happening at any one time in both sound and movement. Choreography and musical lines seem to overlap and blend within the asynchronous structure; I wonder if this is due to Riegger's composition arriving after the dance work was in place, and him being influenced by Humphrey's visual form, structure and dynamic.[9]

The discussion has focused primarily on the Labanotation and music scores because they are core to the first stage of a process for this work in forming the foundation layers of the 'map'. The image of Humphrey as The Matriarch (see Figure 7.3), pictured as an 'other worldly' elongated form, and the Blake text are other component layers that would be factored into subsequent stages of a staging process. As with *Passacaglia*, the translation that will ultimately be conveyed through performance is the transference of a composite meaning created through the interconnection of these component layers.

Conclusions

An important aspect of staging the work of another is to interrogate what it could say now, in our current time, and to consider how that message will be received by an audience. There are no absolutes in the staging of dance and the field has moved on immeasurably from the late 1980s, when reconstruction from a score (such as by Laban, Benesh et al) or the 'handing down' method were the forms of practice that were routinely taking place. There came a flurry of 're'-s – recreation, reimagining, revival, reinvention, re-enactment – in the 1990s/2000s that signalled an expansion of thinking of ways to engage with existing dance works. Other forms still include period performance, co-authoring, transmission. Translation offers yet another, and the benefit of increasing the means of engagement is that new thinking about practice continues to evolve, which is important as the audience appetite for seeing dance works repeatedly over time increases. The *Passacaglia* and *With My Red Fires* examples discussed above offer one set of approaches. The notion of the 'score as map' creates a space from which to consider all variables on equal terms, and to navigate a path through these that may allow fresh discoveries. Such a process, arguably, has the capacity to change how one relates to any given set of documents/evidence and thus could be considered as an evolving, fluid process.

In conclusion, any translation is but one response to a work, hence why a framework of intersemiotic translation with its emphasis on 'transference of sense' seems appropriate as an approach for staging dances in similar ways to those identified for music. As an approach, translation creates a different platform for engaging with a work; a new perspective for exploring the variant properties of a work and, thus, creates the potential for new meanings in a work to be discovered that may not hitherto have been apparent through more established staging practices.

Notes

1 Lucy Venable was an influential figure throughout her professional life in the development of Labanotation as a recording tool. In addition to having a distinguished performing career in New York City with Doris Humphrey and Jose Limon, amongst others, Venable became Director of the Dance Notation Bureau in NYC in the 1960s prior to establishing the DNB Extension at Ohio State University. Venable can be regarded as an authority on *Passacaglia* because of her interconnecting experiences as performer, notator and reconstructor. Humphrey cast her in the leading role for a production at Juilliard in 1955. Doing so acknowledged Venable's skill as both performer and stylistic exponent. In addition, the experience of dancing this particular role under Humphrey's direction gave Venable a close insight into the work which undoubtedly contributed to her notation of the work in 1955. In turn, notating a work of such scale and detail would inevitably inform her reconstruction process for *The Four Pioneers* film recording in 1965 by John Mueller (see also Main 2012).

2 See Main (2012) for a detailed account of issues of co-authorship and authorial intention in relation to staging the work of another.

3 The complete letter is published unabridged in *Doris Humphrey: An Artist First* by Selma Jeanne Cohen (1995) and contains invaluable insights into the choreographer's thought processes and approach to a number of works.

4 Humphrey invited Stokowski to conduct *Passacaglia* in performance in 1940, but he was unable to oblige because of prior commitments (see Main 2012: 82, 85–98, for a detailed exposition on Humphrey's use of Bach and the Stokowski orchestration for this work).

5   See Main (2012), 17, for exposition of Humphrey's 'Fall and Recovery' philosophy that underpins her movement style.
6   MOMENTA is the resident performing arts company of the Academy of Movement and Music in Oak Park, Doris Humphrey's birthplace. Under the artistic directorship of Stephanie Clemens, the company's repertory includes historical works by the legends of American Modern Dance – Doris Humphrey, Loïe Fuller, Isadora Duncan, Ruth St. Denis, Martha Graham and Charles Weidman, and by great classical choreographers like August Bournonville, Mikhail Fokine, Jules Perrot and Marius Petipa. While MOMENTA's home is in Oak Park, the company has performed in festivals in the greater Chicago area, out of state, and internationally.
7   This is an expanded analysis of the Passacaglia 4 example from Main (2012), 93.
8   Humphrey gave the work indicative subtitles as follows: Part One – Ritual: I Hymn to Priapus, II Search and Betrothal, III Departure; Part Two – Drama: IV Summons / Coercion and Escape, V Alarm and Pursuit, VI Judgment.
9   Research to date has not uncovered any direct correspondence between Humphrey and Riegger on the music composition for *With My Red Fires* but there is evidence that Humphrey followed a similar pattern she used for *New Dance*, choreographed a year earlier in 1935 and part of the *New Dance Trilogy* that also included *Theatre Piece* (1936). Like *With My Red Fires*, Humphrey asked Riegger to compose the music after the choreography was complete. In an amusing aside, Riegger wrote the melodic lines for *New Dance* then handed over to Ruth and Norman Lloyd with the request that they write 'my kind of chords for this' (Cohen 1995: 137).

8

Cranko's Reinvention of Pushkin's Text in His Ballet *Onegin* (1965)

Anna Ponomareva

In the spring of 2019, the celestial importance of mirrors was stated at the ceremony of the abdication of the Japanese Emperor, Akihito. His mirror, which may be more than 1,000 years old and is one of the three manifestations of his power, has never been taken from the Ise Grand Shrine in Mie prefecture where it is possibly kept (Jones 2019). This shows that the mirror is sacred and should not be removed from its place even in the case of such an exceptional event as Emperor Akihito's termination of his divine responsibilities. Being hidden from the world, it creates a lot of speculation concerning its superior powers.

Meanwhile, mirrors are not only sacred and powerful in the institution of monarchy in Japan: they are also a significant force in choreography. For example, Cranko's ballet *Onegin* (1965) provides evidence as to the robust use of mirrors in moving the story of Pushkin's novel in verse *Eugene Onegin* (1830s) to its Terpsichorean territory. There, mirrors appear in Scene 1 of the ballet when the girls are involved in reading their fortunes. However, their strength reaches its peak in Part 1, Scene 2, in Tatyana's letter scene. I have selected this episode as my case study because it provides one of the best examples of Cranko's novel choreography in which the text of Pushkin's *Eugene Onegin* plays an even more crucial part than has been suggested before.

By arguing a strong connection between the Pushkin's text and Cranko's *Onegin*, I intend to contribute to a development of the notion of intersemiotic translation (Jakobson 1959), to epxand definitions as represented throughout this volume, and to underline the importance of maintaining stylistic features of the original text in its target translation version expressed by other means rather than word. In looking at the transfer of mode, I do so from the perspective of translation studies.

Several significant terms and concepts are borrowed from current research in translation studies and semiotics for conceptualizing Cranko's decisions. By using them, I am not portraying the choreographer as a translator or a semiotician, but am emphasizing a number of conceptual links between his choices and the translator's procedures in working with signs. The focus is less on terminology than on process (as also discussed in Chapters 2, 3, 4, 5 and 6). In order to do this, first Cranko's interest in Pushkin's novel in verse will be explained. Then the details of concepts of the narrative and the symmetry will be given as they play their crucial role in my claim about the existence of the special bond between *Eugene Onegin* and *Onegin*. Finally, the idea of mirror that frames Cranko's vision of his *Onegin* and adds functionality to his representation of Pushkin's *Eugene Onegin* will be exemplified.

The Three Reasons of Cranko's Being Interested in *Eugene Onegin*

The subject of Cranko's interest in *Eugene Onegin*, the opera and the book, has been already discussed in critical literature. For example, Percival (1983: 174) argues that Cranko reads Pushkin's novel in verse Eugene Onegin (1830s) while this young choreographer from South Africa is working on creating dances for the Royal Opera House production of Tchaikovsky's opera in London in 1952. Meanwhile, Percival does not specify what translation Cranko reads, but it is possible to assume that Cranko has studied one of the following translations into English: by Deutsch (1936), Elton (1937) or Radin and Patrick (1937). These three publications were available as they were published not long ago in order to mark the centenary of Pushkin's death in 1937.

Cranko finds Tchaikovsky's score of *Eugene Onegin* (1879) to be more suitable for a ballet performance rather than opera. He proposed his ideas to the Board of Directors at Covent Garden, noting that he was 'hoping it would be a vehicle for Margot Fonteyn and Rudolf Nureyev' (Craine 2001: 19). His plan is rejected as the Directors consider the music of Tchaikovsky's opera to be sacred, so they do not allow this score to be used for a new ballet performance (Percival 1983: 174). Their decision has its consequences. Soon Cranko moves from London to Germany: he accepts an invitation for a new job, the post of Director in Stuttgart. This job symbolizes a turning point in his career as a choreographer since it opens new perspectives and brings novel elements to his style.

The style is associated with the use of world literature in his work. Cranko's famous ballets, *Romeo and Juliet* (1962), *Onegin* (1965) and *The Taming of the Shrew* (1969), are based on well-known books. According to people who have been close to Cranko or written their reviews on his work, the existence of the narrative (in terms of structure, meaning, dramatic shape and identity, qualities also discussed in Chapter 7) is the essential feature of his choreography. For example, in her obituary on Cranko's death Kisselgoff writes about his gift of producing a great narrative in his work. She points out that 'as a choreographer, Mr Cranko took the risk of reviving the full-evening story-ballet at the time when most audiences favoured the plotless one-act work. It was a gamble he won' (Kisselgoff 1973: 42). With reference to Feinstein, an executive director of the Kennedy Centre for the Performing Arts, Kisselgoff develops her arguments even further and claims that 'he [Cranko] was the greatest story-teller in the history of ballet' (ibid). Other evidence is provided by Tsinguirides in her interview with Bannerman: 'whether it was Pushkin or Shakespeare [Cranko] would say "read the book" so the basis of his ballets was the book [...] it is the story translated into the body-into technique [...] that book is in his steps in his movements [...]' (Tsinguirides 2014).

In the case of *Onegin*, there might also be psychological explanations in choosing this novel. This can be justified by Cranko's personal reasons, for example, the existence of similarities between the choreographer and the main character of the novel.

According to Katseva (2007), a musicologist, if Pushkin and Tchaikovsky considered to name their work as Tatyana and to distance themselves from Onegin, Cranko did not share these ideas. Katseva claims that Cranko could identify himself with Onegin. Mentioning Cranko's interviews during the first tour of the Stuttgart Ballet to the USA, she writes that he was happy to explain his understanding of the main character of the ballet. Katseva provides the following citation of his speech: 'He [Onegin] is young, rich, good looking, but has not achieved anything in his life. Onegin is the drama of rejection. It is a tragedy of loneliness in a crowd. This is frightening and extremely contemporary'[1] (Katseva 2007). She underlines that this quote is Cranko's actual words and argues that, in this specific way, the choreographer emphasizes his closeness to Onegin.

So, on the one hand, Cranko's interest in *Eugene Onegin* might be explained in terms of his looking for a novel style in choreography; on the other hand, it might be interpreted in terms of psychology. Additionally, it could be associated with the time period: the early 1960s provide evidence on the growing popularity of the novel in its new translations into English and their discussion in the press.

First, Arndt's translation of the Pushkin's novel appeared, and the work was awarded the Bollingen Prize for poetry translation in 1963. Immediately after Arndt, in 1964, Nabokov published his four-volume work on *Eugene Onegin*. Nabokov, who did not receive the prize, was devastated, and initiated a dispute between himself and Arndt (later Wilson joined them) on the pages of *The New York Review of Books*. Their battle of words was aimed to discuss possibilities of producing interlingual translation of the Russian masterpiece. It is possible to suggest that these publications, identified as the paratext and epitext[2] of Arndt's and Nabokov's translations, might help Cranko understand better the original text. This issue will be explained later in my chapter.[3]

Thus, the three reasons provided above justify that Cranko's choice of Pushkin's *Eugene Onegin* as his literary source for his *Onegin* is not random: it has been work-related, inspired by the book and personality driven. Out of these three explanations, I am interested to develop my arguments on the new translations of Pushkin's novel which appeared in the time when Cranko was working on his *Onegin*. This will give me a chance to prove my hypothesis that Cranko's ballet might be classified as an intersemiotic translation of Pushkin's novel and to deepen our notion of this type of translation.

Tchaikovsky' Opera *Eugene Onegin* (1879) and Cranko's Ballet *Onegin* (1965)

This section of my article is dedicated to the evaluation of existing links between the opera *Eugene Onegin* and the ballet *Onegin*. The former uses two modalities, music and text, for recreating Pushkin's *Eugene Onegin*. The later adds another modality to its system and operates with the triad of music, text and dance. These three media are interconnected. However, in Cranko's case, it appears to be crucial to search for music first, before solving the issues of dance and text.

It had been earlier mentioned what kind of problems Cranko had when he proposed a new ballet using Tchaikovsky's score of his opera *Eugene Onegin* (1879). Cranko's *Onegin* project was saved by Stolze, a German composer, who created his score for the ballet by arranging and orchestrating different pieces of Tchaikovsky's music, not from his famous opera. In this sense it is possible to argue that Stolze's work might be described as an intralingual translation (Jakobson 1959) of Tchaikovsky's opera score. In this case the aural component of *Onegin* uses the same language (metaphorically speaking), in other words Tchaikovsky's music, but consists of his other compositions. Tchaikovsky's piano pieces in Vols 51–3 of the *Complete Collected Works, the Seasons Opus 37* piano cycle, the *Cherevichki* opera, the *Romeo and Juliet* unfinished opera and the *Francesca da Rimini* symphonic poem were brought into play in Cranko's *Onegin* as its score (Percival 1983: 174). Cranko has made a few adjustments to the libretto of Tchaikovsky's opera in order to make it more suitable for his new ballet. However, these changes are not that dramatic in comparison with the alternations of the music score, but they are important ones.

The libretto is written by Tchaikovsky himself, with his friend and poet Konstantin Shilovsky, after the novel in verse by Pushkin (1830s) which is largely a romantic story. It goes beyond the scope of my article to discuss Tchaikovsky's and Shilovsky's transformations of the novel into his seven scenes of their opera libretto, though that process is also a form of translation. Meanwhile, to provide a brief information on the contextual side of the opera, the summary of the events of the scenes will be given below with short references to the text of the novel.

Scene 1 introduces all the main characters and takes place outside the capital in the manor and estate of Madame Larina, a widow and Tatyana's and Olga's mother. The four first chapters of the Pushkin text contribute to this scene, except the episode of Tatyana's letter which is followed by her meeting with Onegin. To a large extent, the text of Tchaikovsky's and Shilovsky's libretto focuses on the presentation of the main characters of *Eugene Onegin* (1830s) leaving aside Pushkin's general, philosophical and humorous, comments on life. Scene 2 is dedicated to Tatyana's writing her letter to Onegin, a dandy and her new neighbour with whom this romantic girl falls in love at first sight. The scene corresponds to the second part of Chapter 3 of the novel. Scene 3 is a meeting of Tatyana and Onegin in the garden where Onegin rejects Tatyana's feelings. It is based on the first part of Pushkin's Chapter 4. Scene 4 is Tatyana's name-day party which covers the second part of Chapter 5 of the novel. Scene 5 is a duel between Lensky, the bridegroom of Tatyana's younger sister Olga, whose masculine pride and ego were damaged by Onegin, and the offender himself. The scene is after Chapter 6 of the book. The next scene takes place in the capital. It shows Tatyana as a married woman who is the hostess of a grand ball attended by Onegin after several years of his travelling abroad. The content of this scene is provided by Pushkin's text in the first part of his Chapter 8. There is no Onegin's letter scene, however, there is the text of Onegin's letter in the book. The content of Onegin's letter and events happened after in other episodes of Chapter 8 are presented in the final scene of the opera, Scene 7. Just as the novel, the opera ends with Tatyana's rejection of Onegin.

Cranko removes Scene 3 from the libretto of his ballet. This reduction in scene numbers is not related to adaptation, a translation technique usually associated with the maintaining of certain target-text features. It is also not omission in its traditional understanding, in other words, a removal of something from the source text which is untranslatable owing to its complex cultural connotations. It is a 'syntagmatic relationship' (Saussure 1983: 123–5), a transformation concerning positioning, that helps Cranko come back to Pushkin's text, in particular to the preservation of its several stylistic characteristics in which the existence of similarities in the main characters and the mirror reflections in the plot are underlined.

Cranko incorporates other small changes also to the opera libretto. This time he introduces more culture specific elements to his version of the Pushkin's novel. For example, Cranko's Scene 1 briefly mentions reading fortune activities which correspond to the beginning of chapter 5 of the novel. They happen during the time of celebrating the Christmas season in Russia. However, the girls' intention to foresee their future husbands using various magic tricks belong more to pagan-style celebrations: in old English terminology, to the events of the Yuletide Season.

Moreover, by shaping the text of the opera libretto, Cranko makes it to be more suitable to his idea of the narrative in dance. It appears to me that he anticipates some ideas on the figurative dance expressed nearly half a century later by Patel-Grosz at el. (2018), Charnavel (2016), Schlenker (2017) and Abusch (2015). In other words, his anticipates a different way of perceiving the body which emerges from the concept of the work.

As this chapter aims to identify strong connections between Pushkin's novel in verse *Eugene Onegin* and Cranko's ballet *Onegin* by suggesting that the latter is an intersemiotic translation of the former, below I will concentrate on analysing just one facet of their correspondence which only covers a textual domain.

Paratext and Epitext on the Style of the Novel and Its Translation

This section uses several paratextual and epitextual resources which provide new and useful information on Pushkin's *Eugene Onegin* predominately at a time when Cranko works on his ballet. It will be also suggested that these materials might serve as valuable contributions to make more profound his understanding of the stylistic features of the Pushkin's text. If Cranko's choreography relies upon this information, then certain transformations related to substitution in his *Onegin* might be classified as having 'paradigmatic relationship' (Saussure 1916/1983: 121).

Using Genette's terminology (1987), I classify as paratext Nabokov's commentary to his translation of *Eugene Onegin* into English (1964) and Hofstadter's Preface to his *Eugene Onegin* (1999)[4] as these extra materials are attached to their translations. The epitext is formed by Arndt's and Nabokov's correspondence published in *The New York Review of Books* (1964) after Arndt's translation has been awarded the 1963 Bollinger prize. Wilson's article (1965), which has been published after Nabokov's work on *Eugene Onegin* (1964), becomes the peritext of Nabokov's translation as it has been distributed after this translation but is closely related to it.

The formal discussion on translating Pushkin's *Eugene Onegin* was initiated by Nabokov in the pages of *The New York Review of Books* and published in its issue of 30 April 1964.[5] There his opponent was Arndt. Later Wilson, a friend of Nabokov, contributed to the discussion by expressing his views in the article *The Strange Case of Pushkin and Nabokov* (1965).

Nabokov's extreme bitterness and sharp criticism of Arndt's translation of *Eugene Onegin* are presented within every word of his article. This is also depicted in its title, *On Translating Pushkin: Pounding the Clavichord* (1964). What is put after the colon in the title sounds rather odd unless one reads this article with great attention to its details.

To Nabokov, Arndt is the second-rate musician who is capable to produce random sounds different from the original music score. This becomes clear when Nabokov's list of Arndt's mistranslations has been scrutinized. Among several 'glaring mistakes' made by the 1963 Bollinger prize winner he underlines the following:

> 8. [...] In Six: XIX Pushkin has listless Lenski, on the eve of his duel, 'sit down at the clavichord and play but chords on it', a melancholy image which Arndt horribly transforms into: 'the clavichord he would be pounding, with random chord set it resounding'.
>
> Nabokov 1964

Arndt's answers are short and professional. In the title of his article, *Goading the Pony* (1964), he applies the same metaphor, the pony, as his opponent when Nabokov describes his own attempts in translating Pushkin.

Wilson's criticism is centred on Nabokov. Wilson's article *The Strange Case of Pushkin and Nabokov* (1965) clarifies his understanding of what might be behind Nabokov's aggressive attack on Arndt. He concludes: 'There is a drama in his *Eugene Onegin* which is not Onegin's drama. It is the drama of Nabokov himself attempting to correlate his English and his Russian sides' (1965).

The next wave of Nabokov's criticism comes with the publication of his four-volume work on *Eugene Onegin* which consists of one volume of his translation, two volumes of his commentaries and the last volume is a facsimile of Pushkin's text in its version of 1837. On the one hand, Nabokov's foreword to his translation volume looks as if it is the general statement of his views on translation. It has Nabokov's classification of translation types: paraphrastic, lexical and literal. This is followed by a formal verdict: 'To reproduce the rhymes and yet translate the entire poem literally is mathematically impossible' (1964: ix). On the other hand, the foreword might be read as being directly addressed to Arndt. However, his name is not mentioned there; the names of various translators will be mentioned later, in two volumes of Nabokov's commentaries. What is striking in Nabokov's verdict is the adverb 'mathematically'. Are the categories of 'possible' and 'impossible' essentially mathematical? Why there the awkward playing clavichordist from *The New York Review of Books* (1964) has been suddenly promoted to be an accurate statistician?

Foreword materials are followed up by the section of the Translator's Introduction where Nabokov describes the peculiarities of Pushkin's novel. A considerable amount of numerical data is provided: the exact numbers of lines, chapters, pages and stanzas of the original novel are given there. After explaining the form of the Eugene Onegin stanza Nabokov switches to analyse the structure of the novel in verse. This time geometry, another branch of mathematics, is in use: the focus of his arguments is on shapes and reflections. For example, Nabokov compares Pushkin's chapters with 'an elegant colonnade' and talks about a system of subthemes they are linked with. Then he states that these subthemes are 'antiphonally doubled', provide 'a pleasing interplay of built-in echoes' or 'answered' (1964: 16–17). Developing his statements on the structure of the novel Nabokov borrows another concept from mathematics in order to make his points clearer; it is the notion of symmetry. To him the centre of Eugene Onegin is at lines 6 and 7 of Stanza Five in the Fifth Chapter. He writes: 'The entire set of chapters is felt to consist of two parts, with four chapters each, these parts consisting of 2552 and 2676 iambic tetrameters respectively' (1964: 17). Thus, a line of symmetry can be drawn upon 'mysteriously all objects foretold her something' (Ibid). He calls 'the first batch' what is to the left of these two lines, and 'the second batch' occupies what is placed to their right side. Then Nabokov provides examples of various symmetrical combinations.

To a great extent, this deep analysis of the structure of Pushkin's *Eugene Onegin* and other calculations related to the novel in which a plethora of mathematical terminology is used do not agree with Nabokov's verdict in his Foreword. If it is mathematically possible to describe this novel, why is it mathematically impossible to translate it?

Perhaps the lack of logic in Nabokov's use of mathematics in order to justify his translation suggests a quick change in his reasoning when he has been working on his *Eugene Onegin*. Arndt is the first who favours the symmetry of Pushkin in verse and introduces this notion to his translation. Hofstadter, another translator of *Eugene Onegin* (1999), praises Arndt's sensitivity to Pushkin's text and puzzles. He calls Arndt's work on *Eugene Onegin* (1963) as a symmetric translation and specifies his arguments as the following:

> It turns out I'm not the only translator who noticed and opted to respect the novel's мой-моим[6] symmetry; there was one other – the prolific and versatile Walter Arndt. He, too, imitated the gesture, through in a cleverly different manner. Arndt's first line runs, 'Now that he is in grave condition', while his closing line is: 'As I to my Onegin now'. Once again, I'm not sure the symmetry is deliberate, but given Arndt's astuteness, I would bet it is.
>
> 1999: xxiii

It appears from the citation that the idea of symmetry is important in one's understanding of the form of Pushkin's novel in verse and its specific stylistic features. There is a high degree of probability to substantiate that Cranko's ideas of using mirrors in his ballet has been inspired by his reading and evaluating Pushkin's text with the help of Arndt's and Nabokov's translations and their critical reviews of each other works. In other words, using Hofstadter's phrase myself, 'I would bet it is' that paratextual materials, part of Arndt's and Nabokov's translations, help Cranko understand the style of the Pushkin's novel better and create Tatyana's letter scene as a *mirror pas de deux*.

Tatyana's Letter Scene: *mirror pas de deus*

According to Munsterberg, ekphrasis is 'the oldest type of writing about art in the West' (2009). She also states that 'the goal of this literary form is to make the reader envision the thing described as if it were physically present' (ibid). It looks as if Cranko borrows the notion and applies it in his work. For example, let us look at his *Onegin* when it has been stimulated by Pushkin's Tatyana's letter scene and becomes its ekphrastic dance poem.

In Scene 2 of his ballet, Cranko jumps into Pushkin's chapter 5, of which the first part is dedicated to the description of Tatyana's dream. Pushkin's Tatyana sleeps and experiences a dream which looks like a logical continuation of her earlier fortune-telling activities of the day. This episode is notably absent in Tchaikovsky's opera.

At first it appears as if in his interpretation Cranko muddles the events of the original story: instead of seeing how Tatyana's love letter to Onegin is written, the spectator faces the experience in her dreams. Meanwhile, the absence of the physical letter makes room to include some crucial information related to the main characters of the novel in his ballet. Moreover, projecting onto the stage the internal working of her thoughts as dance movements brings the spectator into intimate proximity to Tatyana and Onegin, the subject of her dreams.

This emotional connection between the spectator and the performer and the dream-like effect of the whole scene, to a large extent, are facilitated by positioning a mirror frame on the stage. This object gives its name to the scene: it is called *mirror pas de deux* in the ballet.

Cranko's use of mirrors is also literal, metaphorical and methodological. It is relatively easy to find explanations to justify the appearance of mirrors in *Onegin* as physical objects and methodological solutions. First, mirrors accompany ballet dances all their life: every day they practise in front of mirrors in their rehearsal studios. Second, it has also been previously stated by Percival that Cranko's earlier work *The Forgotten Room* (1952) 'affected the way he staged Tatiana's letter-writing scene' (1983: 92). However, the production of 1952 does not have any mirrors; it is the idea of illustrating what is going on in a young woman's head using the power of dance. Percival describes this in the following way:

> Lancaster's design showed a room in gothic revival style, where a young woman found a book which absorbed her so completely that she began to live its events and was wooed and carried off by the imagined embodiment of its hero. At the end her sister or friend, returning to collect her, found her dead in a chair.
>
> 1983: 92

In Cranko's *Onegin* mirrors appear to be more stylistic devises as symbolic features have been added to them. They are reflective by their origin: they have a special surface. They are however, also reflective because of their projections of the original features of Pushkin's *Eugene Onegin*.

Pushkin's Tatyana writes a love letter to Onegin. In addition to being addressed to him, the text of the letter transforms Onegin to become its subject. Tatyana's writing is more about Onegin rather than Tatyana herself. At the beginning of her letter, she tries to understand who Onegin is and why he has come to their place. This stage might be referred to as an episode in which the self of Tatyana and the self of Onegin have their separate manifestations. Then Tatyana writes about her possible meetings with Onegin in the past. She thinks that Onegin had been with her when she helped poor people, prayed and had dreams. This shows a transition in Tatyana's thinking when she moves herself close to Onegin's self. At the end of her letter, it becomes obvious that she does not need herself as her intention is to be with Onegin's self.

The original play of two selves in Tatyana's letter comes to the stage of Cranko's ballet. There is a big mirror frame on stage in Part 1, Scene 2. Tatyana is in her bedroom, but she is not alone there, rather she is with her identical twin, a double performed by another actress. This provides opportunities for Cranko to emphasize that his Tatyana is dreaming and the mirror surface (it is imaginative, not real on stage) reflects her thoughts.

Then Onegin appears in the frame. He does not move for a second and his image reveals the external situation of Tatyana's deep thinking. Next Onegin comes out of the construction and Tatyana and Onegin dance their *mirror pas de deux*. Khokhlova (2017: 99) states that their dance tells entirely a story of Tatyana's feelings as Onegin does not have any emotions in this scene: he is only an image, an embodiment of Tatyana's dream.

I find it difficult to accept Khokhlova's argument. In my opinion, the role of Tatyana in the *mirror pas de deux* is similar to the part of the Pushkin's character in her letter scene: the whole dance is the play of two selves. When it looks as though Tatyana's self becomes Onegin's self, the subject of her dreams disappears in the frame. The mirror seemingly reflects the process of translation, via the visual representation of such a transfer. The end of the letter scene in the novel is simply the act of Tatyana's finishing her writing. Meanwhile Tatyana's dream in the ballet ends when Onegin uses the mirror frame to disappear from Tatyana's world.

So, in addition to its functions of physical object and methodological solution, the mirror has another task in the ballet: it is a powerful stylistic metaphor which helps Cranko translate Pushkin's *Eugene Onegin* into his *Onegin*. In particular, the frame symbolizes a symmetry line which provides opportunities to draw similarities between the ballet main characters. It also provides two viewpoints, as an encoded summary of what has happened before in the novel and as a decoded sequence of events which Tatyana will face later in her life. Moreover, its imaginative mirror surface serves to maintain the style of Pushkin as its reflective images project what is between lines in the novel.

Conclusion

In my case study, the analysis of Tatyana's letter scene, several statements have been provided to illustrate the kinaesthetic language of Cranko's *Onegin* in which one stylistic feature, the idea of symmetry, takes a metaphorical shape of the mirror frame on the stage and gives the name to the dance scene, *mirror pas de deux*. It has been shown that this mirror image has the same functionality as the notion of symmetry: it reflects and visualizes Tatyana's dreams. Moreover, it communicates the details of the style of Pushkin's *Eugene Onegin*.

However, the communicative role of dance has already been discussed in literature on semiotics: for example, the metaphorical conceptualization of tango and capoeira is provided with the explanations of their semantic domains in Brandt's article *Dance as Dialogue* (2015). Another publication, this time by a team of researchers, O'Halloran, Tan and Wignell (2016), who are interested in intersemiotic translation, analyses a multimodal approach to translating images, videos, non-verbal texts and mathematics. They use systemic functional approaches to multimodal discourse analysis (SF-MDA) and view semiotic resources 'as having a meaning potential which is described in terms of interconnected systems of meaning' (2016: online, section 18). Following Halliday's systemic functional theory (1978) the team groups the meanings of systems into three categories: ideational, interpersonal and textual. In SFT and SF-MDA the societal element in any resources or systems is paramount. However, my case study underlines the importance of maintaining the style of the original in its intersemiotic translation when the peculiar language of Pushkin's novel in verse has been successfully substituted by the various vernaculars of Cranko's ballet.

Thus, further research is necessary to adjust Table 1 from O'Halloran, Tan and Wignell (2016: online, section 25) for the needs of facilitating the process of intersemiotic translation between a text and a ballet. At this stage of my research, I think that it is appropriate to add a subcategory of style to their table which exemplifies the SF-MDA approach to analysing the meanings of a news report arising from its linguistic text and photographs. This new category will be classified as a rank category in language columns and appear in all their three sections on meanings. Adding this extra layer to the existing models of intersemiotic translations on video and image[7] might be a way forward to developing them. Cranko's *mirror pas de deux* from his ballet *Onegin* highlights this opportunity.

Notes

1 It is my translation of the comment that: «Он молод, богат, хорош собой – и ничего не добился в жизни. Онегин – это драма непризнания. Трагедия одиночества в толпе. Это страшно и очень современно» (Katseva 2007).

2 These terms have been introduced by Gérard Genette, a French literary theorist (1930–2018), in his book *Seuils* (Paris, 1987). The book was later translated into English by Jane E. Lewin with a foreword by Richard Macksey and published as *Paratext: Thresholds of Interpretation* (Cambridge and New York: Cambridge University Press, 1997). Genette describes paratrext in his Introduction as 'a *threshold*, a word Borges used apropos of a preface – a "vestibule" that offers the world at large the possibility of either stepping inside or turning back' (Genette 1997: 1) Then he provides the following formulae: '*paratext = peritext + epitext*' (p. 5). This underlines the temporal situation of supplementary materials: peritext covers everything which appears before the text and epitext corresponds to after the text items. Genette is not strict with his definitions. In general, it is possible to assume that peritext and epitext materials might be included in the book or published separately. For more information on Genette's terminology, see his introduction in Genette (1997), 1–15.

3 On the one hand, it looks as if my hypothesis heavily relies on finding evidence to support it, in other words, that Cranko is familiar with Arndt's and Nabokov's translations and other publications related to these translations. The Stuttgart ballet archive has been contacted and there is no document there which names a specific translation of Pushkin's novel in verse *Eugene Onegin* into English that Cranko read. Meanwhile, on the other hand, even without any textual evidence which justifies my hypothesis, I believe it is possible to suggest that Cranko has managed to identify himself the specific features of Pushkin's text and style, the ones which the translators discuss in their works.

4 In spite of the fact that Hofstadter's translation was published in 1999, nearly thirty-five years after Cranko's work on his ballet, I decided to use this source of information on Pushkin's *Eugene Onegin* as in his introductory chapters, the translator shares with his readers a number of valuable outcomes of his close reading of the original text. To me, it is possible to suggest that as Hofstadter Cranko could have an exceptional eye for details in order to find out essential elements of Pushkin's style by himself.

5   Nabokov published his preliminary views on translating the novel in verse nine years earlier, in 1955, in *The New Yorker*. I refer to his publication of 1964 in *The New York Review of Books* as it is more relevant to the subject of my article.
6   The English translation of *мой – моим* is *my – my* as there is no case system in English.
7   For more information, see the Multimodal Analysis Company website, where you can find the following links on image: http://multimodal-analysis.com/products/multimodal-analysis-image/; and on video: http://multimodal-analysis.com/products/multimodal-analysis-video/ (both last accessed 5 July 2021).

Part Four

Institutional Representation

Notation, Archives and the Museum

9

Two National Estonian Ballet Translations of Theodor Amadeus Hofmann's *Coppélia* to Leo Délibes' Music by Mauro Bigonzetti (2002) and Ronald Hynd (2010)

Heili Einasto

Translation as an activity lies at the core of human thinking (Lotman, in Torop 2011: 201): concepts and ideas have to be translated into words, images, and actions for communicative purpose.[1] In order to share thoughts, one has to translate them into ways that enable further processing. Though originally translation referred to the movement of words from one verbal-textual language to another, nowadays translation as a concept is used to refer to the movement of ideas and meanings from one language to another, from one medium to another, from one culture to another, from one time to another, and, depending on who the translator is, from one gender to another. In every translation, some meaning from the original gets lost, and some other meaning is acquired due to interpretations made by translators and readers of translated texts. Even more so when translation is intersemiotic (Jakobson 1959; Torop 2011: 130), when one sign system is interpreted via the signs of another, a literary text translated into a musical-choreographic form as is the case in narrative ballet like *Coppélia* (1870). I am going to discuss here, it is, due to a change of medium, even a more complex cultural, economic, ideological activity (Torop 2011: 204) than is the case when literary texts are translated from one language into another.

Ballet is a unique form of dance that has, since its very beginning in the sixteenth century, relied heavily on literary works to be translation into ballet's peculiar kinetic (non-verbal) idiom, which is built around a specific system of steps, positions, movement sequences, and procedures. Usually, ballets focus on the emotions and feelings of the characters by showing them via imagery that has its roots in bodily sensations. Thus the 'fluttering of the heart' may be translated into movements that use fluttering of legs, feet, arms or hands. Often emotional highs are translated into movement patterns that use high jumps or lifts, whereas episodes of turmoil are depicted via various turns and pivoting patterns. Events in ballets are often only triggers to show the human condition in various emotional states. To be successful, these balletic translations must display the virtues of the system, in which bodies move in a highly determined way. Music and choreography are fundamental in determining ballet movements, and these are usually the responsibility of people (composer, choreographer) who do not appear in the ballet. It is up to dancers to translate into bodily movements on stage what the composer and the choreographer have translated into musical notes and instructions inspired by the libretto, that is the translation of the original text. In ballet, dancers function somewhat like mechanical dolls, insofar as they are the creations of external powers. This is somewhat like what happens in E. T. A. Hoffmann's story *The Sandman* (1816, see 1999), the main source for the ballet *Coppélia*: choreographers create dancers and dances in a manner similar to Dr Coppélius, who makes mechanical lifelike dolls.

Conception of *Coppélia*

Ballet *Coppélia* was conceived around 1867 when the Paris Opera director Emile Perrin approved plans for a new ballet as a collaboration between Charles Nuitter (scenario), Arthur Saint-Léon (choreographer) and Léo Delibes (composer), who had worked successfully together before (Guest 1970: 18). It is not clear how or why Hoffmann's macabre *The Sandman* was chosen as a source material for the new ballet, but it did have some necessary elements that could serve as a basis for a successful ballet of the time. As any translation is a decision-making process of what is to be translated as the context of the source and the translated addressee are different (Torop 2011: 179), let us have a glimpse at the key elements of romantic ballet stories.

While narrative ballets of the seventeenth and eighteenth centuries used primarily antique Greek mythology for their source material, nineteenth-century Romanticism leaned towards fairy tales, legends and mysterious stories that allowed the depiction of supernatural elements, distant lands and cultures. Most ballets of the Romantic era depicted a male poetic character of a poetic nature who is torn between two women: his practical, down-to-earth fiancée representing 'known' values such as secure home, family and position in the society, and an otherworldly creature who embodies yearning for unknown, adventure and transcendence of the mundane. The technical advances of ballet training – standing and dancing *en pointe*, high and light jumps – supported the depiction of supernatural creatures such as airborne sylphides in *La Sylphide* (1832) or spirits of dead maidens in *Giselle* (1841), mermaids or fire-spirits with this kind of out-of-the-ordinary movements.

By 1860s, however, when the idea of a new ballet that would become *Coppélia* was put forth, the fantasy element had lost its appeal, and ballet was being treated more and more as a secondary entertainment to fill the programme after the opera or inserted between its acts (Guest 1960: 49). The influential audience of Paris Opera ballet was composed of Jockey Club members who wanted to see lovely girls doing pretty dances, and anything too serious was an anathema for them – and that had a major effect on how Hoffmann's story was translated into ballet. It was the ballerinas portraying the main characters (the males were danced *en travesti* at the time) that mattered most: the story had to enable the display of their special skills and personality to guarantee the success of the box office (Guest 1970: 19).

The Sandman (1816) and *Coppélia or The Girl with the Enamel Eyes* (1870)

Hoffmann's *The Sandman* is a multilayered story with many narrators, offering multiple was of reading and interpretation. Below I have picked out the line of the story most relevant to the ballet. *The Sandman* portrays a young student, Nathanial, who, engaged to a lovely Clara, is attracted to the mysterious daughter of a mystical Mr Coppola (Coppélius). The latter asks Nathanial to visit his home and the young student becomes enraptured by the daughter Olimpia (actually a mechanical doll) who plays a musical instrument, sings and dances. He starts visiting her, reading her his poems and stories that had bored his fiancée Clara, and receiving single syllabus exclamations as a response which he interprets as admiration. The day Nathanial decides to propose to Olimpia, he discovers that she is a doll. He becomes mad initially, but seems to be cured later, and decides to marry Clara. However, on the verge of their marriage Nathanial, when climbing the tower of their hometown to take a view from above, imagines seeing Mr Coppola and Olimpia again, and he jumps down the tower to his death. Later Clara gets married to a less poetic man, has children and lives a happy family life.

Hoffmann's *The Sandman* was a macabre story with mysterious visitors (alchemists, engineers), emphasis on the eyes as the location of a person's soul, processes of making artificial humans (women), the differences between the mechanical woman and a real one in their response to the male protagonist's artistic aspirations, the protagonist's different states of mind (hallucinatory and real). Hoffmann was not only a romanticist but is also considered a science fiction and fantasy writer, interested in the scientific ideas and human psychology. For Nuitter, Saint-Léon and Délibes it provided a romantic love triangle, and suitable characters – the rest had to be adjusted to suit the expectations of the audience of the time.

This process of translating the story into a three-act ballet with original music and choreography took three years. The idea was conceived in 1867, and in January 1868 choreographer Arthur Saint-Léon wrote to the librettist Charles Nuitter, laying out a detailed plan for the ballet, referring probably to an earlier version that he had decided to adjust: 'I will write the scenes without the music, indicating the links. We shall have to prepare Delibes for this amputation, or rather this adjustment' (Guest 1981: 111).[2] From Arthur Saint-Léon's correspondence, it is clear that the translation-adaptation was done in close collaboration between the librettist, choreographer and composer who fed ideas to each other and adjusted their ideas to meet the other's demand. In this kind of collaboration, the choreographer often prescribed the manner and length of the music, and not the other way round, as has often been the case a century later. Twentieth-century choreographers like George Balanchine followed the music so that 'dance movement parallels the structure of the music, often translating musical dynamics, changes in pitch, rhythmic patterns, phrasing, and orchestration into sequences of movement [...] reiterations in the music accompany a recurrence of corresponding movement sequences' (Foster 1986: 14–16). In the nineteenth century, the idea that translation is sequential (literary source translated into ballet libretto, translated into music and then translated into choreographed movements) as has been the case with many twentieth-century ballets, had not become predominant. The reason for this lies in the expectations of the times. Ballet as a light-hearted entertainment required *musique dansante*; that is, music that was rhythmically precise and simply organized, square phrases, and having flowing melodies (Wiley 1985: 1–10; Upkin 2015: 37). Critics also expressed in no uncertain terms their expectations of ballet composers, revealing an assumption that music must explain the story (Smith 2011: 139), an idea quite alien to the present-day composer.

Classical *Coppélia* in the version of Ronald Hynd

The original choreographic version of the ballet by Arthur Saint-Léon in which the male protagonist was danced *en travestie* by a female dancer, has not survived. Though Pierre Lacotte has offered his reconstruction of the work in 1976, *en travestie* was not used. Most of the modern productions, including that of Ronald Hynd for the Estonian National Ballet in 2010, are usually based on late-nineteenth-century revivals staged by Marius Petipa, Lev Ivanov and Enrico Cecchetti for the Imperial Ballet of St. Petersburg (Naughtin 2014: 176).

Coppélia or *The Girl with the Enamel Eyes* has become a comic story instead of a tragic one. The ballet is set in a Galician small town of unidentified period. Swanilda (Hoffman's Clara) and Frantz (Hoffmann's Nathanial) are engaged but Franz has started to pay attention to a lovely girl (Coppélia, Hoffman's Olimpia) reading a book on the balcony of the doll-maker Dr Coppélius' house. Swanilda and her friends find a key to Dr Coppélius' house that the man has lost when he left, and they go in to see the girl. In the house, they find human-sized dolls in different national clothes (allowing to present different 'character dances') and realize that the mysterious girl on the balcony is also a doll. Their discoveries are interrupted by the return of Dr Coppélius, who throws them out. Only Swanilda has hidden herself and secretly changes into the clothes of the doll. Meanwhile, Franz has found a ladder via which he climbs into the house of Dr Coppélius so he could find the beautiful girl. Dr Coppélius who wants to make his doll alive, requires a human sacrifice and decides to drug Franz with wine and use him for this purpose. When Franz sleeps, he uses a magic book and hopes to transpose Franz's soul to the doll, and to his pleasure the doll awakens. The mechanical-doll choreography in this scene that is preserved in all versions based on the Saint-Léon one, was probably inspired by eighteenth- and nineteenth-century travelling vaudeville shows that featured mechanical automatons (Naughtin 2014: 176). It is a deception, however: it is not the doll, but rather Swanilda in the doll's dress who moves (see Figure 9.1).

The girl awakens Franz, who learns that he has been duped, and the lovers get reconciled when leaving the house of Dr Coppélius, who grieves seeing his doll as 'dead' as before. The happy couple gets married when the new clock for the town is being blessed, the mayor of the town placates angry Dr Coppélius (who wants compensation for damages) with a bag of money, and all the little town's people rejoice.

Delibes, who was the youngest of the collaborating team, wrote music that met the expectations of the ballet audience and critics, and continued the

Figure 9.1 *Coppélia*. Choreography by Ronal Hynd following the original ballet of 1870. Estonian National Ballet production of 2010. Coppélius (Vitali Nikolayev) is bringing to life the doll Coppélia who is actually a village girl Swanilda (Eve Andre). Photo by Harri Rospu, courtesy of the Estonian National Opera.

tradition begun by Adolphe Adam, César Pugny and Ludwig Minkus: the numbers are arranged for colour and contrast, and characters have their *leitmotifs* – themes that express and identify mood and the character (Smith 2011: 148). Thus, all protagonists are presented through their themes (two in the case of Franz, these taking note of the fact that the roles were first danced by a woman *en travesti*): Dr Coppélius' rhythm is off-kilter and his sonorities thin and peculiar, emphasizing his (harmlessly weird) strangeness; Franz's music sounds eager and boyishly impetuous, Swanilda's is light, slightly coquettish and flowingly melodious. To meet the demand for the display of different character dances danced by the dolls and Swanilda when impersonating Coppélia, Delibes composed music featuring the musical tropes that were used to represent different nationalities: bolero for Spain, *gigue* for Scotland, *csárdas* for Hungary, mazurka for Poland (ibid., 144). The finale with its *Fete de la cloche* displayed a range of dances: *valse des heures,* and occasions for which the clock would chime: dawn, prayer, work, village weddings, and then *grand pas de deux*, an obligatory ending of the late-nineteenth-century ballets enabling the ballerina to display her skills in adagio and variations. And finally, the *galop générale* for the whole ballet company expressing the townspeople's joy in the new clock and the newlywed.

It is primarily Delibes' music and late-nineteenth-century style choreography that makes *Coppélia* a family entertainment that parents take their children to see. Hoffmann's sinister alchemist, Coppola-Coppélius, has in this translation become a weird doll-maker, Nathanial's desire for a woman who would respond to his strange artistic aspirations with admiring exclamations, who would dance and sing rather than be occupied with mundane tasks, and his moment of confusion when he cannot distinguish his real fiancée from a doll (imagining Clara being one) has become a comical delusion induced through drugged wine. The ballet stresses the idea that it is a folly to believe that a machine can replace a human as a source of erotic desire – exactly the opposite of what Hoffmann's story implies.

Post-Modern Translation of *Coppélia* by Mauro Bigonzetti

Post-modernism places emphasis on a non-linear, fragmentary narrative that follows the rationale of associations more than logic, stressing often the negative, non-central, uncertain and diversified concepts. Post-modernism translation theories include inputs from deconstruction, post-colonialism, gender studies, and allow a diversified way of treating the subject of translation. Post-modern translation is aware of its interpretative nature, and thus is highly self-reflexive. Mauro Bigonzetti's version of *Coppélia* in the Estonian National Ballet in 2002[3] can be interpreted as a feminist return to Hoffmann's original narrative in the story line and in the names of the characters. The choreographer rewrote the libretto,[4] but kept the title of the ballet and used Delibes' music. There was one addition, though: musical director Aivo Välja composed a *vocalize* using Delibes' melodies[5] that becomes the *leitmotif* for Olimpia. While the classical version was a very close collaborative adaptive translation of the story between the librettist, composer and choreographer and thus different layers of the translation (plot, music, dances) fitted well together, the new version faced the difficulty of suiting the sombre narrative to the general light-heartedness of the music.

When the curtain opens to the *vocalize*, we see two characters: a woman in a silvery grey dress and a man in black. The woman's movements are simultaneously angular and soft, she combines alive organics and insensitive mechanics, bringing forth association with cyborgs – man-made beings who are a reminder humans of their appearance but who also have acquired via new technologies the features common only to machines: tirelessness, enhanced durability and perfect appearance. The woman on stage is subjugated to the man, her state and movements betray her subordination to the man on the one hand, while on the other bring forth her condition as the object of the man's desire and admiration – the latter is demonstrated in this and later scenes by the kisses and caresses covering the body of the woman. According to the programme, the people on stage are Olimpia, a *homonculus*, a doll and her creator and maker, Coppélius – contemporary versions of Hoffmann's characters.

The theme of a perfect machine who is functioning blamelessly in any situation has risen as a phoenix at the beginning of the present biotechnological age – in this sense, Bigonzetti's *Coppélia* is very much a twenty-first-century translation of the original story. Nevertheless, it maintains some of the secrecy of Hoffmann's story in its presenting questions while not giving direct answers to them: mystery shrouds not only Olimpia, the silvery-grey human doll, but also her human rival, Clara; unanswered questions about Coppélius the doll-maker, and Nathanial the poet haunt us throughout the ballet (as they do in the original story), not to speak of other, minor characters. The greatest challenge for the ballet is the discrepancy between the new, Hoffmannesque libretto, the generic contemporary style of choreography of broken lines and filling every musical note with some movement, and Delibes' music with its own characterizations and themes (mentioned in the previous section) suited for the 1870 version but harder to subjugate to the new translation.

Bigonzetti's Coppélius is full of force and nobility, a man mysterious and incomprehensible. On the one hand, he represents a powerful masculinity: his movements are space-covering, large and commanding, and of the men depicted in the ballet he is by far the most powerful. In his own kingdom of mechanical female dolls (the first scene of the second act), Coppélius is the omnipotent father and master, *padre padrone*, whose single gesture can either bless or condemn. He is also an alchemist-mechanic who conducts strange experiments, combining in his creation – constructed women – both nature and *techne*. We do not know what the basic material of his cyborgs is: we see only beautiful, similar looking females whose movements display more softness than do those of the 'real' humans living in the town. The peak of Coppélius' endeavours is Olimpia: 'a very tall and slender lady, extremely well-proportioned and most splendidly attired'.[6] Differently from townspeople who dance *en pointe*, Olimpia moves on demi-pointe, which makes her foot and movement line softer. Olimpia represents the ideal towards which to aspire: her movements are the most fluid, the most liquid of the ballet's female characters – she can be shaped as liquid metal, she is as pliant and flexible – both literally and figuratively – as can only be a perfected human, who is not any more the result of nature's contingency but a master work of high technological precision (see Figure 9.2).

Olimpia can easily be moulded – be that by smith Coppélius or Nathanial – in both hands Olimpia is what they like, thus seeming to be for men a *tabula rasa*, a clean sheet they can write upon at their will. Nevertheless, Olimpia has her own nature unknown to both Coppélius and Nathanial – it is revealed in the lengthy second act solo, the movements of which emphasize longing and aspiration – can it be a cyborg's wish to be a human? A woman's wish to be something else but a man's toy? A slave's desire to make her own choices? The ballet gives no answers, as there is no answer in Delibes' light-hearted ballet music which squeezes this

Figure 9.2 *Coppélia*. Choreography by Mauro Bigonzetti. Estonian National Ballet production of 2002. Coppélius (Ervin Green) can mould Olimpia (Eve Mutso) in any way he wishes. Photo by Harri Rospu, courtesy of the Estonian National Opera.

solo into a traditional ballet frame that in the name of perfection shapes a three-dimensional human body into a flat and two-dimensional figure. But then, ballet as a training system was born out of the baroque ideal of 'cultivated' nature: just as trees and plants had to be trimmed to geometric figures in a baroque park, so bodies had to be trained and disciplined so they could depict 'improved' movements and postures not found in natural settings. Dance masters and choreographers remind Coppélius: they too mould perfected beings from nature-provided material, enhancing them so they would strive for some unattainable ideal. In ballet, training the dancer's body acquires thing-ness, and dancing specializes 'in the most intricate maneuvering of this newly objectified body' (Foster 1998: 254), and dancers, in particular female dancers from the nineteenth century onwards, were seen as upgraded and enriched versions of nature. The trained ballet body is like a perfect machine: disciplined, operating blamelessly in any situation, without unpleasant smells and bodily functions, and Hoffmann in *The Sandman* obviously picked up from this tradition when describing Olimpia.

Despite the title of the ballet, the real mystery in both the story and their different translations, is Coppélius and his motives. At the beginning of the ballet, he seems to push Olimpia into Nathanial's arms, but when the young man 'takes the hook' and makes advances to Olimpia, Coppélius meets him in a forbidding way, even more – he fights with the poet and wins. Does he seek for a soul for his beloved, his Olimpia, that would enable his creation to cross the temporal borders as is the case in the classical version? Bigonzetti provides no answer just as there is no clear and single explanation to Coppélius' relationship to Olimpia in any of the stories, including Hoffmann's. On the one hand, the man mauls his creation – the best example for this is the beginning of the second act, where Olimpia tiptoes into Coppélius' doll-world in an especially awkward position, the body twisted into horizontal, back to the floor, head somewhat lifted. On the other hand, Coppélius desires the silvery body of Olimpia as is revealed by his persistent caresses.

Coppélius' motive in creating the dolls is obscure in all versions of the story. Hoffmann treats Coppélius (Coppola) as a kind of Faustian figure testing the limits of his capacity to create art and life, regarding the dolls as a technology for eliminating the institution of marriage. He needs no wife to create new lives, and Olimpia destroys Nathaniel's desire to be married (to his fiancée). The problem for Nathanial in Bigonzetti's treatment is that he cannot compete with Coppélius for control of Olimpia. Nathanial's self-destructive delusion is that he can awaken Olimpia's desire for him, but Bigonzetti failed to give Olimpia any desire, as is evident from the vaguely articulated attitude of longing and aspiration in her solo dance, which really should not be a solo if she is to reveal a desire for anyone. The solo dance could reveal her desire to be alone, independent of all humans, free of desire and desirability, but an independent Olimpia would move the story in a different direction. The problem for Bigonzetti is how to translate into movement the supreme desirability of the mechanical doll: most choreographers rely on tropes of 'robotness', but these seldom persuade the viewer that the doll is worth dying for.

Questions also pile up in the human world: about the nameless town with its staircases leading to nowhere, and its glassless windows, and in which we know by name only Nathanial and his girlfriend Clara. The latter is dressed into black-and-white costume and wears point-shoes that make her foot line sharper and the movements more rigid than those of the cyborg Olimpia. Clara's movements in the first act remind one of a folding knife and they are much more mechanical than those of Coppélius' dolls. But Clara is not dolly – she is a great deal more independent and self-conscious than the easily mouldable Olimpia as is revealed by her bold initiations into dialogues with Nathanial and her requests for clarification of the man's behaviour in the second act after the poet has perceived Olimpia as his female ideal. It is Clara who initiates all dialogues with Nathanial, thus stepping over the borders of subordinating, obediently reacting womanliness. Nevertheless, she retreats behind these borders as soon as she has achieved contact with her boyfriend – in all the duets' lifts and partnerings, Clara is the passive and assisted side. Is this a womanly wit – to be the neck turning the head, as says an Estonian proverb? Clara is much more tenacious, durable and keeping her own line than is Olimpia – which can be one reason for Nathanial's desire for Olimpia.

Nathanial's romantic poetic nature is expressed in movement language differentiated from other people's dance by its fluid character, emphasizing his sensitivity and less stable nature. Though less powerful and mighty than Coppélius, he has his share of vigorous and beautiful elements in ground-covering leaps and witty body throws directed to Clara. But his sufferings and suicide (if it is he who throws himself down from the tower and is not 'helped' to it by Coppélius, also a possibility) – the reason for which cannot be understood in the ballet, if it is not the mechanicalness of the environment surrounding him – refer to romantic sensibility.

The people of the nameless town are a nameless, uniform group – as is the case in classical versions – moving with wonderful precision and machine-like orderliness. If we ask which ones are dolls and which are humans, it is the townspeople who seem to represent the first category. Women dressed in black enter with small steps on pointes, forced standard grins on their faces, and fall then into Olimpia's withered pose, reminding one of sex-dolls that are 'almost alive'. Girls in white shirts and black shorts remind waitresses in bars where besides drink, sex services are offered for clients – this is emphasized in *enchainement* finishing with a pose in which women have wrapped their legs around men's hips and lower their upper bodies as if in ultimate orgasm. The women's movements contain a great deal of small, tapping steps, bringing into mind ladies walking on high heels, and spatially their movement range is more confined than that of men. Male dances are energetic, contain several open jumps and powerful *entrées*; nevertheless, they are not dignified bourgeois, but rather young pranky men, revealed in their bodily bends, boyish somersaults and comically twitching arms. Male world is much more playful than the female one, but this play is still standardized and unified, none of the characters is brought forth as an individual.

Translation as an Ideological and Political Activity

Translation is a political and ideological activity, and a ballet translation of a literary work entails political decisions that theatre directors, choreographers, dancers and audiences are responsible for, even if they claim a lack of intentionality. The example of the ballet *Coppélia* and its two different versions presented in the Estonian National Ballet (in 2001 and 2010) provide an exciting case of this.

Both versions use the same music but display a different 'reading' of Hoffmann's *The Sandman* that ballet used as its inspirational source. The classical version with Ronald Hynd's choreography follows the ideology of the 1870 original in its light-hearted treatment of the central theme (falling in love with a mechanical doll), whereas Mauro Bigonzetti's contemporary version made an attempt to return to its original source, written in 1816. The translation of the story into ballet was strongly impacted by ballet-goers of the time: the influential Paris ballet audience (who were predominantly male) preferred operetta-like productions that showed ballerinas' skills and characters to their very best, presented humorous or witty stories by easily danceable and memorable tunes, and punctuated classical variations and duets of couples with character dances to 'national' tunes. Thus, ominous scientist and *homunculus* creator Coppola becomes a powerless doll-making freak, and a volatile poet Nathanial into a boyish Franz; only Clara-Swanilda maintains her practical side, though in ballet she is more ethereal than in the story. Hoffmann's many-layered story of complicated twists of love, desire and artistic creation becomes a simplified version of a couple in quarrel that gets easily resolved.

By the late twentieth century, the theme of artificial humans had strongly emerged again, thus enabling Mauro Bigonzetti to return to Hoffmann's novella without the need to make it light and comic. His ballet translates Hoffmann's story into a conventional feminist idiom that would meet the expectations of the largely female audience for ballet. This audience probably finds consoling a story that emphasizes the destructive power of male desire to perfect femaleness through technology: men should be more appreciative of female imperfection and what non-ideal nature defines as human femaleness.

Both versions followed the casting traditions of the time of their conception: the Paris 1870 *Coppélia* cast was overwhelmingly female with the male character *en travesti* – the predominantly male audience desired to see female bodies; the 2001 casting was more even in casting but still followed conventions in terms of sexes playing the roles – the doll-maker (Coppélius) and the poet (Nathanial) are still men desiring the opposite sex, although they could have been women with male dolls or dolls of both sexes, and thus displaying a wider range of desire. But such casting choices are very difficult for ballet companies to pursue because their ensembles have more female dancers than male, and a ballet company must provide roles for the people it has. Thus, by sticking to a conventional feminist translation of the story, Bigonzetti's Coppélia conforms to a rather timid feminist idea of female empowerment achieved through criticizing male desire and proposing that men be more accepting of female desirability as nature has provided it.

Coppélia is a useful example to illustrate how ballet can translate complex ideas into bodily movements and in indicating the limitations of these ballets in translating Hoffmann's manifold ideas. The latter is not due to the constraints of ballet and bodies to render those ideas – rather they are due to the limited, stifled translational imagination of the theatre directors, choreographers, and their basic audiences. Translation in ballet is often a process of preventing ideas from becoming too complicated and novel; a form of internal, unacknowledged censorship is exerted by the respective societies on the minds of the choreographers and their audiences. The choreographers, in particular ballet choreographers, tend to translate stories in a particular way to be in tune with their societies rather than to open up their societies to more imaginative ways of understanding relations between sexes, human and artificial beings, words, music and bodies.

Both the 1870 and the 2002 ballets show the fantasy of choreographers for an ideal human (body) without linking it to any critique of ballet as a delusion or pathology of its Coppélius-like creators. The music limits following this line of thought. It was composed to meet the operetta expectations of the 1870 translation for a Second Empire audience eager to discard Romantic ideas about revolutionary genius determined to overturn the natural order of bourgeois reality. In retaining this music for his revisionist *Coppélia*, Bigonzetti treated Delibes as a binding level of translation that succeeds in getting the revolutionary implication of the original Romantic story 'lost in translation'. Delibes' music has no life outside of its use in this ballet, but ballet dancers and audiences like it because it is easy to move to and does not require them to listen to any complexities in its harmony or instrumentation. To use more modern pieces of music or at least different pieces of music to tell the story would indicate that the classics of ballet history do not translate well in the twenty-first century. Delibes' music signifies respect for a classical ballet and reassures the audience that the feminist translation of the story fits comfortably within nineteenth-century values, in which the idea of female robots is no more disturbing than the bland operetta tunes that accompany the story. It is the music that provides the strongest layer of Hoffmann's translation into ballet, tying it and its audience to the Parisian world of 1870.

Notes

1. Special thanks to Professor Emeritus Karl Toepfer of San José State University, California, whose insights contributed significantly to this article.
2. Saint-Léon's letter from 30 January 1868.
3. The world premier of the ballet was in Rome in 1995, see https://epl.delfi.ee/kultuur/b-estonias-lavastub-uudne-coppelia-b?id=50916405 (accessed 18 February 2023).
4. Information and fact which is detailed in the ballet's programme.
5. Personal communication with Aivo Välja and Alison Kruusmaa (2020). The programme of the ballet did not mention the additional music or its author.
6. Olimpia as described by Nathanial in Ernst Theodor Amadeus Hoffmann's *The Sandman*. See https://germanstories.vcu.edu/ (accessed 18 February 2023).

10

Fruitful Intersemiotic Transfers between Music and Choreography in the National Ballet of Canada's *Romeo and Juliet*

Denise Merkle

This chapter sets out to explore how a choreographer in collaboration with a ballet master or mistress, a choreologist or stager, dancers and the conductor transform ballet music into narrative dance, and how dance and music exchange and transfer their 'dramatic essence' and 'thematic core' (Reardon 2007) during both the creative and the interpretative process. The transfer of such essence is the core theme of this book, and this chapter takes the perspective of specific collaborative voices which are different voices to those of Chapter 5. The focus is on the critics' and dancers' perspectives of transference, exchange and dialogue witnessed and felt between the art forms.

The transformation of Shakespeare's *Romeo and Juliet* (1597) into ballet, generally considered to be his tragedy most suited to the ballet (Crompton 2015) because of its 'continuous momentum' (Stenning Edgecombe 2006: 75), is an example of both adaptation (Cattrysse 2014) and intersemiotic translation, or the transfer of a cultural artefact from one sign system to another (Jakobson 1959/1966). Rather than focusing on the words when performing intersemiotic translation, the 'translators', from the composer to the ballet mistress, must focus on the overall message to be conveyed. Sergei Prokofiev created an intersemiotic translation when, in 1935, he transformed Shakespeare's tragic play into ballet music, which was then successfully translated into performed choreography in 1938. Choreographers, stagers and ballet masters have since then continued to work with dancers to transform Prokofiev's musical sounds into movement and guide their interpretation of the musical score. In other words, the movement of the dancers' bodies responds not only to the musical signs, but also to a variety of linguistic signs or cues. To quote Karen Bennett, 'a ballet production is a very complex work of art in its own right, involving an elaborate system of multiple semiotic codes that in turn add their own interpretation of the musical and linguistic texts' (Bennett 2003: 314). This is a clear case of 'multi-source text' (Cattrysse 2014: 12), a specificity of adaptation, that will be transformed into a single target cultural product.

John Cranko's 1964 and Alexei Ratmansky's 2011 choreographies of *Romeo and Juliet* for the National Ballet of Canada (NBofC) have been retained for this study. Both choreographers chose Sergei Prokofiev's dramatic *Romeo and Juliet* score that has been transformed into a programmatic narrative ballet by a number of renowned choreographers, including Sir Kenneth MacMillan, Frederick Ashton, John Neumeier, Oscar Ariaz and Rudolf Nureyev.

Sergey Radlov, artistic director of the Leningrad State Academic Theatre of Opera and Ballet, first approached Prokofiev in December 1934 with the idea of producing a ballet inspired by Shakespeare's *Romeo and Juliet*. 'Prokofiev composed intensively over the summer of 1935, with his piano score approved in October and performance scheduled for the following spring' (Bennett 2003: 312), only to be dropped in early 1936, likely because of a perceived 'lack of socialist realist content' (Jaffé, cited in ibid.). Moscow's Bolshoi Ballet took up the project after it was shelved by the Leningrad State Opera and Ballet. Material from the Prokofiev score reworked into the first of three orchestral suites premiered in Moscow at the Bolshoi in November 1936. Finally, the ballet choreographed by Vania Psota was performed, and to critical acclaim, in Brno, Czechoslovakia, in December 1938. The first Soviet version was choreographed by Leonid Lavrosky and performed at the Kirov Theatre, Leningrad, on 11 January 1940. Lead dancer Galina Ulanova wrote in glowing terms of the danceability of Prokofiev's musical score: 'Prokofiev, with his vigorous, dynamic, truly visual music, at once so modern and yet so Shakespearean in spirit and flavour, guided us with a sure hand through the action, investing it with meaning and purpose. His vividly drawn characterizations literally dictated the pattern of the dance, making our task incomparably easier' (Ulanova, cited in Vanderlinde 1998b).

Like the first performances in Brno and Leningrad, many subsequent productions, including Cranko's and Ratmansky's for the NBofC, have been a resounding success. John Reardon explains why choreographers find Shakespeare inspirational:

> If the principal glory of Shakespeare is his poetic genius, an art form that rules outspoken language might appear to be at a distinct disadvantage in the

adaptation game. [...] in a curious way, removing language from the field of play forces the interpreter to look for the dramatic essence of the underlying work and locate its thematic core. This stricture, at once confining and liberating, has led choreographers to create some of the most original, refreshing and powerful approaches to the Shakespeare canon of any of his interpreters.

Reardon 2007: 25–6

It was, in fact, Prokofiev who first successfully translated the play's 'dramatic essence' by composing 'visual' ballet music that was 'so Shakespearean in spirit and flavour' (Ulanova, in Vanderlinde 1998b). The *Romeo and Juliet* musical score had located the play's 'thematic core' thereby inspiring choreographers to create the 'original, refreshing and powerful' ballet adaptations to which Reardon refers above. In Reardon's view, choreographers are interpreters of Shakespeare just like composers and theatre directors, and their adaptations equally legitimate. For her part, Translation Studies scholar Karen Bennett treats Prokofiev's musical score as a 'translation' of Shakespeare's play and the ballet production (she analyses Nureyev's production in her article) as a 'translation' of the musical score (Bennett 2003: 315).

In this chapter, while keeping in mind Reardon's 'dramatic essence' of Shakespeare's play text and its 'thematic core' (Reardon 2007: 25–6), we shall analyse from the perspective of translation studies:

1. choreographical memory, as exemplified by Cranko's choreography and direction, and the creative process;
2. choreology as ballet text, with reference to Robyn Hughes' 1980 and Jane Bourne's 1993 Benesh notations of Cranko's choreography;
3. the transference, exchange and dialogue between music and dance in the creative and interpretative processes, with reference to, among others, NBofC ballet master Peter Ottmann's detailed annotation (2011) of Prokofiev's score (1976), based on his collaboration with Ratmansky, and the work of the National Ballet Orchestra (NBO).

The scope of this study is limited to a general overview and, it is to be hoped, will lead to a more detailed expert study of transference, exchange and dialogue between the musical and the choreology scores in the future. Here we start with the translational perspective detailed by dancers, witnessed by critics and interpreted from a translation studies perspective.

John Cranko's Choreographical Memory and the Creative Process

After receiving early ballet training in Cape Town, South Africa, John Cranko (1927–73) studied with the Sadler's Wells Ballet School in London in 1946, and danced his first role with the Sadler's Wells Ballet (SWB), now the Royal Ballet (RB), in November 1947. Cranko (also explored in Chapter 8) transitioned from a dancing career to that of full-time choreographer, with his last performance at the SWB in April 1950. At 23, he was appointed resident choreographer for the SWB 1950-1 season. In 1961 he was appointed artistic director of the Stuttgart Ballet (SB) (Kisselgoff 1973).

Cranko first staged Shakespeare's *Romeo and Juliet* as a ballet in Venice for Milan's La Scala ballet company, the premiere taking place on 26 July 1958. A new version of the choreography was created for Germany's SB and performed in December 1962 (Kisselgoff 1984). By choosing Prokofiev's musical score, Cranko had to deal with the composer's 'vividly drawn characterizations [that] literally dictated the pattern of the dance' (Ulanova cited in Vanderlinde 1998b) in terms of movement, rhythm, timing, gesture patterning and occurrence. James E. Neufeld agrees that the musical score 'frequently dictates [the] treatment' of 'location and sequence of events', but adds that the score 'consequently becomes so vivid and explicit as to hinder the choreographer's individual realization of the drama inherent in events' (Neufeld 1982–3: 120). We will come back to these constraints in section four, and now consider the choreographic process, generally taken to be composed of three stages that are not necessarily linear.

During the first stage of the choreographic process, many ballet choreographers 'gather [...] together the movement material'. '[They] use as raw material for their pieces the traditional steps and *enchaînements* that dancers learn in class' (Mackrell 2020). This of course presupposes that those choreographers are themselves dancers. The second stage involves 'developing movements into dance phrases'. 'A phrase [...] is a series of movements bound together by a physical impulse or line of energy and having a discernible beginning and end. [...] Dance phrases vary both in length and shape, [...] [and o]nce a phrase has been constructed, it can be built onto in many different ways' (ibid.). During the third stage, the choreographer creates 'the final structure of the work' (ibid.). There are two outside influences on structure: the ballet's 'purpose' and the music. In a story ballet, 'the plot [its purpose] will determine the way in which the dance material is to be structured,' alongside the 'length' of the musical score, the 'arrangement of fast and slow movements, and [the music's] treatment of theme' (ibid.). Influences may also be organic. 'In the case of narrative ballets, choreographic ideas may develop into formal motifs, [...] the representation of emotions and events is heavily stylized, and the ordering of the plot is determined as much by aesthetic as by dramatic logic. [...] Finally, the structure of a dance reflects the tradition in which it is created and performed' (ibid.).

Whether or not Cranko respected the order of these stages when choreographing *Romeo and Juliet* is not known. It is nevertheless self-evident that the three stages were part of his creative process of translating Prokofiev's score into classical ballet, and that stages one and two required him to dance many roles while developing the choreography.

Cranko was an old friend and colleague of the NBofC's founding artistic director, Celia Franca. According to NBofC repertoire notes, Cranko was paid $2,000 to direct the company's first production of *Romeo and Juliet* in the spring of 1964, and he received royalties for every subsequent performance in Canada and abroad when the NBofC was touring (Carreiro no date). Cranko died unexpectedly at age 46 in 1973. His choreography would have died with him if not for the memory of his dancers, a made-for-television film of the ballet and Benesh Movement Notation (herein BMN). Yet, he did not choreograph his ballets using notation, but rather by exploiting what was considered by many to be his outstanding memory, which necessarily involved muscle memory, 'a collection of memories [...] of frequently enacted movements' that are 'stored in your brain' (Integrity Dance Center 2020), initially acquired as a ballet dancer, but fine-turned through his work as a choreographer. However, 'before [dancers] get anywhere near muscle memory, [they] must first [...] get the dance into their bodies' (Solway 2007). The same applies to choreographers, who 'get the dance into their bodies' while interpreting the music. As Gweneth Lloyd, choreographer of *The Rose and the Ring* for the Royal Winnipeg Ballet (herein RWB), explained to *Winnipeg Free Press* arts critic Albrecht Gaub: 'Confronted by all this music [...] [Lloyd's] first feeling was one of consternation. [...] The first bars were sheer torture, she found, and then gradually the spell of the music began to assert itself, and the movement began to take shape' (Morriss cited by Gaub 2013: 94).

Likewise, Cranko, the dancer, got Prokofiev's music 'into [his] body', which helped develop his kinesthetic memory through choreography development. 'Each time the dancer repeats a movement [...], [the sensorimotor information] becomes more deeply anchored or consolidated within the implicit memory and no longer requires as much of the dancer's conscious attention to retrieve it' (Hebert 2016/2017).

Moreover, highly structured dance forms such as ballet are easier to learn and remember. According to Carolyn Hebert:

the ease with which movements are learned and remembered is highly dependent upon how structured the movement sequences are. Structured dance forms are those based on a defined set of body shapes and movements, with commonly accepted names, such as those in ballet. [...] The more structured the dance movements are, the greater the ease of encoding and retrieval.

Hebert 2016/2017

Furthermore, the ability to develop muscle memory is aided by 'calling out verbal cues [...], ballet positions [...] and movements', and describing the 'impetus for the movement' (Solway 2007). Diane Solway explains that choreographers and ballet masters and mistresses not only learn and teach choreography in chunks (the dancers learn one movement at a time; the steps are merged into phrases and the phrases into longer sequences), and describe the movements to be done, they also hum the music and count the beats. Eventually the individual chunks congeal into the full-length ballet. Post-performance, many dancers, for example Angel Corella, do not remember performing specific steps because the movement becomes automatic (ibid.).

In 1975, NBC artistic director David Haber wrote a letter to Dieter Grafe, the SB's lawyer, assuring him of 'a very faithful and honest interpretation of John Cranko's original choreography' (Haber 1975: 2). However, Cranko had passed away two years earlier, and the NBofC did not have a resident choreologist in the 1970s. With only the 1964 two-dimensional CBC film of the ballet, the company had to rely on (muscle) memory to recall with accuracy his *Romeo and Juliet*. While muscle memory ensures that the ballet's creator and dancers successfully translate choreography, both memory – and the choreography they learn – die with them.

Choreology as Ballet Text

Forms of dance notation in the West have existed since at least the seventeenth century, when Louis XIV, founder of France's Académie royale de danse in 1661, commissioned Pierre Beauchamp to devise a dance notation system for ballroom and theatre dance in the mid-1670s (Pierce 1998). Ann Hutchinson Guest detailed the differences in notation system in *Choreo-graphics: a comparison of dance notation systems from the fifteenth century to the present*. In fact, Ann (Hutchinson Guest 1998). However, no notation method prior to the twentieth century reproduced dance movement comprehensively. As a result, dance was generally considered an 'illiterate' art form (Wilke et al. 2003) until Labanotation and Benesh Movement Notation (BMN) were developed.

The Dance Notation Bureau (DNB) was founded in 1940 to preserve choreographic works through Labanotation, a movement notation method first published by Rudolf Laban in 1928. However, BMN is generally considered the more accurate and complete notation system for ballet. 'Devised by Rudolf and Joan Benesh, and first published in 1956, BMN is [...] most widely used in the recording and restaging of dance works' (Royal Academy of Dance 2020). The notation shows movements of the head, shoulders, hips, knees and feet on five lines similar to a music staff. In a time of two-dimensional audiovisual recording, experts consider BMN the more precise three-dimensional representation of a full ballet, offering the possibility of synchronization with the music.

Example 10.1 shows two staves of music, under which four staves of dance notation are 'scored like an orchestral score. The first two movement staves show a pair of soloists, and the third and fourth show respectively eight women and eight men. Details of location, direction of movement, movement of groups, etc., are recorded under the staff' (Hall 1967: 193).

Benesh choreologist Juliette Kando explains that '[j]ust like in a full orchestral score used by a conductor to lead an orchestra, a choreology score describes detailed movements and steps complete with rhythm and phrasing for individuals

Example 10.1 Full score of group dance. Mazurka from 'Coppélia' (Hall 1967: 193).

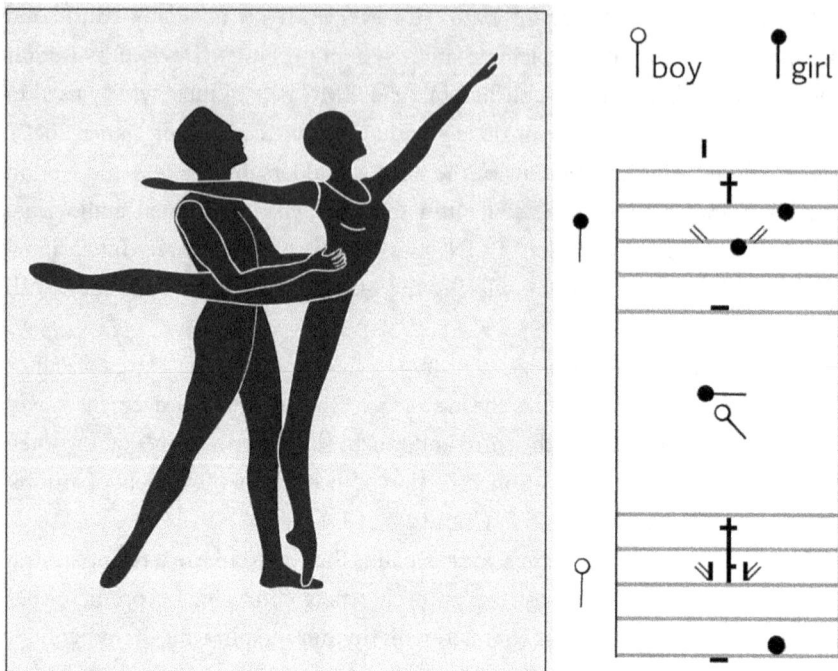

Example 10.2 The notation includes details such as hand holds, many of which are not seen in a photo or video. Credit: Juliette Kando F.I. Chor.

(soloists) and entire groups (corps de ballet), each on their own staves' (Kando 2023). Example 10.2 represents a pas de deux notated on the right on two adjoined staves, one for each dancer.

Apparently, it was choreographer Kenneth MacMillan who advised Cranko to notate his ballets (Landgraf 2015). Consequently, the then artistic director of the SB sent Georgette Tsinguirides (b. 1928), his assistant, ballet dancer, ballet mistress and later choreologist, to study BMN at the Institute of Choreology (herein IC) in London in 1965–6. There, she completed the two-year Benesh course in only one year to become, in 1966, the first choreologist in Germany. Tsinguirides preserved many of Cranko's works in BMN. Retired since 2017 after 72 years with the SB, Tsinguirides taught the works choreographed by Cranko and his successors to several generations of ballet companies around the globe (Hanselmann 2014).

Jane Bourne was born in Lincoln, UK, and also trained at London's IC. She joined the SB in 1974, shortly after Cranko's death, to assist in completing the notation of his repertory (Johnson 2012). Bourne later staged his *Romeo and Juliet*, among other ballets, for companies internationally, including the NBofC.

She had taken the newer three-year course taught by Joan Benesh, who encouraged students 'to apply redundancy theory (that is information which is unnecessary to record)' (Trevien 2015), when notating. Bourne learned on the job in Stuttgart that the theory did not work in a professional environment, because it was inefficient to look up answers to questions. Rather, she quickly learned to write detailed notation. It was a television recording of *Romeo and Juliet* that proved very useful for producing the complete choreological score in 1975, given that Tsinguirides had notated Act 1 only (Landgraf 2015). By 1966 *Romeo and Juliet* had been 'perfected and this [made-for-television] film [with] Heinz Clauss and Marcia Haydée [in the leading roles] was the third or fourth revival' (Trevien 2015). However, the ninety-minute television time slot required major cuts to the ballet. '[I]n order to notate the cut sections [Bourne] had to ask each individual dancer what they had done' (ibid.). Bourne returned to England after six years in Stuttgart, although she was still asked by the company to notate ballet scores and was sent to various companies to teach ballets.

'Then Reid Anderson [formerly with the SB] was asked to teach *Onegin* for [the] first time with the [NBofC], and he needed someone to assist him to teach it. So [Bourne] went and learnt [...] from him. Later he felt confident to send [her to teach] alone' (ibid.). But her work with the NBofC was not limited to teaching choreography, she also notated it. *Romeo and Juliet* was updated by the NBofC in 1995 for a new production staged by Anderson using Bourne's 1993 BMN (Vanderlinde 1998a). Her choreography was the basis of numerous NBofC productions of *Romeo and Juliet* spanning the period from 1995 to 2009, its quality applauded by, for example, dance critic Bill Watt in his review of the 1995 revival of the ballet (Watt 1995: no page).

However, the first BMN of Cranko's *Romeo and Juliet* had in fact been produced for the NBofC by Australian-born Robyn Hughes Ryman in 1980. In London, she studied advanced BMN before earning an MA in Dance at Toronto's York University in 2010. She worked as a (character) dancer or choreologist for such companies as SWB/RB, the Bayerisches Staatsballett, the RWB and the NBC (1980–82) (Ryman 2019). Nevertheless, Bourne's notation of *Romeo and Juliet* was the one finally retained by Anderson and the NBofC for the 1995 revival. More recently, Hughes Ryman taught Benesh notation as part of the National Ballet School's teacher training programme, as well as co-authoring with Rhonda Ryman-Kane a series of four iBooks on BMN and creating a website 'to disseminate information about [...] (BMN)' (ibid.).

The copyright of both the Hughes Ryman and Bourne BMN of Cranko's choreography located in the NBofC archives is privately owned. According to the DNB website, '[n]otating a work does not change the fact that the choreographer owns his/her dance and has the right to restrict its use' (Dance Notation Bureau 2020). Anderson staged Cranko's choreography in 1995; he did not produce a new choreography of the ballet.

Transference, Exchange and Dialogue between Music and Dance, and the Interpretative Process

Karen Bennett writes that Prokofiev and Radlov conceived the ballet scenario together. The 120-scene, five-act Shakespearean tragedy was abridged to a three-act scenario, composed of fifty-eight short episodes, each with a descriptive title. The order of the scenes was essentially the same as Shakespeare's, although the groupings differed, scenes lending themselves to dance (the ball scene, for example) having been lengthened. Leitmotifs were used to create narrative structure by associating musical themes with characters (see Bennett's detailed analysis of the way rhythm, pitch, volume and orchestration contribute to the depiction of complex emotional states) (Bennett 2003: 314–21). NBofC principal dancer Sonia Rodriguez confirms the power of the music that 'takes you through ever [sic] single emotion; just listening to the score you can feel what you should be expressing at that moment' (Rodriguez, in Anon. 2001: Childlike Joy).

As a result, according to James E. Neufeld, Prokofiev's programmatic score gives choreographers very little creative leeway:

> [Cranko was] faced with the same initial restrictions of Shakespeare's well-known dramatization of the story and Prokofiev's explicitly programmatic score. Most of the important decisions about the libretto [had] been made by Prokofiev, working from Shakespeare [...]. To begin with, the score allows for little variation or transposition, aside from the mandolin dance, which Cranko places in the bedroom scene, just before Juliet's unconscious body is discovered [...]. There is little left for the choreographer to do but comply with the demands of the music. Furthermore, Prokofiev's score, at its most powerful, suggests the poetry of Shakespeare's play more than the events of his story. [...] In Prokofiev's music, something has gone wrong in the basic relationship between music and dance. Music, which should provide a strong support for movement, has become dictatorial.
>
> Neufeld 1982-3: 120-1

Neufeld's assertion that 'something has gone wrong in the basic relationship between music and dance' is, however, open to question when one considers the many *Romeo and Juliet*s ever so successfully choreographed to Prokofiev's popular score. Rather than criticizing the composer's work in her 8 February 1995 critique of the ballet production, Deirdre Kelly blames 'Cranko's choreography [for responding] inappropriately to the Sergei Prokofiev score' (Kelly 1995: no page). Kelly's opinion is nevertheless not shared by the majority of ballet aficionados (Clark 2001). Furthermore, Bob Verdun writes of Cranko's choreography staged by Anderson that '[he] ha[d] never seen a ballet as beautifully presented' and '[m]ost important, Prokofiev's music is ideal for dance' (1995: no page). Sarah Crompton concurs, writing, with reference to MacMillan's choreography of the ballet, that '[i]t might seem a strange way to perform Shakespeare – without words. But when dance finds that level of expressiveness, it speaks as loudly as any sonnet' (2015). In addition, she cites dance coach Irek Mukhamedov, who affirms: '[The music] is very dramatic, touching and expressive,' so '[young dancers] must understand the music, learn to sing it, and then the words in [their] heart or [their] mind will speak through [their] body' (cited by ibid.), thanks at least in part, as we have seen, to muscle memory and its response to musical cues.

Alexei Ratmansky also appreciates the music score, which inspired him to produce a new choreography of the ballet, commissioned by the NBofC to premiere at the Four Seasons Centre for the Performing Arts in November 2011. According to critic Paula Citron, 'Ratmansky's greatness lies in his ability to mirror music in dance. There is absolutely no mime. The emotional arc of the characters is cunningly shown in movement. In fact, the music and the dance seem inseparable' (2013: no page). Clearly, what is perceived as a constraint by some, is an inspiration for others.

In a 2012 interview, Elena Lobsanova, who was chosen to dance the role of Juliet in Ratmansky's world premiere, described how the choreographer worked with the dancers: '[h]e studie[d] the music while listening to a recording of it on an mp3 player. At almost every break, he relate[d] some choreographic sequences or moments in the music or scene literally to the text' (2012). Indeed, 'the Bolshoi-trained Ratmansky is [...] [k]nown for his musicality and physical inventiveness' (Re-imagined 2011: no page). Citron explains that Ratmansky's *Romeo and Juliet* is 'watching in dance what one is hearing in the music. It's practically uncanny; Ratmansky and Prokofiev become one. It's a joy [...], aided and abetted by visiting conductor Ormsby Wilkins and the National orchestra' (Citron 2013: no page). Moreover, the choreographer limits the rearrangement of the musical score by, for example, 'putting back the Dance of the Knights in the Capulet party as Prokofiev intended' (ibid.). Lobsanova adds that:

[Alexei's version] has similarities to Rudolph Nureyev's version in that both choreographers fill the music with as much meaningful movement as they can. In most versions the score is cut or rearranged in different places. [...] in Cranko's [version], the music is rearranged in Romeo's solo in the ballroom. We haven't finished creating it yet, but so far I think all the music is there and in its original order.

2012: no page

While collaborating with Ratmansky and working with the dancers in the rehearsal studio, NBofC ballet master Peter Ottmann pencil annotated in detail L. Atovmyan's piano reduction of Prokofiev's score. This version of Opus 64 was a ballet in four acts with a nine-scene libretto. Since Prokofiev's descriptive episode titles of the scenes were in Russian, Ottmann first translated them into English and then annotated the musical score in pencil. For example, above the Russian title of episode 13 'ТАНЕЦ РЫЦАРЕЙ,' he wrote 'Ballroom' and below the Russian, 'Oppression of Power (prevents love from flourishing – heavy, > walks)' (Prokofiev 1976: 37). He also includes verbal references to the orchestra, to the placement and movement of dancers, in addition to some very summary BMN outside and inside the staves. The resulting document is a hybrid piano reduction-choreology score.

And what is the role of the orchestra in the dialogue between music and dance? The NBofC can count on its own orchestra, the National Ballet Orchestra (NBO) – 'the only dedicated ballet orchestra in Canada' (National Ballet of Canada 2020) – to add to the ballet experience during a performance. Other companies, such as the RWB, work with the city's symphony orchestra. According to 'James DePreist [...], "conducting for ballet [is] about suiting the dance and the demands of the choreographer"' (Sulcas 2006). By contrast, current NBofC artistic director and principal conductor, David Briskin, stresses the contribution of live music to inspiring dancers and enriching the ballet performance: 'The [NBofC] has an unwavering commitment to live music and its transformative power. It's not only a priority but a necessity, inspiring the dancers and contributing to the audience's full experience of dance' (National Ballet of Canada 2020). The music not only inspires, it helps to 'keep up the proper tempo for dancers' so that they are not left 'in mid air or behind [their] movements' (Gaub 2013: 95). In fact, when reviewing NBofC productions of *Romeo and Juliet*, critics often refer not only to the quality of dancing, but also to the music, which are considered inseparable. Indeed, the NBO is praised by ballet critics and the ballet-going public alike.

Dance critic Deirdre Kelly writes that Prokofiev's 'score [was] performed Wednesday [8 February 1995] with sensitivity and passion by maestro Ormsby Wilkins and the [NBO]' (Kelly 1995: no page). In his lengthy and revealing review of the performance, Bob Verdun writes:

> [T]he performance of a ballet score [has never] sounded as good! In fact, it was the music that tipped the balance for me and [...] (symphony violinist Nuala Freund) to make a fast trip to Toronto [...].
>
> Music is absolutely crucial to the success of a ballet performance, because it conveys so much of the meaning of a wordless story that lasts almost two and a half hours. [...] powerful music such as Prokofiev's can almost rival Shakespeare's text in helping to tell the famous story of the ill-fated lovers.
>
> Not only is this music very well written, but it was extraordinarily well performed by the [NBO], under the direction of Ormsby Wilkins. I am almost tempted to say that the evening was worth attending just for the music – but that would be misleading, because of the outstanding presentation on the stage.
>
> Verdun 1995: no page

Wilkins was the music director and principal conductor of the NBO from 1990 to 2005, when he was replaced by Briskin. His effective collaborative work with dancers contributed unquestionably to the success of the NBofC. 'Wilkins took a job straight out of school as a rehearsal pianist at the Australian Ballet and learned his craft under John Lanchbery, one of the most important ballet conductors of the 20th century' (Sulcas 2006). As a rehearsal pianist he learned to work closely with dancers, and he continued to do so on the podium while working with the NBofC:

> [T]he dancers want to know what I'm going to do on the podium, 'Can you help me here or not?' [Wilkins] added: 'I'm always trying to work with the dancers to make the phrasing better musically. I actually enjoy that collaboration, listening to preferences but making it a valid musical interpretation. Eventually you get to know individual dancers and to anticipate their needs.'
>
> Ibid.

Briskin adds three skills shared by successful ballet orchestra conductors: (1) 'a very secure sense of tempo – it's analogous to perfect pitch – being able to conduct an exact metronome mark out of thin air'; (2) 'a working knowledge of ballet vocabulary and terminology' (see, for example, Wilkin's use of the term 'phrasing', in the above quotation); and (3) 'a real eye for movement' (ibid.).

Transference and exchange between music and dance are once again evident through ongoing respectful dialogue between the NBO under the leadership of its conductor and NBofC dancers. This dialogue, combined with the dialogue between the composer or musical score, and the choreographer, ballet master or mistress and the dancers, contribute to the interpretative process that will translate into a successful ballet performance.

Conclusion

In 1949, *Winnipeg Free Press* arts critic, Frank A. Morriss, described the collaboration between music composer and ballet composer required to create *The Rose and the Ring* for the RWB:

> The story, too complicated for ballet form, had to be simplified [...] After [a] meeting, which took hours of time, Mr. Kaufmann [the music composer] went home and made a preliminary sketch of the score. Miss Lloyd [the ballet composer] then joined him and listened to the music to catch the idiom to which she would have to adapt her steps. Certain points were discussed, small alterations made, the type of instrumentation was indicated, and the musical motif for each character was set. The next step was for Mr. Kaufmann to record the piano score.
>
> Gaub 2013: 94

While transference, exchange and dialogue between the music and ballet composers may occur during the process of 'writing [...] ballet', the example of *Romeo and Juliet* has clearly demonstrated that transference, exchange and dialogue occur at all stages of the creation of a story ballet, from the conception of the musical score and the choreography, through to the interpretation of the music and the choreography on stage during the ephemeral performance that is ballet.

Many actors are involved in the creation and interpretation processes, intervening at various stages: composer, choreographer, stager, ballet master or mistress, coaches, orchestra conductor, dancers, not to mention set and costume designers, confirming that 'we cannot understand ballet without broadening our horizons to appreciate music's relationship with its contingent arts' (Mawer 2012: 77). The successful production of a story ballet relies on the nonlinear contribution of these many actors to translating convincingly the dramatic essence and thematic core of the source text (Reardon 2007). Its production as a cultural product thus clearly requires the interpretation and adaptation of a multi-source text (Cattrysse 2014).

Evidently, creativity and interpretation are intimately interwoven with multiple iterations in the Kaufmann-Lloyd collaboration, and the same applies to the many collaborations that have produced successful intersemiotic translations of *Romeo and Juliet*. Prokofiev interpreted Shakespeare, Cranko and Ratmansky interpreted Prokofiev's musical score as well as Shakespeare's text during the creative process, and dancers allow Prokofiev's music to embody them, as well as often returning to Shakespeare's text. Neither the exchange between music and dance, nor creativity and interpretation operate in isolation; they are all interconnected and nurture one another to produce the final intersemiotic cultural product.

11

Dancing Symbols

Movement Notation as a Form of Translation

Mary Wardle

This chapter will analyse how dance notation, exemplified by the two arguably most widely used systems – Labanotation (1928) and Benesh Movement Notation (1955) – sets about translating physical movement into a form of written documentation, recording all manner of elements such as the part(s) of the body involved, directionality, the height at which the movement develops, its speed, the dancer's gaze, weight-bearing, the positions across the stage, the number of dancers appearing simultaneously and any potential interaction, such as in a *Pas de deux* or the more choral movements of the *Corps de ballet*. The fact that, since the seventeenth century, the Western classical dance tradition has produced around one hundred different dance notation systems (Hutchinson Guest 1984: xi) is indicative of the perceived importance of recording choreography in a written form. These transcription codes exist for a number of reasons most of which are pragmatic – accessing older works no longer in a company's repertoire; passing new choreographies on to future generations; allowing dancers to learn and practice their parts without the presence of a teacher; affording copyright protection for the choreographer's creative work – but they can also, perhaps inadvertently, contribute to alleviating some of the stigma attached to dance as a 'lesser' artform due, in part, precisely to the limited way in which dance can be studied, archived and handed down, a stigma consolidated by a cultural environment that prioritizes written records over oral transmission. After an initial overview of dance notation and its history, issues traditionally debated in Translation Studies such as authorship, originality, reproduction, creativity, interpretation and (un)faithfulness will be investigated in relation to dance notation.

One of the recurring motifs in academic discussions of dance as an art form is the lowly status to which it is often relegated (inaccurately), obscured by the long shadow of literature and fine art as well as of its fellow performing arts, theatre and music. Joseph Margolis writes: 'I think it is accurate to say that the dance is the single principle art that is [...] very nearly unmentioned in comprehensive overviews of aesthetics' (1984: 70), while Graham McFee describes dance as 'a "Jenny-come-lately" to the aesthetic feast, trying to find its own elbow room' (2013: 649). Perhaps the single most influential reason for this is dance's intrinsic ephemeral nature (already mentioned in previous chapters, see especially Chapters 5, 6, 8 and 9): 'choreographic works do not seem as ontologically robust, easily identifiable or stable as (say) paintings or novels. As a performing art, dance generates moving objects that have always been difficult to identify across time and space, and a feature of whose being is their disappearance' (Pouillaude 2017: xi). In painting or sculpture, the creative act results in a tangible artefact, while dance, as Marcia Siegel observes, 'exists at a perpetual vanishing point. At the moment of its creation it is gone [...] [it is] an event that disappears in the very act of materializing' (van Zile 1985: 42), and yet the traces of the dance text and the documents which record it become vital for research in this field.

The point can be illustrated with the example of *The Dying Swan*. The dance, the shortest complete ballet at two and a half minutes, came about in 1905 after Anna Pavlova asked dancer and choreographer Mikhail Fokine to write a *pièce d'occasion* for her to perform at a gala. The dancer had been inspired by seeing the swans during her walks in the park and by her reading of Alfred Lord Tennyson's 1830 poem *The Dying Swan* – the poet was extremely popular at the time in Russia and Pavlova would have read his poems in translation. Fokine proceeded to write the piece, setting it to *Le Cygne*, a piano and cello composition from Camille Saint Saëns' suite *Le Carnaval des animaux* written in 1886. Pavlova would go on to perform the ballet herself thousands of times and it has become a set piece for dancers of all nationalities ever since. Its cultural legacy can be detected, for example, in the reference to Pavlova that Ogden Nash inserts in his 1950 poem, 'Verses for Camille Saint-Saëns' *Carnival of the Animals*', and, also, posthumously, we might say, in the way many dancers, even today, choose to incorporate certain features of *The Dying Swan* into their interpretations of *Swan Lake*, a ballet that predates Fokine's choreography by almost thirty years.[1]

From this brief example, we can see how many acts of creative expression can be integrated into one dance but, of all the texts mentioned, the literary texts, their translations and the musical scores are the only ones for which we have easily accessible, tangible records. The choreography does not fare as well. Already, within Fokine's lifetime, *The Dying Swan* was becoming so popular and being staged by so many different dancers and companies, that the choreographer decided to produce a written document detailing his version of the ballet, as best he could, to preserve it for posterity: 'I wish to record this dance and by all possible means make clear its composition, its technique and plan' (Fokine 1925: 4). He was following in a long, if often unnoticed, tradition of dance transcription. Practices for the written recording of dance and movement – graphic, iconic, symbolic documentations – date back to the fifteenth century in Europe, including famous choreographers such as Raoul Feuillet, who under Louis XIV, published *Chorégraphie, ou l'Art de décrire la Dance* in 1700. This work was very popular and translated throughout Europe. Since most head and body movements would have been standardized and known by heart, Feuillet's book only transcribed the footwork and the patterns traced on the floor by the dancers. There have been several other transcription systems adopted over the centuries by different choreographers or dance instructors, with many functioning along the same lines as that created by Feuillet.[2]

With *The Dying Swan*, however, Mikhail Fokine was creating a new kind of dance, what came to be known as the *Ballets Russes*, dances 'of the whole body', as he describes them, and not only of the limbs. He was interested in 'the significance of plastic expression' and going beyond the 'ordinary physical exercise': he sought the 'poetry in the movements of the dance [...]. It is not an appeal merely to the eye of the onlooker, but to his soul, emotions and imagination' (Fokine 1925: 4). And so, in 1925, twenty years after Pavlova had first performed it, he produced a booklet setting out his choreography, integrated with photographs of each of the different positions, performed by his wife, Vera Fokina. He proceeded by dividing the musical score into fifty-three sections, each corresponding to a photograph and a description of the movements. This is complemented with diagrams indicating the dancer's movements across the stage and further information regarding the scenery, the lights, the costume, the music and the curtain. At around the same time, Vaslav Nijinsky was developing his own notation system, based on Stepanov notation,[3] the system then used at the Imperial Dance Academy of St Petersburg. Unlike Fokine, who had simply used words and photographs, Nijinsky notated his choreography of *L'Après-midi d'un faune* (1912) with symbols on a music score-like stave, a bold enterprise, since – as in the case of Fokine – the movement patterns of *Faune* depart so radically from all the elements of classical style which had, up until then, been so codified and therefore more straightforward, relatively speaking, to consign to paper. It is precisely because of the innovations of style and expression in dance in the opening decades of the twentieth century that two new, groundbreaking notation systems were developed and, to varying degrees, are still used today: Labanotation was devised in 1928 by the highly influential Hungarian dance theorist, and choreographer, Rudolf von Laban which is arguably the most widely used system still today. Benesh Movement Notation, on the other hand, was developed in 1955 by Joan Benesh, a British dancer with the Royal Ballet, and her husband, Rudolf and is still used today by that company and the Royal Academy of Dance.

Benesh notation – marginally more intuitive for a novice to decipher than Labanotation – is transcribed on a five-line stave – allowing the use of regular music manuscript paper – in parallel with the actual musical score, where each line corresponds to different levels along the vertical axis of the dancer's body: respectively, the floor, the height of the knees, of the waist, the shoulders and the head. Because movement develops in three-dimensional space, there are further symbols indicating whether hands, arms, feet or legs are in line with the body, in front of it or behind. Labanotation, while also using abstract symbols to represent the parts of the body, is developed in column-like patterns up the page, under the horizontal musical notation. Neither of these systems represents the dance in a mimetic fashion: the notation is a graphic system through which embodiment is encoded and can later be re-enacted. It is important to stress that both transcribe the experience of moving rather than illustrating what the dancer 'looks like' while performing. The symbols, therefore, are not 'artistic impressions' of the dancer's body: they are not illustrations or drawings but can be considered a new 'language'. It is beyond the scope of this chapter to describe how either of these systems works in any detail but the words of Hutchinson Guest – one of the preeminent authorities on dance notation in general and Labanotation in particular – will suffice to appreciate the levels of complexity involved:

> The [notated] actions, concentrations and aims are: flexion, extension, rotation, direction and level, traveling, change of support, absence of support, balance, loss of balance, and relationship to the environment. Each of these elements has subdivisions, the various possibilities of which are combined to produce movement sequences. Progression develops from the simplest of examples to the more intricate.
>
> 2008: xxxiii

Marguerite Causley outlines how Benesh notation can precisely indicate:

> rhythm and phrasing, dynamics and all other qualities of movement; twists, inclinations and displacements of the head and various parts of the trunk; complex positions of hands, fingers, feet, eyes, eyebrows and so on; patterns of

movement by groups of varying numbers; support of one person by another, contact with objects; contact with the ground in sitting, lying, kneeling, et cetera.

1967: 76

While these notation systems are more closely associated with recording dance, be it ballet, contemporary, ballroom, folk, etc. – and this will be the emphasis throughout this discussion – it should be pointed out that movement notation also has great potentialities in many other fields, such as physical education, neurology, physiotherapy, ethnology. It is also employed to record original choreographies for the correct attribution of copyright.[4] Indeed, notation finds a place in any context where the precise recording and analysis of human movement-patterns is of import. As a field of study – 'the scientific and aesthetic study through notation of all forms of movement – it is known as choreology, a universal kinetic language' (Causley 1967: 77).

Historically, classical ballets have been transmitted from one generation to the next through a combination of oral and gestural tradition. Before video recordings, and still today in many companies, the traditional way in which choreographies are handed down from one cohort of dancers to the next is through the figure of the *répétiteur* or stager, often former dancers themselves, whose role it is to pass on not only the steps but also their execution in the form judged to be the closest to the wishes of the original choreographer. Often, *répétiteurs* are elevated to the repositories of otherwise unavailable knowledge, the incarnation, it might be said, of authenticity: as Temin puts it 'répétiteurs are the delegates of the choreographers or their estates' (2009: 73). In some cases, like that of Merrill Ashley and the *Ballo della Regina*, a work created for her by George Balanchine, the ballet is bequeathed to the dancer who then holds the copyright and the accompanying freedom to stage it as they see fit (Temin 2009: 74). One of the drawbacks with this can be the apparently idiosyncratic interpretation of what constitutes the 'text' to be transmitted. For example, Francia Russell, another of Balanchine's alumni, feels that having worked directly with the master, she 'picked up the specific shadings of each gesture, and believes she's able to give the choreography a period authenticity that later dancers who performed the same ballet cannot' (Temin 2009: 74). Advocates of notation argue that transcription systems avoid what can be highly subjective interpretations by *répétiteurs*. The task of passing on the dance is even more fraught when continuity of memory is lost and subsequent re-stagers are confronted with disparate source materials such as 'newspaper reviews, collaborators' correspondence, the choreographer's drawings and plans, an annotated musical score, class notebooks, models of the scenography, and personal accounts by the original participants' (Pouillaude 2017: 235), without necessarily having witnessed the dance themselves.

Typically, a dance survives through its instantiation. Through being performed repeatedly, it 'has the potential for a dynamic existence: ever changing, but capable of living through those changes' (Duerden 2007b: 130). This repetition, however, requires that the identity of the work be established which begs the question as to what exactly constitutes the identity of a dance. As Sarah Rubidge asks: 'Is a work's identity tied to our ability to recognize its instantiation?' (2000: 205). Just as with productions of Shakespeare, spoken in present-day English, staged in modern settings with contemporary costumes, so with dance, there is some discussion as to what constitutes the 'core' of the work. What has to remain the same and what can be changed for *Swan Lake* to still be *Swan Lake*? Is it the narrative, the bravura steps, the costumes, its division into acts, the music? Nelson Goodman divides art forms into two categories: autographic, such as painting, where the artist produces one piece, a unique painting, and any further instances of that work are considered forgeries or fakes; and allographic, such as literature or music, where there are multiple copies or reproductions of the same work across space and time (1968: 113). It is, however, much easier to claim that one copy or edition of *Wuthering Heights* is the same as another – paratextual elements may change but the words themselves remain identical – than it is to claim similarity between different performances of Beethoven's *Fifth Symphony*. In this sense, dance can be equated with music as another such allographic art form. In his discussion of the topic, terming them 'multiple arts', McFee introduces a distinction, widely referred to in such varied fields as logic, linguistics and computer science, to differentiate between the abstract concept of what might be understood by *Swan Lake* on the one hand, in a sentence such as '*Swan Lake* is my favourite ballet' and, on the other, what *Swan Lake* actually looks like in any one specific staged performance: 'The technical device I propose to use is a distinction between type and token, where the token is the specific object in front of me and the type is the general object' (McFee 1994: 24). In terms of dance notation, McFee's concept of type is what would be recorded in the dance score whereas the token would be any resulting performance. We can conclude therefore that, 'there is a similar relationship between the text and the performance of a theatre piece to the relationship between the dance score and performance of choreography, and the traditions of each performance art share the convention of the passing-on of ideas from one generation to the next' (Duerden 2007b: 131).

If we follow Roman Jakobson's famous tripartite definition of translation (1959: 233) as explored already in Chapters 1 and 4 in particular, then most classical ballets can be categorized as examples of intersemiotic translation or 'transmutation', representing as they do a choreographed, kinetic interpretation of some earlier text: *The Sleeping Beauty* (1890), choreographed by Marius Petipa, is based on the classic fairytale of the same name. Indeed, as is often the case, a number of different sources and influences converge to give rise to the new text: Petipa includes references from the Grimm Brothers' version of the tale, *Dornröschen*, as well as the earlier *Conte* by Charles Perrault, *La Belle au bois dormant*,[5] although, for good measure, he opts to throw in a number of characters from other stories – Puss in Boots, Tom Thumb, Little Red Riding Hood and Cinderella, among others. There is also, most obviously, a parallel intersemiotic translation of the tale into the musical score of Tchaikovsky, specifically commissioned for the ballet. The translation process that interests us more closely here, however, is that between notation and dance. It is important to remember that, unlike literary translation, dance notation operates in both directions, as it were: the dance is notated into a written score – either at the time of its inception or at a later stage – and then, subsequently, the same score becomes the 'source text' for returning to the 'original' dance steps.

Furthermore, unlike music and theatre, where the originator of the text – the composer and the playwright respectively – is usually the person who transcribes the work onto paper, in the form of the musical score and the play-text, with dance the choreographer and the notator are most commonly two separate people, sometimes working in different time periods or geographic locations. Even in the best-case scenario of the notator working alongside the choreographer, 'recording not only the steps but also the imagery, motivation, and characterization given to the dancers by the choreographer or stager',[6] there is considerable leeway for different notators to notate differently. This is one of the first similarities with literary translation, where the author of the source text very rarely corresponds with the translator: the translator, therefore, has to interpret the text and, just as with literary texts, one original can give rise to a number of possible versions, as clearly illustrated by the ongoing research into retranslation within Translation Studies.[7] The example below highlights how different translators can approach the same source text and, while the resulting translations are clearly dissimilar, focusing on different aspects and choosing to emphasize certain features over others, they are both undeniably translations of the same text:

> C'était agaçant, cette manie qu'avaient les gens richissimes de ne faire jamais, jamais que des affaires.
>
> Sagan 1965: 51
>
> It was irritating, this mania that the ultra-rich had for always, always getting a bargain.
>
> Sagan 1966: 52
>
> God, it was a drag, this obsession of the super-rich for doing nothing but swinging deal after deal.
>
> Sagan 2009: 59

In this respect, the source text can be likened to a musical score, and the translation becomes the individual interpretation, changing from artist to artist, from performance to performance. This same performative, interpretative element is present, obviously, also in dance. Mikhail Fokine recognized the scope for variety in how dancers might choose to interpret *The Dying Swan*, and sought to provide guidelines:

> Making the dance an imitation of the bird is a mistake which has been made by many performers. The more unrealistic and emotional the execution, the loftier and more beautiful will be the impression conveyed. The execution may be more lyric or more dramatic. I admit both interpretations and I leave to the performers to follow the course which their individuality dictates.
>
> 1925: 14

Still today, dancers interpret the piece according to their individual temperaments and training. Trinidad Vives, artistic associate for Boston Ballet, reflects on her coaching of three different ballerinas, for the role of *The Dying Swan*:

> They come from entirely different backgrounds. Karine [Seneca] was the most reserved. She's having this intimate moment with herself that pulls the audience in. Lorna [Feijóo] is more expressive. She has no fear about doing things her own way. Romi [Beppu] is the youngest and least experienced. She was more hesitant [...]. The three dancers responded differently to the music. It depended on when they wanted to take a deep breath or make a big arm gesture.
>
> Temin 2009: 65

Other factors influencing the outcome include the dancers' preparation: Beppu, we are told, chose to watch recordings of great ballerinas such as Maya Plisetskaya and Natalia Makarova dancing the role, focusing on the 'simple' and 'emotional' characteristics of the part and rejecting the more melodramatic interpretations. The dancers' performances can also be affected by factors for which there can be no rehearsal such as the atmosphere created in the theatre by the presence of the live audience. All of these elements can be considered as facets of the dance 'text': the notator's role is to distinguish the elements that determine the unique 'type' from the multiple 'tokens', or to couch the conundrum in more pragmatic terms, the notator is faced with the unenviable task of sorting the untouchable core from the movable feast that is the individual interpretation: 'Inevitably, there are steps that don't suit a particular dancer. There are some steps that should never be touched, but sometimes modifying things slightly isn't the end of the world' (Temin 2009: 77).

Just as in any other form of translation, therefore, the process of intersemiotic translation that underpins dance notation is susceptible to varying degrees of possible interpretation, in its initial transcription phase and in the subsequent transition back from notation to physical movement and ultimately performance. In this respect, therefore, 'the notated dance score shares important similarities with a music score or a play-text – offering a sense of the author's intentions but requiring reconstruction and interpretation. [...] dance, music and theatre all become manifest as artworks through performance' (Duerden 2007b: 128). The significant difference between dance notation on the one hand and theatre scripts and musical scores on the other, however, is that scripts and scores conventionally precede the performance whereas, in dance, a performance can precede the notation, rendering the relation between source text and target text a complex one. As mentioned above, typically the dance notator is not the person who choreographed the dance and, therefore, the concept of authorial intention is something that the notator needs to take into consideration. In 'reconstructing and interpreting' to pick up on Duerden's words, what are the elements that a notator needs to be aware of and to what extent is the outcome affected by different 'translation' strategies? To begin with, not all notation systems are the same, with each reflecting different aspects of movement. Benesh Movement Notation, for example, emphasizes the end position of movements whereas Labanotation tends to focus on the movement itself: 'This distinction is just one of the ways in which movement can be conceptualized differently and in which notation can vary in capturing this conceptualization' (Youngerman 1984: 102). Traditionally, companies tend to adopt one specific system, allowing for a homogenous archive of their repertoire.

Once a notation system has been chosen, 'decisions need to be made about *how* a movement is achieved, not simply what it looks like' (Duerden 2007b: 131). The same gesture can be recorded in a number of different ways, notating 'the general idea' of a movement, on the one hand and writing down every single detail of it, on the other – and any degree of detail between the two extremes. One example of such divergence is that of a dancer descending to the floor where, in the first instance, little indication is given of how this should be achieved. The notation reflects the following movements: 'the knees bend a lot, and the supports change from feet to hips and then the back – so you sink right down until you are sitting on the floor, then lie back' (Duerden 2007a: 13). In the second version of the notation, however, the instructions are far more precise in describing how the movement should be executed, adding a degree of constraint to the individual dancer's interpretation: alongside the previous symbols, the notator has also added notation for 'a step backwards, dropping the centre of weight, sliding the hands out along the floor as you roll down the spine to a lying position' (Duerden 2007a: 13). To describe the principle at the root of his notation system, Rudolph von Laban himself explained how, in deciding to draw a wheel, we can choose whether to represent its outward appearance or the inner workings: 'The representation of a wheel by a circle gives its outer form, as it is seen from the outside, so to speak. The representation of the wheel by the spokes shows us the inner tension forces which keep the wheel spokes apart. The wheel is seen from within here' (Youngerman 1984: 114).

Notation therefore does not seek to impose how a dance must be, but rather to provide a basic text on to which a dancer/re-stager can project their own version and creation of a particular role. Most notators would concur that the score actually gives the dancer freedom to create their own interpretation of the part, knowing that the underlying text is true to the choreographer's original vision. Once the dance has been notated, there is then the question of how it is 'translated' once again, back into movement. A number of factors can influence the restaging: the choreographer and/or notator may no longer be present, the stage on which the dance is to be performed may be larger or smaller than that used initially, the dance company and the soloists may no longer be the same. Joan and Rudolph Benesh acknowledge that there may have to be changes 'due to physique and temperament – the former permitting a higher arabesque or more arched back, and the latter small changes of accent and rhythm. Differences, such as the precise height of a leg, or whether an accent is up or down, can be shown in the notation' although they also add that when these changes depend on 'the personality of the performer or current fashion, they go beyond the scope or purpose of a notation' (Benesh and Benesh 1956: 44). At this point, they conclude that 'only a true interpretive artist can breathe back into the paper-frozen notes or steps the life and magic conceived by the creator' (ibid., 44).

Thus, again, as with literary translation, the hermeneutic process underlying the transfer from one code to another cannot be reduced to a mechanical process whereby content A automatically corresponds to content B. As we have seen, the notation represents only certain elements of the dance, those elements considered to be the essential characteristics or the core components of the piece, the defining features that distinguish it from other dances. The individual dancer or re-stager then has varying degrees of freedom to further characterize and customize the piece, as can be seen in a recently filmed practice session with three dance students taught by Mei-Chen Lu in Nanjing, China.[8] Each was given the same notated score and asked to perform the series of steps. The results, seen in the clip as the notation scrolls down the side of the screen, are strikingly different as the three individual dancers perform, while still adhering to the same 'script'. To the outsider, the lack of familiarity with notation and how it functions make this example all the more intriguing: 'the importance of the score or text is understood in relation to drama and music, but sometimes seems to be regarded with suspicion in dance, as if notating a dance inevitably restricts its dynamic existence and pins it down to a single interpretation' (Duerden 2007b: 128). The point is that notation, far from being prescriptive, is able to accommodate a variety of circumstances and interpretations. As well as literary translation, therefore, another useful analogy for understanding some of the characteristics of dance notation is the process undergone by (audio)visual material in the case of audio description: here a narration track is produced primarily for blind or sight-impaired consumers of video material, live performances or events such as guided tours of art galleries and sporting events. There is therefore a transfer from the visual mode – as with dance – to another code: verbal in the case of audio description and graphic in dance notation and, as in all cases of translation, the translator must choose which of the many elements, each with its own references and associations, to privilege for their new audience.

Reminiscent of issues raised in the much-debated question of (un)faithfulness in translation practice, dance notation claims to record an authentic, objective version of the work. Indeed, advocates speak of recording the original choreography 'correctly': 'notation allows objective documentation of dance in the same way that a musical score allows a composer to specify the intent of a musical composition' (Wilke et al. 2005: 201). It is precisely for reasons of authenticity that many practitioners favour notation over video recording. In the age of sophisticated digital equipment for filming performances and reliable storage solutions, dance notation may appear anachronistic to the uninitiated.

Indeed, some dance companies do now film their choreographies and rely on video recordings to access performances no longer in their repertoire, however, generally speaking, dance notation has not been superseded and is still employed by many companies. From a pragmatic point of view, notation can indicate information which cannot be captured by the visual recordings, such as grips and the position of hands and parts of the body hidden to the back of the stage or obscured by other dancers. The primary failure of film, however, is that it is a record of one specific performance and thus contains the idiosyncrasies of individual performers and, possibly, performers' errors. Proponents of notation explain that the use of a dance score allows performers to learn the choreography without being influenced by previous dancers' artistic interpretations of the work: 'studying a score does focus the attention on the detail as well as the larger picture, detail that is frequently lost or misinterpreted in watching video or film, but that can hold the key to full embodied understanding as the dancer works at achieving the subtleties as well as the overall shape and "flow"' (Duerden 2007b: 128).

Just as nobody would suggest studying or learning to play a new piece of music solely by listening to a recorded performance, whatever the standard of the recording, so dance notators believe that any ballet – or other form of movement – should be recorded using notation for accuracy and impartiality. As one notator, Anna Trevien, puts it: 'Would you ask an actor preparing Shakespeare's *Hamlet*, to learn the role, the words, the intention behind those words, from a DVD of Mel Gibson's version of *Hamlet*? Or would you hand a recording of Beethoven's *Ninth Symphony* to a musician, expecting them to learn their part in the orchestra by listening to it?'[9] Today, many of the major dance companies rely on both video and choreology to accurately stage the classical repertoire, on the one hand, and preserve the originality of new ballets, on the other. While it is important to emphasize that one of the greatest achievements of dance notation is precisely that it allows the retrieval of historical pieces and can give a clue to works no longer in a company's repertoire, it also, potentially, means dancers can arrive at first rehearsals with some familiarity with the choreography, or, in the case of national dance competitions, the pieces to be performed can be sent out to schools ahead of time, for the dancers to learn their parts – although, in practice, knowledge of dance notation is mostly limited to specialized dance notators and a small number of choreographers. In an attempt to promote familiarity with the various systems, courses in notation training – including online courses – are now widely available in a variety of languages[10] and, more recently, software programs for both recording and reading dance notation have been developed.[11]

To summarize, one of the defining characteristics of dance is its ephemeral nature, it exists through repetition rather than as one single 'authenticated' original as we have in literature or fine art (Pouillaude 2017: xi): there is still a degree of debate as to whether it is desirable to aspire to permanent stability for an artform whose very essence is transient movement. However, as Goodman stresses, the primary function of the written record is not as 'a practical aid to production'. It is rather 'the authoritative identification of a work from performance to performance' (1968: 127–8). On this basis, Parker and Macmillan conclude that 'given a necessity of choice, it is thus preferable to consult the notated record rather than the moving image' (Parker and Macmillan 1990: 93), whether this be in the tradition of the *répétiteur* or video. Parallels are perhaps most easily drawn between the relationship of dance to notation on the one hand and music and the music score on the other. One significant difference, however, is that in the vast majority of cases, it is the composer herself who produces the musical score, which is therefore the direct result of the creative process and can lay claim to containing the author's intention. In dance notation, however, this is hardly ever the case.

Dance notators can intervene centuries after the choreography was first created: they are specialized practitioners and tend to be the only figures who can either write or read the notated score. There is also the additional problem of to what extent the choreographer can be considered as the sole originator of the dance, with little or no acknowledgment of the dancers' contribution. In this sense, notation is closer to literary translation, where the translator is tasked with communicating a text they did not write themselves and whose author may no longer be available to consult over hermeneutic quandaries. Any translation practice requires an act of close reading of the source text and an understanding of how the specific medium communicates to its audience. Literary translators must first appreciate the stylistics of the author if they are to attempt to transfer the writing of Jane Austen or Haruki Murakami into another language and be able to deploy alliteration, irony, flamboyance and any number of other devices in their own writing. Music notation can be introduced 'as an aid to understanding pitch, time structure, time values, and manner of performance' (Hutchinson Guest and Curran 2008: xxxiv). All this is also applicable in the case of dance notation in connection to movement studies. As Hutchinson Guest and Curran point out:

> The act of dancing is a physical one, but behind it must be an intelligent awareness of what one is doing. Communication requires clarity based on a comprehensive understanding of the nature and facts of movement. The Language of dance, like all languages, has the purpose of communication, communication through a common terminology and vocabulary supported by the written form.
>
> Ibid.

There appears to be a general consensus among theorists and practitioners that dance notation should not be approached as a prescriptive straitjacket, subjugating the creative talent in choreographers and dancers alike. Youngerman clarifies that 'notation systems are more than tools for documentation; they are systems of analysis that can be used to illuminate many aspects of the phenomenon of movement. Notation scores embody perceptions of movement' (1984: 101). For Goodman, the fact that notation does not record each and every detail of a dance should not detract from its merits but rather be valued as a feature that allows the work to survive while being imbued with the style and creativity of each new performance:

> a [dance] score need not capture all the subtlety and complexity of a performance. [...] The function of a score is to specify the essential properties a performance must have to belong to the work; the stipulations are only of certain aspects and only within certain degrees. All other variations are permitted; and the differences among performances of the same work ... are enormous.
>
> Goodman 1968: 212

It seems appropriate to conclude, therefore, with a quotation about translation *tout court* and, more specifically about how any meaningful code – in our case the dance – can be translated (back) into another code – here, notation – with all the variations that such a transfer entails:

> A 'theory' of translation, a 'theory' of semantic transfer [...] is an intentionally sharpened, hermeneutically oriented way of designating a working mode of all meaningful exchanges, of the totality of semantic communication (including Jakobson's intersemiotic translation or 'transmutation'). [...] all procedures of expressive articulation and interpretative reception are translational, whether intra- or interlingually.
>
> Munday 2016: 269

Questions of meaning, equivalence, interpretation, variation and translatability have long preoccupied the academic field of translation studies. Widening the debate to include the transfer from movement to dance notation and back provides a challenging and, hopefully, stimulating addition to the ongoing debate.

Notes

1 *Swan Lake* premiered in Moscow in 1877.
2 For a detailed discussion of the history of notation systems, see Hutchinson Guest (1989).
3 Vladimir Stepanov, a dancer with the Mariinsky Theatre, had published his volume, *L'Alphabet des Mouvements du Corps Humain*, in Paris in 1892.
4 For more on copyright and dance, see Pavis and Wood (2020).
5 See Sweeney (1999), 513: Petipa, the choreographer, was French and therefore worked principally from the Perrault version. The identification of Sleeping Beauty with a rose, however, derives from the Grimms' version, *Rose Briar*.
6 From the homepage of the Dance Notation Bureau website: http://dancenotation.org/notating/frame0.html (accessed 4 July 2020).
7 For further discussion, see the issue of *Cadernos de Tradução*, 39, no. 1 (2019), dedicated to Retranslation.
8 See: https://www.youtube.com/watch?v=0arnlCyUQ8I (accessed 4 July 2020).
9 From: https://beneshinaction.wordpress.com/2018/03/23/preserving-the-dance-heritage-film-or-notation/ (accessed 4 July 2020).
10 For Benesh courses, see: https://www.royalacademyofdance.org/about-us/benesh-international-benesh-movement-notation/benesh-training-centre/; and for Labanotation courses, see: http://www.dancenotation.org/studying/frame0.html (both accessed 4 July 2020).
11 For Benesh Notation Editor, see: https://ca.royalacademyofdance.org/benesh-international-benesh-movement-notation/benesh-notation-editor/; and for Laban Writer, see: https://dance.osu.edu/research/dnb/laban-writer (both accessed 4 July 2020).

Bibliography

Abusch, Dorit (2015), 'Possible Worlds Semantics for Pictures', *A Handbook Article, College of Arts and Sciences, Cornell University Library*, Ithaca, NY. Available online: http://hdl.handle.net/1813/44654 (accessed 30 July 2020).

Acocella, Joan (1993), *Mark Morris*, New York: Farrar Straus Giroux.

Albright, Daniel (2014), *Panaethetics: On the Unity and Diversity of the Arts*, New Haven, CT: Yale University Press.

Anderson, Earl R. (1998), *A Grammar of Iconism*, Madison, NJ: Fairleigh Dickinson University Press.

Anon. (2001), 'Childlike Joy: Sonia Rodriguez Celebrates National Ballet's History by Searching Her Own Past', *Onstage*, 11, 13–19 September. Print. National Ballet of Canada Archives.

Anon. (2011), 'Re-imagined, *Romeo and Juliet* Opens the National Ballet of Canada's 60th Season', *Globe and Mail Arts Supplement*, 6 October, n.p. Print. National Ballet of Canada Archives.

Apollinaire, Guillaume (1917), 'Parade et l'esprit nouveau', *Souvenir Program, Mai 1917*, Library of Congress, 19–20. Available online: https://www.loc.gov/resource/ihas.200181871.0?st=gallery (accessed 11 April 2021).

Arndt, Walter (1964), 'Goading the Pony', *New York Review of Books*, 2 (6). Available online: https://www.nybooks.com/articles/1964/04/30/goading-the-pony/ (accessed 7 April 2020).

Bachman-Medick, Doris (2009), 'Introduction: The Translational Turn', *Translation Studies*, 2 (1): 2–16.

Bakst, Leon (1917), 'Chorégraphie et Décors des Nouveaux Ballets Russes', *Souvenir Program, Mai 1917*, Library of Congress, 25–6. Available online: https://www.loc.gov/resource/ihas.200181871.0?st=gallery (accessed 11 April 2021).

Ballets Russes à Paris, Les (1917), *Souvenir Program, Mai 1917*, Library of Congress. Available online: https://www.loc.gov/resource/ihas.200181871.0?st=gallery (accessed 11 April 2021).

Bannerman, Henrietta (2014), 'Is Dance a Language? Movement, Meaning and Communication', *Dance Research*, 32 (1,): 65–80.

Bannerman, Henrietta (2015), 'John Cranko's Antigone (1959): A Ballet Lost and Found', *Dance Research*, 33 (1): 1–15.

Barr, Alfred H. (1946/1980), *Picasso: Fifty Years of His Art*, New York: Museum of Modern Arts.

Barry, Peter (2022), 'Contemporary Poetry and Ekphrasis', *Cambridge Quarterly*, 31 (2): 155–65.

Bassnett, Susan (1993), *Comparative Literature: A Critical Introduction*, Oxford and Cambridge, MA: Blackwell.

Bassnett, Susan (2014), *Translation Studies*, 4th edn, London and New York: Routledge.

Batchelor, Kathryn (2018), *Translation and Paratexts*, Abingdon and New York: Routledge.

Béjart, Maurice (1961), *Boléro*, Théâtre de la Monnaie, Brussels. Available online: https://www.youtube.com/watch?v=bflVYdssyAc (accessed 20 June 2022).

Béjart, Maurice (1979), *Un instant dans la vie d'autrui*, Paris: Flammarion.

Béjart, Maurice (1983), 'Une vierge nietzchéenne', in *Grand Théâtre de Genève. Salomé*, Grand Théâtre de Genève, Fonds Maurice Béjart. SAPA. Copyright Maurice Béjart Foundation, pp. 31–35.

Béjart, Maurice (1988), *Béjart Ballet Lausanne*, Palais des Congrès. Fonds Maurice Béjart. SAPA. Copyright Maurice Béjart Foundation.

Béjart, Maurice (1990), 'Interview de Maurice Béjart à propos de "La Mort Subite", "Pyramide" etc', Interview by Jean Pierre Pastori. Fonds Maurice Béjart. SAPA.

Béjart, Maurice (1991). *La Mort subite*. Paris: Palais des Congrès.

Béjart, Maurice (1996). *La vie de qui? Mémoires 2*, Paris: Flammarion.

Béjart, Maurice (1998), 'Interview de Maurice Béjart à propos de son non-intérêt pour les mises en scènes lyriques', Interview by Jean Pierre Pastori, April. Fonds Maurice Béjart. SAPA.

Béjart, Maurice and Gaston Berger (1991), *La Mort subite: Journal intime*, Paris: Librairie Séguier.

Béjart, Maurice and Jean-Pierre Pastori (1992), *Cap Rudra*, Lausanne: Editions Plume.

Benesh, Rudolf and Joan (1956), *An Introduction to Benesh Movement-Notation: Dance*, London: Adam and Charles Black.

Benjamin, Walter (1923/1971), 'Die Aufgabe des Übersetzers', in Tillman Rexroth (ed.), *Gesammelte Schriften* IV:1, 9–21, Frankfurt a.M.: Suhrkamp.

Bennett, Karen (2003), 'Star-cross'd Lovers: Shakespeare and Prokofiev's "pas de deux" in *Romeo and Juliet*', *Cambridge Quarterly*, 32 (4): 311–47.

Benthien, Claudia and Gabriele Klein, eds (2017), *Übersetzen und Rahmen. Praktiken medialer Transformationen*, Paderborn: Wilhelm Fink.

Bentley, Toni (2002), *Sisters of Salome*, Lincoln, NE, and London: University of Nebraska Press.

Berman, Antoine, Isabelle Berman and Valentina Sommella (eds) (2018), *The Age of Translation: A Commentary on Walter Benjamin's 'The Task of the Translator'*, translated and with an introduction by Chantal Wright, Abingdon and New York: Routledge.

Bigliazzi, Silvia, Peter Koffler and Paola Ambrosi (2013), 'Introduction', in Silvia Bigliazzi, Peter Koffler and Paola Ambrosi (eds), *Theater Translation in Performance*, 1–26, New York and London: Routledge.

Blain, Martin and Helen Julia Minors (eds) (2020), *Artistic Research in Performance through Collaboration*, Basingstoke: Palgrave Macmillan.

Boase-Beier, Jean and Michael Holman (1999), 'Introduction: Writing, Rewriting and Translation. Through Constraints to Creativity', in Michael Holman and Jean Boase-Beier (eds), *The Practices of Literary Translation: Constraints and Creativity*, 1–17, Manchester: St. Jerome Publishing.

Bochet, Marc (2007), *Salomé: Du voilé au dévoilé: métamorphoses littéraires et artistiques d'une figure biblique*, Figures bibliques, Paris: Cerf.

Boria, Monica, Ángeles Carreres, María Noriega-Sánchez and Marcus Tomalin, eds (2020), *Translation and Multimodality: Beyond Words*, London: Routledge.

Buckle, Richard (1979), *Diaghilev*, London: Weidenfield and Nicolson.

Burnard, Pam, Valerie Ross, Laura Hassler and Lis Murphy (2018), 'Translating Intercultural Creativities in Community Music', in Brydie-Leigh Barleet and Lee Higgins (eds), *The Oxford Handbook of Community Music*, 229–42, Oxford: Oxford University Press.

Caddy, Davinia and Maribeth Clark (eds) (2020), *Musicology and Dance: Historical and Critical Perspectives*, Cambridge: Cambridge University Press.

Cage, John (1965), *Variations V*, New York: Henmar Press.

Cage, John, David Tudor and Gordon Mumma (musicians); Merce Cunningham Dance Company; Stan VanDerBeek and Nam June Paik (film/projections) (1966/2013), *Variations V*, film recording produced by the NDR Hamburg on DVD, New York: Mode Records.

Call, Josep and Michael Tomasello (2005), 'Reasoning and Thinking in Nonhuman Primates', in Keith Holyoak and Robert G. Morrison (eds), *The Cambridge Handbook of Thinking and Reasoning*, 607–32, Cambridge: Cambridge University Press.

Carreiro, Assis (n.d.), *Repertoire Notes*. The National Ballet of Canada. Print. National Ballet of Canada Archives.

Carroll, Noel and Margaret Moore (2008), 'Feeling Movement: Music and Dance', *Review Internationale de Philosophie*, 4 (246): 413–35.

Cattrysse, Patrick (2014), *Descriptive Adaptation Studies: Epistemological and Methodological Issues*, Antwerp and Apeldoor: Garant Publishers.

Causley, Maugarite (1967), *An Introduction to Benesh Movement Notation*, London: Max Parrish.

Chandler, Daniel (2007), *Semiotics: The Basics*, 2nd edn, London and New York: Routledge.

Charnavel, Isabelle (2016), 'Steps towards a Generative Theory of Dance Cognition', Manuscript, Harvard University, Cambridge, MA. Available online: http://ling.auf.net/lingbuzz/003137 (accessed 21 August 2019).

Chen, Zhe, Rebecca Polley Sanchez and Tammy Campbell (1997), 'From Beyond to Within Their Grasp: The Rudiments of Analogical Problem Solving in 10- and 13-Month-Olds', *Developmental Psychology*, 33 (5): 790–801.

Citron, Paula (2013), 'Ratmansky's *Romeo and Juliet*: Everyone will love his National Ballet production', *Globe and Mail*, 13 March, n.p.

Clark, Bob (2001), 'Perfect Wedding of Music and Story', *Calgary Herald*, 21 September, n.p. Print. National Ballet of Canada Archives.

Cocteau, Jean (1917a), 'La Collaboration de Parade', *Nord-Sub*, 4–5 (June–July), 29–31.
Cocteau, Jean (1917b), 'La Parade: Argument', *Souvenir Program, Mai 1917*. Library of Congress, 40. Available online: https://www.loc.gov/resource/ihas.200181871.0?st=gallery (accessed 11 April 2021).
Cocteau, Jean (1918), *Le Coq et l'arlequin*, Paris: Éditions de la Sirène.
Cocteau, Jean (1989), *Lettres à son mère, Vol. 1: 1898–1918*, ed. P. Caizergues, Paris: Gallimard.
Coessens, Kathleen, ed. (2019), *Sensorial Aesthetics in Music Practice*, Leuven: Leuven University Press.
Cohen, Selma Jeanne (1995), *Doris Humphrey: An Artist First*, Princeton, NJ: Princeton Book Company.
Cook, Nicholas (2013), 'Foreword', in Siu-Lan Tan, Annabel J. Cohen, Scott D. Lipscomb and Roger A. Kendall (eds), *The Psychology of Music in Multimedia*, v–vii, Oxford: Oxford University Press.
Cooper, Douglas (1967), *Picasso: Théâtre*, New York: Abrams.
Coppélia (2002), Premier March 7, Choreography by Mauro Bigonzetti, musical director Aivo Välja. Recording of the premier by the courtesy of the company.
Coppélia (2010), Premier March 13, Choreography by Ronald Hynd, musical director Mihhail Gerts. The Estonian National Ballet DVD.
Cox, Arnie (2016), *Music and Embodied Cognition: Listening, Moving, Feeling, and Thinking*, Bloomington and Indianapolis, IN: Indiana University Press.
Craine, Daniel (2001), 'A Trial of Broken hearts', *The Times*, 20 November, 19.
Cripps, Charlotte (2004), 'Sitting Out the Dance', *The Independent*, 4 November, 18.
Crompton, Sarah (2015), '*Romeo and Juliet*: How Ballet Gets to the Heart of Shakespeare', *The Guardian*, 17 October. Available online: http://www.theguardian.com/stage/2015/oct/17/romeo-and-juliet-ballet-shakespeare (accessed 20 June 2022).
Cronin, Michael (2020), *Across the Lines*, Cork: Cork University Press.
Cruttwell-Reade, Ninfea (2012), 'Intrusions and Inversions: Morton Feldman's For John Cage at Ether', 11 October. Available online: https://bachtrack.com/review-southbank-centre-ether-festival-feldman-for-john-cage-tilbury-morgan (accessed 10 May 2022).
d'Udine, Jean (1917), 'Couleurs, mouvements, et sons: Les Ballets Russes en 1917', *Le Courrier musical*, June, 239.
Damsholt, Inger (2006), 'Mark Morris, Mickey Mouse, and Choreomusical Polemic', *Opera Quarterly*, 22 (1): 4–21.
Dance Notation Bureau (DNB) (2020), New York, USA. Available online: http://www.dancenotation.org/ (accessed 16 February 2023).
Davies, James Q. (2003), 'Dancing the Symphonic: Beethoven-Bochsa's Symphonie Pastorale, 1829', *19th-Century Music*, 27 (1,): 25–47.
Davis, Mary E. (2006), *Classic Chic: Music, Fashion, and Modernism*, Berkeley, CA: University of California Press.

Davis, Mary E. (2007), *Erik Satie*, London: Reaktion Books.
Dayan, Peter (2011), *Art as Music, Music as Poetry, Poetry as Art: From Whistler to Stravinsky and Beyond*, Farnham: Ashgate.
De Keersmaeker, Anne Teresa and Bojana Cvejić (2012), *A Choreographer's Score: Fase, Rosas danst Rosas, Elena's Aria, Bartók*, Brussels: Fonds Mercator.
De Keersmaeker, Anne Teresa and Bojana Cvejić (2014), *Drumming & Rain. Carnets d'une chorégraphe*, Brussels: Fonds Mercator.
Deacon, Terrence W. (1997), *The Symbolic Species: The Co-Evolution of Language and the Brain*, New York: W. W. Norton & Company.
Deacon, Terrence W. (2003), 'Universal Grammar and Semiotic Constraints', Morten H. Christiansen and Simon Kirby (eds), in *Language Evolution*, 111–39, Oxford: Oxford University Press.
Deacon, Terrence W. (2006), 'The Aesthetic Faculty', in Mark Turned (ed.), *The Artful Mind: Cognitive Science and the Riddle of Human Creativity*, 21–53, New York: Oxford University Press.
Derrida, Jacques (1968), 'La Différance', *Bulletin de la Société française de philosophie*, 62 (3): 73.
Desblache, Lucile and Helen Julia Minors (2014), 'Translating Music'. Available online: http://www.translatingmusic.com (accessed 30 June 2022).
Dimova, Polina (2013), 'Decadent Senses: The Dissemination of Oscar Wilde's *Salome* across the Arts', in Clair Rowden (ed.), *Performing Salome, Revealing Stories*, 15–47, Farnham: Ashgate.
Dollfus, Ariane (2017), *Béjart: Le démiurge*, Paris: Arthaud.
Duerden, Rachel (2007a), 'Dancing in the Imagined Space of Music', *Dance Research*, 51 (1): 73–83.
Duerden, Rachel (2007b), 'Dancing Off the Page? Notation and Its challenges', in Rachel Duerden and Neil Fisher (eds), *Dancing Off the Page*, 128–37, Alton: Dance Books.
Duerden, Rachel (2010), 'The Mis-Shapen Pearl: Morris, Handel, Milton, and "L'Allegro, Il Penseroso Ed Il Moderato"', *Dance Research*, 28 (2): 200–17.
Engel, Johann Jakob (1998), 'On Painting in Music [1780]', in Wye Jamison Allanbrook, Oliver Strunk and Leo Treitler (trans. / eds), *Source Readings in Music History*, 954–65, New York: W. W. Norton & Company.
Eugene Onegin: A Novel in Verse / Alexander Pushkin (1999), translated, with a preface and notes, by Douglas Hofstadter, New York: Basic Books.
Fauconnier, Gilles (1994), *Mental Spaces: Aspects of Meaning Construction in Natural Language*, with a foreword by George Lakoff and Eve Sweetser, 2nd edn, Cambridge: Cambridge University Press.
Fauconnier, Gilles and Mark Turner (2002), *The Way We Think: Conceptual Blending and the Mind's Hidden Complexities*, New York: Basic Books.
Fitzpatrick, Jacob (2020), 'Stravinsky, Balanchine, and Agon: An Intersection of Musical Movement and Dance', PhD thesis, University of Wisconsin, Madison, WI.

Fokine, Mikael (1925), *"Dying Swan"*, *Music by C. Saint-Saens, Detailed Description of the Dance*, New York: Fischer.
Foster, Susan (1996), *Reading Dancing: Bodies and Subjects in Contemporary American Dance*, Berkeley and Los Angeles, CA, and London: University of California Press.
Foster, Susan (1986), *Choreography and Narrative: Ballet's Staging of Story and Desire*, Bloomington and Indianapolis, IN: Indiana University Press.
Foster, Susan Leigh (2008), *Reading Dancing: Bodies and Subjects in Contemporary American Dance*, Berkeley, CA: University of California Press.
French, Peter A., Howard K. Wettstein and Patrick Londen (2020), *Philosophy of Dance*, Boston, MA: Wiley Periodicals.
Frizot, Michel (2008), 'Notation als graphische Darstellung und ästhetischer Sprung', in Hubertus von Amelunxen, Dieter Appelt and Peter Weibel (eds.), in collaboration with Angela Lammert, *Notation. Kalkül und Form in den Künsten*, 55–66, Berlin and Karlsruhe: Akademie der Künste/ZKM Zentrum für Kunst und Medientechnologie.
Gaub, Albrecht (2013), 'Walter Kaufmann and the Winnipeg Ballet: A Fruitful Collaboration Soon Forgotten', *Société québécoise de recherche en musique*, 14 (2): 89–99.
Genette, Gérard (1987), *Seuils*, Paris: Editions du Seuil.
Genettte, G. (1997), *Paratext: Thresholds of Interpretation*, translated by Jane E. Lewin, with a foreword by Richard Macksey, Cambridge and New York: Cambridge University Press.
Gentner, Dedre (1983), 'Structure-Mapping: A Theoretical Framework for Analogy', *Cognitive Science*, 7 (2): 155–70.
Gentner, Dedre (2003), 'Why We're So Smart', in Dedre Gentner and Susan Goldin-Meadow (eds), *Language in Mind: Advances in the Study of Language and Thought*, 195–235, Cambridge, MA: MIT Press.
Gentner, Dedre and Kenneth J. Kurtz (2006), 'Relations, Objects, and the Composition of Analogies', *Cognitive Science*, 30 (4): 609–42.
Georges-Michel, Michel (1917), 'The Opening of "La Parade"'. Drawing, oil on cardboard, Achenbach Foundation, T&D1962.13, Fine Art Museums, San Francisco, CA. Available online: https://art.famsf.org/michel-georges-michel/opening-la-parade-td196213 (accessed 14 July 2021).
Gonçalves, Stéphanie (2019), 'Le Boléro comme "lieu de mémoire". Généalogie, temps et mémoire', *Recherches en danse*, 7: 1–20.
Goodman, Nelson (1968), *Languages of Art*, Indianapolis, IN: Bobbs-Merrill Company.
Goswami, Usha (2001), 'Analogical Reasoning in Children', in Dedre Gentner, Keith J. Holyoak and Boicho N. Kokinov (eds), *The Analogical Mind: Perspectives from Cognitive Science*, 437–70, Cambridge, MA: MIT Press.
Grigoriev, S. L. (1953/1960), *The Diaghilev Ballet 1909–1929*, translated by Vera Bowen, Harmondsworth: Penguin.
Gross, Valentine (1952), 'Le Socrate que j'ai connu', *La Revue Musicale*, 214: 139–44.

Guest, Ivor (1960), *The Dancer's Heritage: A Short History of Ballet*, London: A. & C. Black.

Guest, Ivor (1970), *Two Coppélias: A Centenary Study*, London: The Creative Press.

Guest, Ivor, ed. (1981), *Letters from a Ballet Master: The Correspondence of Arthur Saint-Leon*, London: Dance Books.

Gut, Serge (1990), 'Le Phénomène répétitif chez Maurice Ravel. De l'obsession à l'annihilation incantatoire', *International Review of the Aesthetics and Sociology of Music*, 21: 29–46.

Gutsche-Miller, Sarah (2015), *Parisian Music-Hall Ballet 1871–1913*, Rochester, NY: University of Rochester Press.

Haber, David (1975), *Letter to Dieter Grafe, c/o the Stuttgart Ballet*, 2 June. Print. National Ballet of Canada Archives.

Hall, Fernau (1967), 'Benesh Notation and Ethnochoreology', *Ethnomusicology*, 11 (2): 188–98.

Halliday, Michael (1978), *Language as Social Semiotic: The Social Interpretation of Language and Meaning*, London: Arnold.

Hanselmann, Ulla (2014), 'Die Stuttgarter Choreologin Georgette Tsinguirides. Die Hüterin des Tanzerbes', *Stuttgarter Zeitung*, 28 November. Available online: https://www.stuttgarter-zeitung.de/inhalt.die-stuttgarter-choreologin-georgette-tsinguirides-die-hueterin-des-tanzerbes.c5bcf2af-deb5-42c2-8b53-33b3ddaca041.html (accessed 30 April 2022).

Harding, James (1975), *Erik Satie*, London: Secker and Warburg.

Hebert, Carolyn (2016), 'Movement Memory: How We Learn, Retain and Remember Dance', *The Dance Current: Canada's Dance Magazine*, November/December.

Hebert, Carolyn (2016/2017), 'Movement Memory: How We Learn, Retain and Remember Dance', *The Dance Current: Canada's Dance Magazine*, November/December 2016, posted 17 February 2017. Available online: https://www.thedancecurrent.com/feature/movement-memory (accessed 19 May 2020).

Herman, Louis M. (2002), 'Exploring the Cognitive World of the Bottlenosed Dolphin', in Marc Bekoff, Colin Allen and Gordon M. Burghardt (eds), *The Cognitive Animal: Empirical and Theoretical Perspectives on Animal Cognition*, 275–83, Cambridge, MA: MIT Press.

Hilton, Wendy (1997), *Dance and Music of Court and Theater: Selected Writings of Wendy Hilton*, Dance & Music Series, no. 10, Stuyvesant, NY: Pendragon Press.

Hinton, Leanne, Johanna Nichols and John Ohala (1994), 'Introduction: Sound-Symbolic Processes', in Leanne Hinton, Johanna Nichols and John Ohala (eds), *Sound Symbolism*, 1–12, Cambridge: Cambridge University Press.

Hodgins, Paul (1992), *Relationships between Score and Choreography in Twentieth-Century Dance: Music, Movement and Metaphor*, Lewiston, ME: Edwin Mellen Press.

Hoffmann, Ernst Theodor (1999), 'The Sandman', in Robert Godwin-Jones (ed.), *19th-Century German Stories*, Virginia Commonwealth University, Richmond, VA. Available online: https://germanstories.vcu.edu/ (accessed 30 September 2019).

Hofstadter, Douglas R. and Emmanuel Sander (2013), *Surfaces and Essences: Analogy as the Fuel and Fire of Thinking*, New York: Basic Books.

Hollander, John (1988), 'The Poetics of Ekphrasis', *Word & Image*, 4 (1): 209–19. Available online: https://doi.org/10.1080/02666286.1988.10436238 (accessed 23 July 2020).

Holland, John H. (1998/2010), *Emergence: From Chaos to Order*, Oxford: Oxford University Press.

Holyoak, Keith J. (2005), 'Analogy', in Keith Holyoak and Robert G. Morrison (eds), *The Cambridge Handbook of Thinking and Reasoning*, 117–42, Cambridge: Cambridge University Press.

Holyoak, Keith J. and Paul Thagard (1995), *Mental Leaps: Analogy in Creative Thought*, Cambridge, MA: MIT Press.

Humphrey, Doris (1959), *The Art of Making Dances*, New York: Rhinehart.

Hutchinson Guest, Ann (1984), *Dance Notation: The Process of Recording Movement on Paper*, London: Dance Books.

Hutchinson Guest, Ann (1998), *Choreo-Graphics: A Comparison of Dance Notation Systems from the Fifteenth Century to the Present*, London: Gordon and Breach.

Hutchinson Guest, Ann and Tina Curran (2008), *Your Move*, London: Routledge.

Integrity Dance Center (2020), Website. Available online: http://www.integritydancecenter.com/the-importance-of-muscle-memory-and-ballet/ (accessed 14 June 2022).

Jäger, Ludwig (2004/2012), 'Die Verfahren der Medien: Transcribieren – Adressieren – Lokalisieren', in Jürgen Fohrmann and Erhard Schüttpelz (eds), *Die Kommunikation der Medien*, 69–79, Tübingen: De Gruyter.

Jäger, Ludwig (2010), 'Intermedialität – Intramedialität – Transkriptivität', in Arnulf Deppermann and Angelika Linke (eds), *Sprache intermedial. Stimme und Schrift, Bild und Ton*, 301–24, Berlin and New York: De Gruyter.

Jäger, Ludwig and Georg Stanitzek, eds (2002), *Transkribieren – Medien/Lektüren*, München: Wilhelm Fink.

Jakobson, Roman (1959), 'On Linguistic Aspects of Translation', in Reuben Arthur Brower (eds), *On Translation*, 232–9, Cambridge, MA: Harvard University Press.

Jakobson, Roman (1959/1966), 'On Linguistic Aspects of Translation', in Reuben Arthur Brower (ed.), *On Translation*, 232–9, Cambridge, MA: Harvard University Press.

Jakobson, Roman (2004), 'On Linguistic Aspects of Translation', in Lawrence Venuti (ed.), *The Translation Studies Reader*, 138–43, New York and London: Routledge.

Johnson, Edward (1973), *Bach Transcriptions* (sleeve notes), London: Decca Record Company.

Johnson, Robert (2012), '"Onegin," A Tale of Remorseful Love, Returns to American Ballet Theatre', *The Star Ledger*, 4 June. Available online: https://www.nj.com/entertainment/arts/2012/06/onegin_a_tale_of_remorseful_lo.html (accessed 12 June 2021).

Jones, Anna (2019), 'Akihito and Japan's Imperial Treasures that Make a Man an Emperor', BBC News, 27 April. Available online: https://www.bbc.co.uk/news/world-asia-47931671 (accessed 23 August 2019).

Jordan, Stephanie (1996), 'Musical/Choreographic Discourse: Method, Music Theory and Meaning', in Gay Morris (ed.), *Moving Words*, London and New York: Routledge.

Jordan, Stephanie (2000), *Moving Music: Dialogues with Music in Twentieth-Century Ballet*, London: Dance Books Ltd.

Jordan, Stephanie (2012), 'Mark Morris Marks Music, or: What Did He Make of Bach's Italian Concerto?', in Stephanie Schroedter (ed.), *Bewegungen zwischen Hören und Sehen: Denkbewegungen über Bewegungskünste*, 219–36, Würzburg: Königshausen & Neumann.

Jordan, Stephanie (2015), *Mark Morris: Musician—Choreographer*, Binsted: Dance Books, Ltd.

Jordan, Stephanie (2018), 'Acts of Transformation: Strategies for Choreographic Intervention in Mark Morris's Settings of Existing Music', in Patrizia Veroli and Gianfranco Vinay (eds), *Music-Dance: Sound and Motion in Contemporary Discourse*, 76–90, London and New York: Routledge.

Jordan, Stephanie and Richard Cohn, eds (2021) 'Music and Dance: Special Issue on Choreomusical Analysis', *Journal of Music Theory*, 65 (1).

Kando, Juliette (2020), 'What is Choreology', *Owlcation*. Available online: https://owlcation.com/humanities/what-is-choreology (accessed 14 June 2022, last accessed 13 December 2022).

Katseva, Marina (2007), 'Даль свободного романа (О балетмейстере Джоне Кранко)' ['The Wildness of Casual Novel (On the Choreographer John Cranko)'], *Слово Word*, 54. Available online: https://magazines.gorky.media/slovo/2007/54/dal-svobodnogo-romana.html (accessed 21 August 2019).

Kelly, Deirdre (1995), 'Margaret Illmann Star of Dusty Classic', *Globe and Mail*, 10 February, n.p. Print. National Ballet of Canada Archives.

Khokhlova, Daria (2017), *Балет «Онегин» Джона Кранко: русская поэзия в западноевропейской хореографии* [*Ballet "Onegin" by John Cranko: Russian Poetry in the Choreography of Western Europe*], Moscow: Inturreklama –Teatralis.

Kisselgoff, Anna (1973), 'John Cranko Dies at 45: Stuttgart Ballet Director', *New York Times*, 42, 27 June. Available online: https://www.nytimes.com/1973/06/27/archives/john-cranko-dies-at-45-stuttgart-ballet-director-hurok-pays-tribute.html (accessed 12 June 2021).

Kisselgoff, Anna (1984), 'Dance: Joffrey in Cranko's "Romeo and Juliet"', *New York Times*, C00018, 14 December. Available online: https://www.nytimes.com/1984/12/14/arts/dance-joffrey-in-cranko-s-romeo-and-juliet.html (accessed 12 June 2021).

Klein, Gabriele (2019, English trans. 2020), *Pina Bausch und das Tanztheater. Die Kunst des Übersetzens*; resp. *Pina Bausch's Dance Theater. Company, Artistic Practices and Reception*, Bielefeld: Transcript.

Krebs, Katja (2012), 'Translation and Adaptation – Two Sides of an Ideological Coin', in Laurence Raw (ed.), *Translation, Adaptation and Transformation*, 42–53, London: Bloomsbury Academic.

Kress, Gunther (2000), 'Text as the Punctuation of Semiosis: Pulling at the Same Threads', in U. Meinhof and J. Smith (eds), *Intertextuality and the Media: from Genre to Everyday Life*, 132–54, Manchester: Manchester University Press.

Kress, Gunther (2010), *Multimodality: A Social Semiotic Approach to Contemporary Communication*, London and New York: Routledge.

Kundera, Milan (1988), *The Art of the Novel*, translated from the French by Linda Asher, New York: Grove Press.

Landgraf, Ilona (2015), 'Keeping Cranko's Heritage Vivid', *Landgraf on Dance*, December. Available online: https://www.ilona-landgraf.com/2015/12/keeping-crankos-heritage-vivid-2/ (accessed 12 June 2021).

Larson, Steve (2012), *Motion, Metaphor, and Meaning in Music*, Bloomington and Indianapolis, IN: Indiana University Press.

Launay, Isabelle (2017), *Poétiques et politiques des répertoires. Les danses d'après I. Recherches*, Pantin: Centre national de la danse.

Leaman, Kara Yoo (2016), 'Analyzing Music and Dance: Balanchine's Choreography to Tchaikovsky and the Choreomusical Score', PhD thesis, Yale University, New Haven, CT. Available online: https://www.proquest.com/docview/1923454136?pq-origsite=gscholar&fromopenview=true (accessed 25 November 2022).

Lefevere, André (1992), *Translation, Rewriting, and the Manipulation of Literary Fame*, Translation Studies, London and New York: Routledge.

Lobsanova, Elena (2012), 'Interview with Elena Lobsanova about Her Role as Juliet in 2012 60th Anniversary Production'. Print. National Ballet of Canada Archives.

Loffredo, Eugenia and Manuela Perteghella (eds) (2006), *Translation and Creativity: Perspectives on Creative Writing and Translation Studies*, London and New York: Continuum.

Louppe, Laurence (2004), *Poétique de la danse contemporaine*, Librairie de la danse, 3rd edn, Brussels: Contredanse.

Louvel, Liliane (2002), *Texte/image: Images à lire, textes à voir. Interférences*, Rennes: Presses Universitaire de Rennes.

Mackrell, Judith R. (2020), 'Choreography: The Three-Phase Choreographic Process', *Encyclopedia Britannica*, Available online: https://www.britannica.com/art/dance/The-three-phase-choreographic-process (accessed 16 May 2020)

Macksey, R. (1997), 'Foreword', in J. E. Lewin (trans.), Gérard Genette, *Paratexts: Thresholds of Interpretation*, xi–xxii, Cambridge and New York: Cambridge University Press.

Main, Lesley (2012), *Directing the Dance Tradition of Doris Humphrey: The Creative Impulse of Reconstruction*, Madison, WI: University of Wisconsin Press.

Main, Lesley (2017), 'The Transmission–Translation–Transformation of Doris Humphrey's *Two Ecstatic Themes* (1913)', in Lesley Main (ed.), *Transmissions in Dance*, 85–108, Basingstoke: Palgrave Macmillan

Main, Lesley, ed. (2017), *Transmissions in Dance*, Basingstoke: Palgrave Macmillan.

Main, Lesley, ed. (2018), *Transmissions in Dance*, Basingstoke: Palgrave Macmillan.

Mannoni, Gérard and Maurice Béjart (1985), *Maurice Béjart: L'Avant-scène ballet / danse 16*, Paris: L'Avant-Scène.
Margolis, Joseph (1984), 'The Autographic Nature of the Dance', in Maxine Sheets-Johnstone (ed.), *Illuminating Dance: Philosophical Explorations*, 70–84, London: Associated University Presses.
Martín de León, Celia and Gisela Marcelo Wirnitzer, eds (2021), *Tibon: Estudios Traductologicos 3: En más de un sentido: Multimodalidad u construcción de significados en traducción e interpretación*, Les Palmas de Gran Canaria: ULPGC ediciones.
Massine, Léonide (1968), *My Life in Ballet*, London: Macmillan.
Mawer, Deborah (2000), 'Ballet and the Apotheosis of the Dance', in Deborah Mawer (ed.), *The Cambridge Companion to Ravel*, 140–61, Cambridge: Cambridge University Press.
Mawer, Deborah (2006), *The Ballets of Maurice Ravel: Creation and Interpretation*, Aldershot: Ashgate.
Mawer, Deborah (2012), 'Music-Dance (and Design) Relations in Ballet Productions of Ravel's *Daphnis et Chloé*', *Société québécoise de recherche en musique*, 13 (1–2): 77–85.
McFee, Graham (1994), 'Was that *Swan Lake* I Saw You at Last Night? Dance-Identity and Understanding', *Dance Research: The Journal of the Society for Dance Research*, 12 (1): 20–40.
McFee, Graham (2013), 'Dance', in Berys Gaut and Dominic McIver Lopes (eds), *The Routledge Companion to Aesthetics*, 649–59, London: Routledge.
Miller, Leta E. (2001), 'Cage, Cunningham, and Collaborators: The Odyssey of *Variations V*', *Musical Quarterly*, 85 (3): 545–67.
Milton, John (2012), *The Shorter Poems*, in Barbara Kiefer Lewalski and Estelle Haan (eds), *The Complete Works of John Milton, Volume 3*, Oxford: Oxford University Press.
Minors, Helen Julia (2013a), 'Exploring Interart Dialogue in Erik Satie's *Sports et divertissements* (1914/1922)', in Caroline Potter (ed.), *Erik Satie: Music, Art and Literature*, 115–35, Farnham: Ashgate.
Minors, Julia Helen (2013b), 'Introduction: Translation in music Discourse', in Julia Helen Minors (ed.), *Music, Text and Translation*, 1–6, London: Bloomsbury.
Minors, Helen Julia (2013c), 'Music Translating visual Arts: Erik Satie's *Sports et Divertissements*', in Helen Julia Minors (ed.), *Music, Text and Translation*, 107–20, London: Bloomsbury.
Minors, Helen Julia (2016), 'Mediating Cultures and Musics: An Intercultural Production of *A Midsummer Night's Dream*', in Pamela Burnard, Elizabeth MacKinley and Kimberley Powell (eds), *Routledge Handbook of Intercultural Arts Theory, Research and Practice*, 417–30, London: Routledge.
Minors, Helen Julia (2019), 'Translations between Music and Dance: Analysing the Choreomusical Gestural Interplay in Twentieth- and Twenty-First-Century Dance Works', in Monica Boria, Ángeles Carreres, María Noriega-Sánchez and Marcus

Tomalin (eds), *Translation and Multimodality: Beyond Words*, 158–78, London: Routledge.

Minors, Helen Julia (2020a), 'Opera and Intercultural Musicology as a Mode Translation', in Adriana Serban and Kelly Chan John Benjamins (eds), *Opera in Translation: Diversity and Unity*, 13–33, Amsterdam: John Benjamins Publishing Co.

Minors, Helen Julia (2020b), 'Soundpainting: A Tool for Collaborating during Performance', in Martin Blain and Helen Julia Minors (eds), *Artistic Research in Performance through Collaboration*, 113–38, Basingstoke: Palgrave.

Minors, Helen Julia (2021), 'Music and Multimodal Translation', in Celia Martín de León and Gisela Marcelo Wirnitzer (eds), *Tibon: Estudios Traductologicos 3: En más de un sentido: Multimodalidad u construcción de significados en traducción e interpretación*, 171–90, Les Palmas de Gran Canaria: ULPGC ediciones.

Minors, Helen Julia (2022), 'Music Speaks: The Role of Emotional Expression in Music for Sci-fi Fantasy Films', in Susan Petrilli and Meng Ji (eds), *Intersemiotic Perspectives on Emotions: Translating across Signs, Bodies and Values*, 332–48, London and New York: Routledge.

Minors, Helen Julia (2023), 'Music Speaks: The Role of Emotional Expression in Music for Sci-Fantasy Films', in Susan Petrilli and Meng Li (eds), *The Intersemiotic Perspectives on Emotions Translating across Signs, Bodies and Values*, 332–48, London and New York: Routledge.

Minors, Helen Julia, ed. (2013), *Music, Text and Translation*, London: Bloomsbury.

Montandon, Alain (2017), '"Danse, Salomé, danse!"', in Maria Benedetta Collini and Pascale Auraix-Jonchière (eds), *Voix poétiques et mythes féminins*, Collection Mythographies et sociétés, 187–207, Clermont-Ferrand: Presses universitaires Blaise Pascal.

Multimodal Analysis Company (2020), *Multimodal Analysis for Critical Thinking*. Available online: http://multimodal-analysis.com/index.html (accessed 25 July 2020).

Munday, Jeremy (2016), *Introducing Translation Studies: Introducing Translation Studies*, 5th edn. Milton Park and New York: Routledge.

Munsterberg, Marjorie (2009), *Writing about Art*. Available online: https://writingaboutart.org/index.html (accessed 14 July 2020).

Myers, Rollo H. (1968), *Erik Satie*, New York: Dover Publications.

Nabokov, Vladimir (1964), 'On Translating Pushkin: Pounding the Clavichord', *New York Review of Books*, 2 (6). Available online: https://www.nybooks.com/articles/1964/04/30/on-translating-pushkin-pounding-the-clavichord/ (accessed 23 August 2019).

National Ballet of Canada (2020), 'The Richness of Live Music', *Soaring*. Available online: https://national.ballet.ca/Donate/Soaring/Orchestra (accessed 12 June 2021).

Naughtin, Matthew (2014), *Ballet Music: A Handbook*, Lanham, MD: Rowman & Littlefield Publishers.

Neufeld, James E. (1982–3), 'Two Romeo and Juliets: The National Ballet and the RWB', *Revue d'études canadiennes*, 17 (4): 120–4.

O'Halloran, Kay L., Sabine Tan and Peter Wignell (2016), 'Intersemiotic Translation as Resemiotisation: A Multimodal Perspective', *Signata*, 7: 199–219.

O'Halloran, Kay L., Sabine Tan and Peter Wignell (2019), 'SFL and Multimodal Discourse Analysis', in Geoff Thompson, Wendy L. Bowcher and Lise Fontaine (eds), *The Cambridge Handbook of Systemic Functional Linguistics Cambridge*, 433–61, Cambridge: Cambridge University Press.

Orledge, Robert (1990), *Satie the Composer*, Cambridge: Cambridge University Press.

Orledge, Robert (1995), *Satie Remembered*, with translations from the French by Roger Nichols, Portland, OR: Amadeus Press.

Parker, Monica and Kenneth Macmillan (1990), 'Benesh: The Notation of Dance', in Horice Barlow, Colin Blakemore and Miranda Weston-Smith (eds), *Images and Understanding*, pp. 81–93, Cambridge: Cambridge University Press.

Pârlog, Aba-Carina (2019), *Intersemiotic Translation: Literary and Linguistic Multimodality*, Cham: Palgrave Pivot.

Pastori, Jean Pierre (2017), *Maurice Béjart: L'Univers d'un chorégraphe*, Lausanne: Presses Polytechniques et Universitaires Romandes.

Patel-Grosz, Pritty, Patrick Georg Grosz, Tejaswinee Kelkar and Alexander Refsum Jensenius (2018), 'Coreference and Disjoint Reference in the Semantics of Narrative Dance', in Uli Sauerland and Stephanie Solt (eds), *Proceedings of Sinn und Bedeutung*, 22 (2), *ZASPiL 61*, 199–216. Available online: https://semanticsarchive.net/Archive/GE4MWViN/Patel-Grosz.pdf (accessed 21 August 2019).

Pavis, Mathilde and Karen Wood (2020), 'Creative Industries and Copyright: Research into Collaborative Artistic Practices in Dance', in Martin Blain and Helen Julia Minors (eds), *Artistic Research in Performance through Collaboration*, 165–84, Basingstoke: Palgrave Macmillan.

Pawyza, Fanny (1996), 'Béjart, le désir et la mort', in Mireille Dottin-Orsini (ed.), *Salomé, Figures mythiques*, 151–65, Paris: Autrement.

Peirce, Charles Sanders (1955), *Philosophical Writings of Peirce*, edited by Justus Buchler, New York: Dover.

Perazzo Domm, Daniela (2008), 'Jonathan Burrows and Matteo Fargion's "Both Sitting Duet" (2002): A Discursive Choreomusical Collaboration', in Janet Lansdale (ed.), *Decentring Dancing Texts*, 125–42, New York: Palgrave Macmillan.

Percival, John (1983), *Theatre in My Blood. A Biography of John Cranko*, London: The Herbert Press.

Perteghella, Manuela (2013), 'Translation as Creative Writing', in Graeme Harper (ed.), *A Companion to Creative Writing*, 195–212, Chichester: John Wiley & Sons.

Petrilli, Susan and Meng Ji, eds (2022), *Intersemiotic Perspectives on Emotions: Translating across Signs, Bodies and Values*, London and New York: Routledge.

Pharo, Carol A. (1997), 'Musical Form and Dance Form: The Role of Cadential Formulae in Early 18th-Century Choreographies', in Linda J. Tomko (compli.),

Reflecting Our Past, Reflecting on Our Future: Proceedings, Society of Dance History Scholars, 305–10, Riverside, CA: Society of Dance History Scholars.

Pierce, Ken (1998), 'Dance Notation Systems in Late 17th-Century France', *Early Music*, 26 (2): 286–99.

Potter, Caroline (2016), *Erik Satie: A Parisian Composer*, Woodbridge: Boydell Press.

Potter, Caroline, ed. (2013), *Erik Satie: Music, Art, and Literature*, Farnham: Ashgate.

Pouillaude, Frédéric (2017), *Unworking Choreography: The Notion of the Work in Dance*, translated by Anna Pakes, Oxford: Oxford University Press.

Prokofiev, Sergei (1976), *Op. 64 Romeo and Juliet*. Ballet in four acts. Nine-scene libretto by S. Radlov, A. Piotrevsky, L. Lavrovsky and S. Prokofiev. Piano Reduction by L. Atovmyan. State Publishers Music Moscow, 1976. Distributed by G. Schirmer, publisher copyright, 1976. Annotated by Peter Ottmann, 2011. Print. National Ballet of Canada Archives.

Pushkin, Alexander (1963), *Eugene Onegin: A Novel in Verse*, The Bollingen Prize translation in the Onegin Stanza by Walter Arndt, New York: Dutton.

Pushkin, Alexandr (1964), *Eugene Onegin: A Novel in Verse*, translated from the Russian, with a commentary, by Vladimir Nabokov, London: Routledge & Kegan Paul.

Pushkin, Alexander (1999), *Eugene Onegin: A Novel in Verse*, translated, with a preface and notes, by Douglas Hofstadter, New York: Basic Books.

Quiblier, Marie (2014), 'Ce que la reprise fait à l'œuvre chorégraphique / Subversion et invention', *Marges*, 18: 140–52.

Rajewsky, Irina O. (2002), *Intermedialität*, Tübingen and Basel: Francke/UTB.

Reardon, John (2007), 'Ballet and the Bard', *Performance*. Print. National Ballet of Canada Archives.

Regnault, François (1991), 'La mort subite', 1990. Fonds Eiji Berger. SAPA. Copyright François Regnault and Maurice Béjart Foundation.

Regnault, François and Maurice Béjart (1991), 'La Mort subite'. Fondation Maurice Béjart. Fonds Maurice Béjart. SAPA. Copyright Maurice Béjart Foundation and François Regnault.

Reynolds, Christine (2013), 'Parade: Ballet réaliste', in Caroline Potter (ed.), *Erik Satie: Music, Art and Literature*, 137–60, Farnham: Ashgate.

Richardson, John (2007), *A Life of Picasso: Volume III, The Triumphant Yyears 1917–1932*, London: Jonathan Cape.

Rothschild, Deborah Menaker (1991), *Picasso's Parade*, London: Sotheby's Publications.

Royal Academy of Dance (2019), *Benesh International: Benesh Movement Notation*. Available online: https://www.royalacademyofdance.org/about-us/benesh-international-benesh-movement-notation/ (accessed 10 June 2022).

Rubidge, Sarah (2000), 'Identity and the Open Work', in Stephanie Jordan (ed.), *Preservation Politics: Dance Revived, Reconstructed, Remade*, 205–15, London: Dance Books.

Ryan, Marie-Laure (2012), 'Narration in Various Media', *The Living Handbook of Narratology*, Hamburg: University of Hamburg. Available online: http://www.lhn.uni-hamburg.de/article/narration-various-media (accessed 12 January 2022).

Ryman, Robyn Hughes (2019), *DanceWrite. Resources for Benesh Movement Notation*. Available online: dancewrite.com/wp/ (accessed 10 June 2022).
Sagan, Françoise (1965), *La Chamade*, Paris: Julliard.
Sagan, Françoise (1966), *La Chamade*, translated by Robert Westoff, London: John Murray.
Sagan, Françoise (2009), *That Mad Ache*, translated by Douglas Hofstadter, New York: Basic Books.
Sanders, Julie (2016), *Adaptation and Appropriation*, London: Routledge.
Satie, Erik (1917), *La Parade*, Paris: Rouart, Lerolle & Cie.
Satie, Erik (1924), 'Interview with Pierre de Massot, *Paris-Journal*, 30 May, 2.
Saussure, Ferdinand de (1983), *Course in General Linguistics*, R. Harris (trans. / annotator), C. Bally and A. Sechehaye (eds), collaboration of A. Riedlinger, London: Duckworth.
Schlenker, Philippe (2017), 'Outline of Music Semantics', *Music Perception*, 35: 3–37.
Schroedter, Stephanie (2018), *Paris qui danse. Bewegungs- und Klangräume einer Großstadt der Moderne*, Würzburg: Königshausen & Neumann.
Schroedter, Stephanie (2021), 'Musik als Bewegung. Transformationen musikalischer Energetik im Tanz', in Katrin Eggers and Arne Stollberg (eds), *Energie! Kräftespiele in den Künsten*, Klangfiguren, vol. 2, 369–81, Würzburg: Königshausen & Neumann.
Schroedter, Stephanie, ed. (2012), *Bewegungen zwischen Hören und Sehen. Denkbewegungen über Bewegungskünste*, Würzburg: Königshausen & Neumann.
Serban, Adriana and Kelly Chan, eds (2020), *Opera in Translation: Diversity and Unity*, Amsterdam: John Benjamins Publishing Co.
Short, Rachel (2016), 'Musical Feet: The Interaction of Choreography and Music in Leonard Bernstein and Jerome Robbins's Ballet Fancy Free', PhD thesis, University of California, Santa Barbara, CA.
Smith, Marian E. (2000), *Ballet and Opera in the Age of Giselle*, Princeton, NJ, and Oxford: Princeton University Press.
Smith, Marian E. (2011), 'The Orchestra as Translator: French Nineteenth-Century Ballet', in Marion Kent (ed.), *The Cambridge Companion to Ballet*, 138–50, Cambridge: Cambridge University Press.
Snodgrass, Mary Ellen (2015), *Encyclopedia of World Ballet*, 102–5, New York: Rowman and Littlefield Publishers.
Solway, Diane (2007), 'How the Body (and Mind) Learns a Dance', *New York Times*, 28 May 2007; *International Herald Tribune*, 28 May 2007. Available online: https://www.nytimes.com/2007/05/28/arts/28iht-dance.html (accessed 1 June 2022).
Spies, Werner (2008), *The Continent Named Picasso: The Eye and the Word: Collected Writings on Art and Literature*, New York: Abrams.
Sprigge, Elizabeth and Jean-Jacques Kihm (1968), *Jean Cocteau: The Man and the Mirror*, New York: Coward-McCann Inc.
Steegmuller, Francis (1970), *Cocteau: A Biography*, Basingstoke: Macmillan.

Stenning Edgecombe, Rodney (2006), 'Trans-formal Translation: Plays into Ballets, with Special Reference to Kenneth MacMillan's *Romeo and Juliet*', *Yearbook of English Studies*, 36 (1): 65–78.

Sulcas, Roslyn (2006), 'Dance Conducting: Good for the Nerves, if Not the Career', *New York Times*, 25 June 2006. Available online: https://www.nytimes.com/2006/06/25/arts/dance/25sulc.html (accessed 1 June 2022).

Sweeney, Susan Elizabeth (1999), 'Fantasy, Folklore, and Finite Numbers in Nabokov's "A Nursery Tale"', *Slavic and East European Journal*, 43 (3): 511–29.

Tarantini, Angela Tiziana (2021), *Theatre Translation: A Practice Research Model*, Basingstoke, Palgrave.

Temin, Christine (2009), *Behind the Scenes at Boston Ballet*, Gainesville, FL: University Press of Florida.

Tomasello, Michael (2006), 'Why Don't Apes Point?', in N. J. Enfield and Stephen C. Levinson (eds), *Roots of Human Sociality: Culture, Cognition and Interaction*, 506–24, New York: Berg.

Tomasello, Michael (2008), *Origins of Human Communication*, The Jean Nicod Lectures, Cambridge, MA: MIT Press.

Torop, Peeter (2011), *Tõlge ja kultuur* [Estonian: *Translation and Culture*], Tallinn-Tartu: Tartu Ülikooli kirjastus.

Trevien, Anna (2015), 'Jane Bourne, FI Chor. Benesh in Action', *How Dance Movement Notation is Applied in the Professional World of Ballet*, 16 February. Available online: https://Beneshinaction.com/2015/02/16/jane-bourne-fi-chor/ (accessed 1 June 2022).

Tsinguirides, Georgette (2014), 'Interviews with Henrietta Bannerman', Stuttgart: Stuttgart Opera House, 24–25 April.

Upkin, Triinu (2015), *Rahvuste kujutamine klassikalistes narratiivsetes ballettides. Magistritöö* [Estonian: *Depicting nations in classical narrative ballets. Master Thesis*], Tallinn: Tallinna Ülikool.

van Zile, Judy (1985), 'What is the Dance? Implications for Dance Notation', *Dance Research Journal*, 17 (2): 41–7.

Vanderlinde, Sharon (1998a), *Ballet Notes. Romeo and Juliet*. 1998. Print. National Ballet of Canada Archives.

Vanderlinde, Sharon (1998b), 'Historical Note on the Ballet'. *Ballet Notes. Romeo and Juliet*. Print. National Ballet of Canada Archives.

Venuti, Lawrence (1998), *The Scandals of Translation*, London and New York: Routledge.

Venuti, Lawrence (2008), *The Translator's Invisibility: A History of Translation*, London and New York: Routledge.

Verdun, Bob (1995), 'Superb Music and Dancing: Marvelous New Design Ensures there is Never a Dull Moment in Ballet of *Romeo and Juliet*', *Elora Sentinel*, 13 February, n.p. Print. National Ballet of Canada Archives.

Volta, Ornella, ed. (1989), *Satie: Seen through His Letters*, translated by Michael Bullock, London and New York: Marion Boyars.

Watt, Bill (1995), 'On Your Toes', *Scarborough News*, 15 February, n.p. Print. National Ballet of Canada Archives.

Weber, Gottfried (1825), 'Über Tonmalerei', *Cäcilia*, 3 (10): 125–72.

White, Barbara (2006), '"As if They Didn't Hear the Music," Or: How I Learned to Stop Worrying and Love Mickey Mouse', *Opera Quarterly*, special issue, Simon Morrison and Stephanie Jordan (eds), *Sound Moves*, 22 (1): 65–89.

Wilde, Oscar (2003), *De Profundis*, in *Collins Complete Works of Oscar Wilde*, 5th edn. (with corrections), 980–1059, Glasgow: HarperCollins.

Wilde, Oscar (2006), *Salomé*, edited by Pascal Aquien, Paris: Flammarion.

Wiley, Roland (1985), *Tchaikovsky Ballets: Swan Lake, Sleeping Beauty, Nutcracker*, New York: Oxford University Press.

Wilke, Lars, Tom Calvert, Rhonda Ryman and Ilene Fox (2003), 'Animating the Dance Archives', *VAST03: The 4th International Symposium on Virtual Reality, Archaeology and Intelligent Cultural* Heritage, in David Arnold, Chalmers and Franco Niccolucci (eds), *The Eurographics Association*, doi: 10.2312/VAST/VAST03/093-100.

Wilke Lars, Tom Calvert, Rhonda Ryman and Ilene Fox (2005), 'From Dance Notation to Human Animation: The LabanDancer Project', *Computer Animation and Virtual Worlds*, 16: 201–11.

Wilson, Edmund (1965), 'The Strange Case of Pushkin and Nabokov', *New York Review of Books*, 4 (12). Available online: https://www.nybooks.com/articles/1965/07/15/the-strange-case-of-pushkin-and-nabokov (accessed 2 August 2019).

Youngerman, Susanne (1984), 'Movement Notation Systems as Conceptual Frameworks: The Laban System', in Maxine Sheets-Johstone (ed.), *Illuminating Dance: Philosophical Explorations*, 101–23, London: Associated University Presses.

Zbikowski, Lawrence M. (2002), *Conceptualizing Music: Cognitive Structure, Theory, and Analysis*, Oxford and New York: Oxford University Press.

Zbikowski, Lawrence M. (2008), 'Dance Topoi, Sonic Analogues, and Musical Grammar: Communicating with Music in the Eighteenth Century', in Danuta Mirka and Kofi Agawu (eds), *Communication in Eighteenth Century Music*, 283–309, New York: Cambridge University Press.

Zbikowski, Lawrence M. (2012), 'Music, Dance, and Meaning in the Early Nineteenth Century', *Journal of Musicological Research*, 31 (2–3): 147–65.

Zbikowski, Lawrence M. (2014), 'Dance Topics I: Music and Dance in the *Ancien Régime*', in Danuta Mirka, *The Oxford Handbook of Topic Theory*, 143–63, New York: Oxford University Press.

Zbikowski, Lawrence M. (2017), *Foundations of Musical Grammar*, Oxford Studies in Music Theory, New York: Oxford University Press.

Zbikowski, Lawrence M. (2018a), 'Conceptual Blending, Creativity, and Music', *Musicæ Scientiæ*, 22 (1): 6–23.

Zbikowski, Lawrence M. (2018b), 'Ways of Knowing: Social Dance, Music, and Grounded Cognition', in Patrizia Veroli and Gianfranco Vinay (eds), *Music-Dance: Sound and Motion in Contemporary Discourse*, 57–75, New York: Routledge.

Index

Après-midi d'un faune, L' 165
Academie royale de danse 152
Adam, Adolphe 138
Albright, Daniel 1, 4, 7, 11–12
Allan, Maud 95
American Sign Language 34
Apollinaire, Guillaume 65, 66, 77, 78
Archer, Kenneth 9, 10, 17–25
architecture 19, 50, 61
archives 4, 9, 10, 17, 18, 22, 23, 24, 155
    living archive 22, 25
Arndt, Ernst 120, 123, 124–5
    Goading the Pony 123
Ariaz, Oscar 148
artistic research 14, 49
Ashton, Frederick 148
Auric, Georges 66
authenticity 20, 21, 24, 167, 173

Bach, Johann Sebastian 10, 66, 97, 99, 102, 103, 104
Bakst, Léon 96
Balanchine, George 4, 7, 22, 167
    Le Chant du Rossignol 22
Ballets Russes 17, 61, 63, 69, 71, 77, 95, 165
Ballets Suédois 17
Bausch, Pina xii, 54, 55
    Blaubart 54
    Die sieben Todsünden 54
Beethoven, Ludwig van 30, 81, 168, 174
Béjart, Maurice 10, 81–98
    Boléro 81, 85, 87, 89, 90, 92
    Casta Diva 82, 88
    Gaîté parisienne 87
    La Mort Subite 81, 82, 85, 89, 90, 92
    Le Chant du Compagnon errant 87
    Le Sacre du printemps 87
    Salome 81
Benesh, Joan 166
Benesh Movement Notation 11, 113, 149, 151, 152, 153, 154, 155, 163–77

Benjamin, Walter 52
Bigonzetti, Mauro 11, 133–46
Brecht, Bertolt 54
Bolero 10, 80, 85, 87, 89, 90–6
Bollingen Prize for poetry translation 120, 123
Boston Ballet 170
Burkert, Matthias 54

Cage, John 55, 100
Chaplin, Charlie 76
choreography 4, 7, 10, 11, 19, 24, 29, 30–1, 33, 35, 36, 39, 40, 41, 42, 43, 45, 46, 50, 86, 89, 90, 92, 93, 94, 95, 96, 99, 100, 101, 102, 103, 106, 107, 108, 110, 111, 117, 119, 123, 134, 136, 137, 139, 140, 144, 147, 149, 150, 151, 152, 155, 156, 157, 163, 164, 165, 168, 173, 174, 175
chronophotography 56
Choros 50
Chouinard, Marie 55
Cocteau, Jean 63, 65, 66, 69, 70–6, 77, 78
    Le Coq et l'arlequin 77
Coppélia vii, viii, 11, 133, 137–46
Cranko, John 10, 117
    Onegin 117–30
    Romeo and Juliet 119
    The Forgotten Room 126
    The Taming of the Shrew 119
Cunningham, Merce 55

Dance Notation Bureau, The 152
dance reconstruction 6, 9, 17–25
Dayan, Peter 13, 61, 67
Délibes, Leo 11, 133–46
Derrida, Jacques 61
Diaghilev, Serge 17, 25, 63, 69, 71–2, 73–4, 77, 78
Duerden, Rachel 39, 168, 171

Dufort, Louis 55
Dying Swan, The 164, 165, 170

Eadweard's Ear vii, 9, 55, 58
Einasto, Heili ix, 11, 133–46
Eisenschneider, Andreas 55
entrainement 60
Estonia National Ballet 133, 137, 139, 144
Eugene Onegin 10

Feuillet, Raoul 165
Flaubert, Gustave 84
Fokine, Michel 95, 164, 165, 170
Forsythe, William
   Decreation 54
Fuller, Lois 31, 95
Fullington, Doug 18

Giselle 135
Glasstellar, Joa 10, 56
Grafe, Dieter 152
grammar 32, 36, 41
Grigoriev, Serge 73
Gross, Valentine 69–70, 71, 72, 74, 77

Haber, David 152
Handel, George Frederick viii, 40
   L'Allegro, il Penseroso ed il Moderato 32, 37–9
Henry, Pierre 81
Hodson, Millicent 9, 10, 17–25
Hofmann, Theodor Amadeus
   Coppélia 11, 133–46
   The Sandman 134, 135–6, 142
Honegger, Arthur
   Skating Rink 17, 22
Humphrey, Doris vii, 10, 99, 109
   Passacaglia 99, 100, 101, 102, 103–8
   With My Red Fires 102, 108–13
Hutchinson Guest, Ann 152, 175–6
Huysman, Joris-Karl 84
Hynd, Ronald 133–46

Imperial Dance Academy of St Petersburg 165
intercultural 4, 8, 12, 13, 67
intermedial 7, 52, 55, 83, 84

intramedial 52, 55, 59
intuitive 55, 166

Jaques-Dalcroze, Émile 51
Jakobson 11, 15, 25, 68, 84, 85, 117, 120, 133, 145, 169, 176
   interlingual 8, 14, 84
   intralingual 8, 14, 84
   intersemiotic 8, 10, 11, 15, 68, 75, 78, 84, 85, 99, 100, 102, 106, 108, 111, 112, 114, , 117, 120, 122, 128, 129, 133, 147, 161, 169, 171, 176
Jennens, Charles 37
Jordan, Stephanie 39, 43, 51, 67, 77, 99, 106, 107

Kando, Juliette 153–4
Keersmaeker, Anne Teresa De 59–61
   accumulation 61
   Drumming 60, 61
   mirroring 61
   phase-shifting 61
   Piano Phase 60
   Rain 60, 61
   Violin Phase 60
Kress, Gunther 2, 7, 11, 13, 15, 25, 68

Laban, Rudolf 153, 166
   Labanotation 11, 99, 101, 102, 111, 113, 152, 163–77
language
   bodily/gestural 6, 8, 33, 54, 74, 75, 81, 133, 134, 142, 144, 145
   common 49, 51, 69
   evolution 35
   music 49
   scope 47
   transfer 4, 11
Leningrad State Academic Theatre of Opera and Ballet 148
Lobsanova, Elena 157
Loesch, Juliette ix, 81–98

MacMillan, Kenneth 148, 154, 157
Mahler, Gustave 81
Main, Lesley ix, 10, 99–115
Mallarmé, Stefan 84
Marie, Rolf de 17
Massine, Léonide 22, 63, 65, 68, 73, 74–6, 78

materiality 50, 51, 52 60
meaning 4, 5, 11, 12, 14, 32, 34, 42, 48n, 68, 74, 76, 78, 100, 102, 104, 106, 107, 112–14, 119, 128, 133, 148, 176
mediality 50, 51, 52, 53 59, 60
Merkle, Denise ix, 11, 147–61
Mickey Mousing 51
Milton, John 37
mimesis 93
Minkus, Ludwig 138
Minors, Helen Julia x, 3, 8, 12, 13, 17–25, 49, 52, 63–78, 100, 101, 102
  Music, Text and Translation xiv, 5, 11, 12, 17, 63, 99
mode 3, 9, 11, 12, 13, 25, 52, 68, 75, 78, 176
MOMENTA Dance Company vii, 104, 105
Morris, Mark 9, 29, 99, 106, 107–8
  Gloria 29–48
  Mozart Dances 32, 43–6
Mort Subite, La 10
movement 5, 6, 9–11, 29–32, 45–8, 49–62, 64, 68, 74–6, 89, 91, 93–4, 99–114, 133–4, 136, 140, 143, 147, 150, 152, 153, 158, 163–77
  space and time 50, 94
Mozart, Wolfgang Amadeus viii, 81
multisensory 8
multimodality 12, 13, 15, 75
Muybridge, Eadweard 56

Nabokov, Vladimir 120, 123, 124–5
National Ballet of Canada 147–61
Neumeier, John 148
Nikinska, Bronislava 96
Nijinsky, Vaslav 23, 165
Nureyev, Rudolf 118, 148, 149, 158

paratext 10, 120, 122–5
Paris Opera 134, 135
Pavlova 164, 165
Perrault, Charles 169
Petipa, Marius 19–20, 137, 169
Picasso, Pablo 63, 64, 72, 73, 74, 77
Ponomareva, Anna xi, 10, 117–30
Prokofiev, Sergei 147–9, 156
Pugny, César 138
Pushkin, Alexander 117–30

Radlov, Sergey 148, 156
Ratmansky, Alexei 17, 19, 148, 157, 158, 161
Ravel, Maurice 85, 90, 93–5
reconstruction 18, 17–25, 113
  definition 17
  facsimile 18, 21, 22, 24–5
Regnault, François 86
Reich, Steve 59, 60
  Music for 18 Musicians 60
Rodriquez, Sonia 156
Romeo and Juliet 11, 147–61
Rose and the Ring, The 160
Royal Ballet 166
Royal Academy of Dance 166
Rubenstein 96
Ryman, Hughes 155

Sadler's Wells Ballet 150
Saint-Saens, Camille
  Le Carnaval des animaux 164
Sauguet, Henri
  Le Chatte 21
Satie, Erik 63–78
  La Parade 10, 63–78
  Mercure 64
senses 49, 52, 101
Sert, Misia 69, 70
Sleeping Beauty 19, 169
Smith, Mariam 20
Stokowski, Leopold 101, 102, 103, 104
Strauss, Richard, 82
Stravinsky, Igor 23, 25
  Le sacre du printemps 17, 20, 22, 23, 81
Schroedter, Stephanie xi, 5, 9, 49–62
Shilovsky, Konstantin 121
Smith, Mariam 6
St Denis, Ruth 95
Swan Lake 164, 168
Sylphide, La 135
syntagmatic relationship 122

Tchaikovsky, Pyotr Ilyich 10, 118, 120–1, 169
Tharp, Twyla 9
transcript 52, 59, 161, 163, 165, 167, 171
  transcriptivity 52
transduction 78

translation 133
- artistic 65, 67–8
- analogical mapping / analogical thinking / analogy 31, 32–3, 40, 41, 68–9, 74
- analogical reference 34–7, 42, 46, 47
- choreographic 20, 112
- communication 100–1
- dance 3
- dialogues 63, 149
- embodied 75
- faithfulness 173
- ideological 144–6
- kinetic 81–98, 133
- literal 59, 124
- metaphor 47
- musical 3, 91, 134, 149, 151
- multimodal 3, 5–9, 14
- myths 14
- notation 163–77
- opera 8
- permanent 53
- post-modern 139–44
- process 20, 21, 34, 49–62, 68, 78, 85, 99, 100, 147, 150, 151, 156–7, 160, 169
- sequence of events 30, 136

theatre 7, 99
theories 52
transmediation 85
transcription 21
transfer of sense 64, 127
translation turn 13
translating music 5, 12, 96, 136
Tsinguirides, Georgette 154–155
Tudor, David 55

Variations V
visualization 29, 30, 31, 36, 40, 43, 45, 68, 107
Vivaldi, Antonio viii, 29

Wagner, Richard 81
Wardle, Mary xii, 163–77
Wehrli, Penelope 10, 55, 56
Weidman, Charles 103
Weyergans, François 82
Wilde, Oscar 81–98
- *De Profundis* 83
- *Salomé* 82, 88
With My Red Fires 10

Zbikowski, Lawrence xiii, 9, 29–48, 51, 69

www.ingramcontent.com/pod-product-compliance
Lightning Source LLC
Chambersburg PA
CBHW052113300426
44116CB00010B/1645